SCREAM

SCREAM

CHILLING ADVENTURES
in the SCIENCE *of* FEAR

MARGEE KERR

PUBLICAFFAIRS
NEW YORK

Published in the United States by PublicAffairs™,
a Member of the Perseus Books Group

Book design by Jack Lenzo

Library of Congress Cataloging-in-Publication Data
Kerr, Margee.
Scream : chilling adventures in the science of fear / Margee Kerr.
pages cm
Includes bibliographical references and index.
ISBN 978-1-61039-482-6 (hardback)—ISBN 978-1-61039-483-3 (e-book) 1. Fear. 2. Emotions. I. Title.
BF575.F2K47 2015
302′.17—dc23
2015018426

First Edition
10 9 8 7 6 5 4 3 2 1

Dedicated to the Simmonses and the entire ScareHouse cast and crew. Thank you for the support and for the scares.

Terror is a passion which always produces delight when it does not press too close.

—*Edmund Burke*

CONTENTS

LIST OF THRILLS AND CHILLS

NOTABLE HAUNTED PLACES

* Moundsville State Penitentiary, Moundsville, West Virginia
* Trans Allegheny Lunatic Asylum, Weston, West Virginia
* Eastern State Penitentiary, Philadelphia
* Penfield Reef Light House, Bridgeport, Connecticut
* Hill View Manor, New Castle, Pennsylvania
* Hotel De Salto, Tequendama Falls, Colombia
* Cathedral de Sal de Zipaquirá, Zipaquirá, Colombia
* Guatavita Lagoon, Colombia
* La Candelaria, Bogotá, Colombia
* Central Bogotá Cemetery, Bogotá, Colombia
* Aokigahara Forest, Mount Fuji, Japan

NOTABLE HAUNTED HOUSES AND SCARY ENTERTAINMENT

* ScareHouse, Pittsburgh
* Terror Behind the Walls, Philadelphia
* Factory of Terror, Canton, Ohio
* Ghostly Manor, Sandusky, Ohio
* Haunted Hospital, Fuji-Q Highland, Japan
* Ultimate Fort, Fuji-Q Highland, Japan
* Daiba School Horror, Tokyo
* Ghost Bar, Tokyo

- Lock Up, Tokyo
- Castillo Del Terror, Bogotá, Colombia

NOTABLE THRILL RIDES AND ACTIVITIES

- Skydiving, Grove City, Pennsylvania
- CN Tower EdgeWalk, Toronto
- Fuji-Q Highland: Takabisha, Dodonpa, Eejanaika
- Cedar Point: Millennium Force, Corkscrew, GateKeeper, Gemini, Blue Streak, Raptor
- Universal Studios: Hollywood Riptide Rocket, The Amazing Adventures of Spiderman, Simpsons Ride, Transformers 3D, Harry Potter and the Escape from Gringotts
- Six Flags New Jersey: Batman, Green Lantern, Kingda Ka, Nitro, Superman, Slingshot

PREFACE

Room of Doors at ScareHouse in Pittsburgh, Pennsylvania. Photo courtesy ScareHouse. Copyright Rachellynn Schoen.

It's about nine on a Friday night in mid-October. It's cold, but it's still the refreshing cold of autumn, not yet chilly enough to see your own breath. After surveying the line of people wrapped around the building for the length of about two city blocks, I start walking back up the hill to the main entrance of ScareHouse, a haunted attraction (or "haunt") in Pittsburgh.

As I walk, a customer shouts at me: "Hey! Hey! How scary is it?" I shout back, "Did you bring a change of pants?" and keep on walking. I give a passing nod to one of our security guards as I go through the front doors and weave my way around customers toward the heavy black curtains at the back of the lobby. As soon as I pass the curtains, the temperature increases by what seems like 20 degrees. I can feel a growing sense of anticipation as I make my way back to the Barn through the secret actor hallway that stretches down the middle of the haunt. On my left the growls and snarls coming from a zombie apocalypse grow louder and then fade as I pass. I smile as I hear a loud "splat" followed by high-pitched screams as one of our actors, a particularly energetic zombie, throws himself against a Plexiglas pane just inches away from a customer's face (he'll do this at least once a minute for the next five hours). On my right I hear the gargling, incomprehensible ranting of a deranged priest as I pass by the Chapel.

I finally get to the last stretch of the back hallway, and already I can feel the vibrations from the sliding and banging of the Serial Killer door. I say "door," but it's actually a wall of the room attached on a slider with a metal plate on the end that amplifies the sound. I hear "WHAT ARE YOU DOING IN MY ROOM?" followed by several different voices screaming and shouting, "Oh my God," and other expletives. Though I can't see our serial killer yet, I know what he is doing: holding up his butcher knife, bare chest puffed out, stepping just far enough into the space to intimidate but not impede the customers as they go running forward. The serial killer pulls back and slams the door closed. Just as the customers catch their breath and start to collect themselves, the serial killer's "victim" character appears and begs for their help. Confused, startled, scared to death, they continue to run forward, into the Barn. The entrance is quiet, eerie, and filled with stuffed animals (not the fluffy kind), and just around the corner wait a butcher, a scarecrow, a chainsaw, and well, someone we just call Hayloft. This stretch of the haunt—from the Basement to the Barn—is one of my favorite places in the world.

I give a high five to the serial killer and ask how the scares are tonight. With a big smile he responds, "Awesome." The crew in this stretch of rooms has worked together for over three years. The energy and intensity they build are nothing short of magical. I sneak into a drop panel (a window cut into a wall with a heavy door that you can drop open and pop through) right next to the sliding door and peer through a penny-sized hole in the wall, and I watch. These peepholes pepper the entire haunt and are built for actors and security guards watching for cues, customer flow, and, of course, troublemakers. For sociological observation, not so much.

The first time I did this I felt creepy, and if I'm honest, it still feels creepy. Peering through a hole in the wall is hardly a socially sanctioned and acceptable thing to do. To say it's taboo is an understatement. I spent over six years working in research with oversight of the institutional review board (IRB) at a local university, which set strict parameters on human subject research. The IRB is pretty serious about informed consent, especially when dealing with sensitive situations. And while all customers are repeatedly warned and notified they will be on camera once entering the haunt, this kind of voyeurism still feels unfair, dangerous, and yes, powerful. Making it feel even more awkward, I'm watching people in a moment of pure terror and vulnerability. I see the expressions on their faces, I hear their screams, and occasionally I see the tears in their eyes. They run, trip over each other, and instinctively push back, forward, any direction that is away from the serial killer and his knife. I've seen men push their girlfriends out of the way as they try to move and others drop to their knees and scream for God.

There is usually a minute or so break in between groups. It's a quiet and surreal minute. The screams from the previous group now entering the Barn can be heard as they are introduced to our scarecrow. I crouch there, peering through the hole, and catch sight of the first person in the next group. She's young, probably mid-twenties, and looking around at everything. There is a lot to hold her attention. The room is scattered with photos on the wall, a sink filled with blood and guts, a 3-D projection of maggots crawling over garbage. She scans the floor, the corners, trying to see ahead, completely unsuspecting that at any moment the entire wall to her left will slam open. I feel anxious, even though

I've watched this many times. The anticipation builds, and I feel my heart start beating faster. I wonder *when*—when is he going to slide the door? I watch as the customer moves slowly forward, her attention distracted by a mirror placed right in front of her on an opposing wall, the wall I'm hiding behind. For a moment I think she can see me, but I know it's impossible. Just as she realizes it's her own reflection in the mirror, the door slams open, and the serial killer delivers his scare. The young woman, along with the rest of her group, screams as they stumble forward and to the right. I turn to watch them round the corner and see their screams have turned to hysterical laughter right before reverting back to screams as the killer's victim delivers *his* scare. As the group moves into the Barn, I congratulate the actors on their highly successful one-two setup. They smile and laugh and reset their positions at their own peepholes, waiting for their cue.

Again in this moment of quiet I find myself in awe. Something amazing is happening in this space. Each time I walk away I feel as if I've witnessed humans at their most basic and primal state. It's a privilege. How often in life do we actually see each other stripped of pretense and social scripts? So I continue to crouch, staring through a peephole, watching customers scream in terror, actors poised on their toes watching and lying in wait to jump out and go "boo," and I wonder how we got to this point and why all these people are standing in line for two hours to pay money for the chance to scream.

> > >

I've been a fan of haunted houses since my first trip at age six through a tiny, shabby, thrown-together haunt with toilet paper mummies and black plastic bats on a gymnasium stage. Not only were they in line with my general interest in scary stories and fascination with the macabre, but Halloween was the best holiday, in my opinion, because it was all about friends, monsters, and candy, rather than family and responsibility. I found the excitement and anticipation of haunted houses exhilarating, realizing pretty early in life that I was a thrill seeker. Of course I didn't use that language or know what a thrill seeker was, or an adrenaline junky, or a daredevil, or the academic concepts for these terms: sensation seeking, novelty seeking, benign masochism, hedonic reversals. I didn't know what stress sensitive versus stress resilient meant; I just knew I really enjoyed things like haunted houses, scary movies, riding my horse bareback with abandon across fields, roller-skating fast, and going on the steepest roller coasters. I never really stopped to think about why I enjoyed it. I just figured it was fun and funny and an all-around good time.

My thrill seeking led me to ScareHouse, a nationally recognized haunted attraction in Pittsburgh. ScareHouse was the scariest haunt I'd ever been through (and I've been through a lot). In the midst of one particularly scary moment there, I actually ran into a wall and hurt my shoulder; it was sore for weeks. It was also the weirdest haunt I'd seen: there was no Freddy or Jason or Leatherface, and it wasn't all gore and blood and guts, like so many popular haunts these days. Instead it had rooms where you wore 3-D glasses and everything was painted in neon colors, and there were strange and unusual original characters. The mood was unsettling and uncanny. After going through the haunt I felt energized but also relaxed and even calm. I decided I wanted to be there as much as possible, which was crazy because I was in the middle of writing my dissertation, and I had a full-time job with the Veterans Administration working in the Center for Health Equity Research and Promotion.

After finishing my first tour of ScareHouse, I found one of the owners, Scott Simmons, and I told him I would do whatever they needed to be part of their team. An actor, still covered in blood, had been stalking us. He asked in jest, "What can a sociologist do for a haunted house?" "I can analyze data!" I replied. So that's what I did.

My dissertation advisor gave me the side eye upon learning my plans to work at ScareHouse, but I didn't care. Every year, on their customer survey, ScareHouse asked, "What do you find scary?" What an opportunity! This data, though not exhaustive or controlled enough to be published in the *American Journal of Sociology*, was a rare glimpse behind the curtain, into fear as it looks in the real world. Since 2008 I have had the pleasure of reading people's reports of what they fear, and it is not only entertaining but enlightening.

As I continued to study fear in my work both at the University of Pittsburgh and at ScareHouse, I found I had questions that weren't being answered with theory and stacks of lab research. Everything I read focused on the negative side of fear. Scholars show how panic, anxiety, worry, and fear have taken hold of the American psyche and become the driving emotions behind a majority of our actions and decisions, to our great detriment. Numerous authors dissect and condemn the rampant "fear profiteering" in contemporary American society, arguing (correctly) that fear is used to sell products and shape political debates. Viewer-hungry news outlets manipulate our fear response and our brain's inability to distinguish "real" threats from the abstract and anomalous terrors across the globe that appear within seconds on our smart phones and TVs. We live in an objectively safer world than ever before, but we're bombarded with fear-triggering messages and worried about issues that likely won't affect us and are far from our control. We are arguably consumed with fear.

And yet lots of people enjoy fear. They *love* screaming their heads off, and they proudly post pictures of their wet pants on Twitter and Facebook. They exit haunted houses smiling, laughing, hugging, and giving each other high fives.

My observations at ScareHouse (not to mention the commercial success of scary material from TV to video games) were not matching up to the literature. There were questions that needed to be answered. Some of them were fun: Why do some people like haunted houses and others don't? What's the difference between physical thrills like roller coasters and psychological chills like being alone in the dark? But some were serious: What can we learn from scaring ourselves? How do biology and culture influence what we're afraid of and how we engage with scary and thrilling material? And why, in a world where people perceive themselves to be in ever-greater danger, are we seeking out even more fear— in record numbers? I discovered a story about fear that needed to be investigated, experienced, and shared.

So I went about trying to do just that. And it wasn't going to happen in a lab.

> > >

For the past two years I've been all over the world trying to understand fear from inside out. I've been to the world's scariest haunted houses and on its steepest roller coasters. I've dangled, suspended by a cable, from one of the tallest human-made structures in the world. I've jumped out of a plane and spent the night at an abandoned prison—twice. I've been handcuffed and forced to crawl through a tunnel in the pitch dark—and yet I was more terrified by something that happened to me in broad daylight. I've cried a few times, including once by myself in the middle of a forest in Japan and once in a crowd in Colombia. I've spoken to a long list of experts and scientists studying all things thrilling, scary, and haunting. These experiences have changed my life for the better.

This book is the result of what I learned. These are my adventures in fear.

PART I
PHYSICAL THRILLS

The world was to me a secret which I desired to divine.
—*Mary Shelley,* Frankenstein

1

THE STOMACH DROP

Sunset at Fuji-Q Highland, Japan. Photo by the author.

There's nothing quite like gazing up through a roller coaster's vast web of iron and steel.

My first ride was at age eleven on the Comet, Hershey Park's oldest roller coaster, where I couldn't stop tying and retying my ponytail because I was convinced my Rapunzel-like hair, which at the time extended below my waist and almost down to my knees, would get caught in the tracks. (In hindsight, this concern still seems reasonable.) There had been many more rides since then, and I can remember every one, each unique and exciting in its own way. But I knew the roller coaster I was about to get on was special: it's the steepest one in the world and located at the base of the tallest mountain in Japan. The Takabisha at Fuji-Q Highland amusement park is a 3,300-foot, two-minute ride that takes guests 141 feet in the air and then drops them over a 121-degree-beyond-vertical, record-breaking plunge. I had come halfway around the world to ride it.

Thrill rides offer a unique type of scary experience. Rather than being frightening because of their content, they take our "thinking" brain off-line and deliver a quick and powerful jolt directly to our body. Their swift nature—they last no more than a few minutes—is part of what makes them so much fun. Unlike hanging off the side of a tall building for almost an hour (more about that later), thrill rides leave little time for our brain to critically think about what is happening or struggle to conquer our fear. Instead we surrender all control to the machine that flips, flings, twists, turns, and throws us around in ways the human body wasn't designed to handle. Strapped into seats and at the mercy of the ride, our body is launched into a high arousal state in a matter of seconds, triggering the chemical cascade collectively known as fight or flight, or the threat response—what most people just call "fear."

What we call fear isn't as simple as it sounds. In fact, the National Institutes of Health recently developed a thirty-four-page document outlining the many facets of not just fear but all emotion. For example, what most call "fear" is divided into several negative valence systems, which include acute threat, potential threat, sustained threat, loss, and frustrative nonreward. The document then goes on to identify the genes, molecules, cells, and circuits in the body to study along with the physiological and behavioral tests to administer. It is an impressive cataloguing, and all of this to try to understand this thing most of us just call a *feeling*.

Most people talk about fear as an emotion, which sounds sensible—but emotions are hard to explain. Imagine trying to tell an alien, who knows nothing of the human experience, how to distinguish fear from other emotions, like anxiety. What is the difference between happiness and surprise, anger and frustration, guilt and shame? For that matter, how do you tell an alien what an emotion is at all? What is a *feeling*? Is it a collection of physical reactions (like an increased heart rate and sweating) that result in specific kinds of behavior (like screaming and covering your eyes)? If so, which physical reactions map onto which specific kinds of behavior? And are they the same for all humans? Does "happy" feel the same for me as it does for you?

Maybe. Well, sort of. The theory of universal emotions gained traction in the 1970s, when Paul Ekman identified six facial expressions he claimed all people agreed were representative of specific emotions, regardless of time and place: fear, surprise, anger, happiness, sadness, and disgust. He later expanded this list to include amusement, contempt, contentment, embarrassment, excitement, guilt, pride, relief, satisfaction, sensory pleasure, and shame. But new research from Erika Siegel and Lisa Feldman Barrett (a distinguished professor and director of the Interdisciplinary Affective Science Laboratory who literally wrote the book *How Emotions Are Made*), who recently conducted a meta-analysis of emotion studies, found there are "no consistent and specific changes in physiology during discrete emotions," meaning that you can't guess someone's emotional state from a list of their physical symptoms, like sweating or heart rate or body temperature. Rather, there is a range of behaviors and meanings tied to a range of physiological responses that can and do change based on person, time, and place. So fear for me might not be the same as fear for you, and it probably isn't.

Still, there are certain universal biological facts about fear. Every organism, from the fruit fly to the human, has a defense or threat response; it's one of our survival circuits.* In humans the threat response works like this: a stimulus (for example, the thundering roar of a roller coaster) sets off the alarms, triggering two warning signals—what neuroscientist and fear expert

---

*Other survival circuits are responsible for energy and nutrition, fluid balance, thermoregulation, and procreation.

Joseph LeDoux calls the "low road" and the "high road." The low road bypasses the gathering of contextualizing information to get quickly to the brain structure that processes threat: the almond-shaped amygdala, found deep in the middle of our brain. The amygdala then triggers a whole host of reactions throughout the brain and body (in other words, activation of the sympathetic nervous system), preparing the body for fight or flight. The high-road signal, arriving not even a full second after the low-road signal, is slower because it is collecting information from other parts of our brain—particularly neocortical regions that are responsible for critically evaluating information and that involve slow, conscious processes like deliberation. For example, the high-road signal brings together visual information and any information in our stored memory that might be useful. This second signal can either reinforce the first—a neurological version of Monty Python's famous exhortation to "run away, run away"—or debunk the signal as a false alarm and send a message to return the body to a relaxed state (activating the parasympathetic nervous system). In the case of the amusement park, as soon as that second signal arrives letting you know you've done this before and are safely belted into a steel machine, the real fun can begin.

Evidently, our threat-response systems have been busy, because these are good times for thrill seekers: the attraction and amusement park industry is booming. Over 290 million people visited four hundred amusement parks in the United States in 2010, up from 145.5 million two years prior. And there is no sign of it slowing down, with an average growth rate of about 6 percent per year for the last seven years and an impressive economic impact through sales, job creation, and consumer spending of $219 billion in 2011.* The growth of attractions and amusement parks internationally is even bigger, especially in Asia and South America. A

---

*In 2011 there were thirty thousand attractions in the United States. Economic impact includes $91 billion in direct impacts and $127 billion in indirect and induced impacts, $67 billion in total labor income, and 2.3 million total jobs, according to analysis by the International Association of Amusement Parks and Attractions' 2014 study *The Economic Impacts of the US Attractions Industry*.

recent poll from the International Association of Amusement Parks and Attractions (IAAPA) shows 67 percent of respondents plan on visiting an amusement park or attraction in the coming year—and for good reason. Amusement parks offer a variety of activities for a range of palates, with something to excite everyone from the smallest toddler to the adventurous grandparent. The king of the amusement park, though, has always been the roller coaster.

> > >

Since that first adventure at Hershey Park, I had ridden Apollo's Chariot at Busch Gardens, Harry Potter and the Escape from Gringotts at Universal Studios, Phantom's Revenge at Kennywood (about twenty times), and the dozens of rides at the self-proclaimed roller coaster capital of the world—Cedar Point, in Sandusky, Ohio. So I felt confident I had experienced the most extreme and spectacular rides out there. Inevitably, I was wrong. In typical American fashion I'd assumed my country had the best thrill rides in the world, an assumption that was quickly disproven by a little research. Extreme rides are all over the globe: Dubai, China, Finland, Australia, Japan. Fuji-Q Highland, where I was standing, has broken over fourteen Guinness World Records, and by the end of that day I would get to experience three current record-holders: the steepest in the world (Takabisha), the one with the highest acceleration at launch time (Dodonpa), and the tallest, fastest 4-D coaster, with the most inversions in the world (Eejanaika).*

My trip to Fuji-Q could not have been on a more perfect day: the air was crisp and cool, the sun bright and low in the sky. Behind the dazzling human-made roller coasters, Ferris wheels, and towering inversion rides that looked like giant steel monsters; behind the

---

*A bit of roller coaster trivia here: a 4-D coaster is one with rotating cars, so that riders can be "inverted" even when the track is right side up. This has led to some dispute about which roller coasters have the most inversions. The Roller Coaster Database credits England's the Smiler with the most, but the Guinness Book of World Records recognizes Eejanaika, even though some of its inversions are 4-D. Regardless, to ride Eejanaika is to spend a lot of time upside down.

house-sized golden *maneki-neko* "fortune cats"; behind the crowds and food vendors and ticket booths stretched the majestic Mount Fuji. The park was otherworldly: I felt as if I were in a mythical land where anything could happen. I marveled at the park and the snowcapped peak that surely inspired it, a testament to humans' incredible intelligence, creativity, and hard work, and all for the purpose of making ourselves scream. How in the world did such a ridiculous machine as the roller coaster come into existence?

> ﹡ ﹡ ﹡

Roller coasters have a long history that follows the tracks of industrialization, consumerism, and political and economic transitions. The first coasters were inspired by something called the Russian Ice Slides, which were popular in seventeenth-century Russia. Designed after the local ice-covered mountains, which people had been sledding down for fun since at least the fifteenth century, the Russian Ice Slides were built out of wood and were as tall as eighty feet, with long slopes covered in ice. Much as they do on today's coasters, riders would sit in sleds or carts made of wood and speed down the mountain, which sometimes included additional human-made bumps to make it a little more exciting.

Initially, Europe was the leader in building thrill rides, experimenting with various railway experiences throughout the mid-1800s. The Centrifugal Railway, built in 1846 in the Frascati Gardens in Paris, was a single-loop coaster entirely dependent on centrifugal force to carry the cart up and around. These early coasters were terrifying not only because of the physical experience but because their reliability and safety were at best questionable. In the early days of thrill rides, death was not out of the question.*

In the United States the roller coaster was improved and then took off into the stratosphere with the invention of the electric

---

*Thrill rides are incredibly safe today, as Charles C. W. Cooke, a reporter for the *National Review*, stated: "Americans are 5,000 times more likely to be legally executed by their own government than to die on a roller coaster." However, there is still no federal oversight of amusement parks; they voluntarily follow standards by the American Society for Testing and Materials.

trolley car and some help from clever capitalists. Electric trolley cars, designed and used to move coal and material from one location to another, ran on electricity purchased at a flat rate from the emerging electric companies. Recognizing that it didn't matter if one or a hundred cars were in rotation on the tracks, trolley companies took the opportunity to make more money by encouraging the public to ride the trolleys—in exchange for a small fee—for leisure and pleasure. Families began taking the trolley cars out of town for excursions to parks and an escape from the cramped and bustling city. The result: the public enjoyed the ride as much as the destination, especially when the trolley ascended steep peaks and took deep dips into the valley.

Steadily the masses were discovering the joy of the commercially marketed thrill, and soon entrepreneurial and engineering visionaries were creating a new generation of roller coasters and rides, starting with the Gravity Pleasure Switchback Railway, which opened at Coney Island in 1884. Developed by LaMarcus Thompson, the railway carried passengers down a six-hundred-foot track and up the other side to a tower, where it reversed direction and rolled back down and up. The coaster became the most popular ride at Coney Island, and others were soon being built across the country; by 1920 there was an impressive 1,500 to 2,000 coasters in the United States. But it was not just roller coasters titillating guests at the turn of the twentieth century. Ferris wheels (introduced at the World's Columbian Exposition in Chicago on June 21, 1893), carousels, and swings were all being designed and built to trigger those glorious sensations.

The quickly expanding industry came to a halt, however, with the Great Depression. The public did not have the disposable income or the desire to seek out thrilling experiences, as all their energy went toward collecting and preserving resources. Between 1930 and 1939 over 1,500 amusement parks closed, their rides demolished and scavenged for any valuable materials. Still, those early days of thrilling fun had not been forgotten. During the postwar boom, a generation sought to re-create for their children the joys they'd experienced. Amusement parks began making a comeback, breaking new ground in 1955 with the opening of Disneyland in Anaheim, California. Disneyland was not only the first theme park but the birthplace of the steel roller coaster. Opened in 1959, the Matterhorn Mountain was not particularly scary; it mostly just went up and down hills. But its steel design and construction provided the foundations for what became the multiloop, suspended, and stand-up coasters we know and love today, including the record-breaking Takabisha.

> . > . >

Walking through the gates at Fuji-Q, I instantly felt my heart rate increase. I heard the telltale click-click-click as the coasters climbed the track, the screams growing louder and then fading as riders twisted and turned through loops and inversions, and finally the ground-shaking thunder as they sped around through the web of rails.

I immediately ran to the Takabisha and got in line. Usually waiting in line is filled with growing anticipation, and all around me I watched as friends and couples jumped up and down with excitement, struggling to control their nerves as they talked and laughed. Amusement parks are made for friends and family, and they prove the truth of the saying "A happiness shared is a happiness doubled." Indeed, research from Arthur Aron and colleagues found that participants reported an increase in relationship quality after participating in something novel and exciting together. Recent research by Garriy Shteynberg at the University of Tennessee found through a series of social experiments that "simultaneous co-attention," or participating in something with others, leads to a more intense emotional experience. He and his colleagues showed that scary advertisements felt scarier, negative images made people feel sadder, and happy images made people feel happier when people knew they weren't experiencing them alone.*

---

*The impact of the presence of others during emotional experiences is a bit more complicated; as I'll show in later chapters, the presence of a friend, loved one, or even a stranger can make scary experiences *less* scary and even hills appear less steep. The difference may be in the motivation of the friend—is he or she there to support and offer a life preserver, or are you both in the same boat?

We enjoy experiences with others not only because of our own emotional responses, but because when we watch someone experience something, we experience it ourselves—it's how we empathize and connect to each other. Kyung Hwa Lee and Greg Siegle from the University of Pittsburgh conducted a meta-analysis of existing studies that used neuroimaging to measure emotional evaluation of the self and others. They found similar or overlapping patterns of brain activity when we experience an emotion and when we evaluate others' emotions. For example, the part of our insular cortex (a brain structure located in the left and right hemispheres inside the cerebral cortex—more on that later) that processes pain is active when we experience pain ourselves *and* when we are simply observing something that causes pain, as in "I could *feel* my teeth hurt watching that dentist drill into her tooth!" This could be why you scream when your friend is startled and why you cry when you see your loved one cry. Of course seeing someone else do something, or even imagining doing something ourselves, is not exactly the same as experiencing it directly (as I would repeatedly learn). For example, we mostly only experience the affective part of the physical pain of others; we really don't have the same intense physical sensations in our body. This means that you'll suffer along with the character on screen trying to cut off his foot, but won't be screaming in agony as though your foot really was being sawed from your leg (but it might ache a little).

The mechanisms behind this process of creating overlapping layers of representation is still debated, but researchers like neuroscientist V. S. Ramachandran and Lindsay Oberman believe it is likely a result of mirror neurons, or what Ramachandran calls the discovery responsible for the great leap forward in human civilization. The mirror neuron was discovered by an Italian research team in the premotor cortex of macaques in 1992. They noticed that this new class of neurons was active not only when the monkey was carrying out a task but when it watched another monkey do the same thing. The media interpreted this as the discovery of the neurological basis of empathy, birthing a tornado of headlines claiming everything from the discovery of God in the brain to the human soul. But as cognitive neuroscientist and science writer

Christian Jarrett pointed out in his critical article, "A Calm Look at the Most Hyped Concept in Neuroscience—Mirror Neurons," the hype was largely just that: a chance to grab attention and headlines. Researchers James Kilner and Roger Lemon, through their careful review of research on the topic, show that there are more questions than answers about mirror neurons. They do work in the motor cortex and likely play a role in our ability to mimic expressions and gestures, but they are not the "soul" source of human empathy (pun intended).

> > >

Watching the faces light up around me, I found myself wishing I had someone to share this experience with. Just the night before, on the train to Mount Fuji, I had thought about how amazing it was to be so far away from everything and everyone. No one knew where I was; no one could reach me; no one expected anything from me. I felt free from all responsibilities, as if I had been given a hall pass in life. But as I stood in line, those same thoughts took on new meaning, and instead of smiling like those around me, I felt a wave of sadness. I was alone. All of a sudden I felt heavy and tired. I wanted to go sit in my room and stare at the wall.

As my turn approached, the ride attendant walked over, held up one finger, and asked, "One?" Embarrassed at forcing the couples around me to separate, I nodded my head. Sharing a car with three strangers, I felt self-conscious and burdensome—not your typical emotional state before a roller coaster ride. I should have been sweating bullets and feeling anxious and exhilarated, as I had while riding coasters all day with my friends at Cedar Point. I tried to shake it off. Finally, after instructions in Japanese, English, and a few other languages, the car took off—accelerating to sixty-two miles per hour in only two seconds—and then dropped into total darkness. Instantly my whole body came alive, and before I knew it, I was screaming.

> > >

Humans have sophisticated systems of prediction, and when our predictions don't match our experience, it raises a red flag and puts us in a state of uncertainty.* Perhaps the most important are the systems that tell us what to expect from changes in gravitational force: namely, our vestibular system and our proprioception (or our awareness of our body in the space around us). Our brain brings together information from these systems to help us determine things like balance, acceleration, and direction. An incorrect prediction is profoundly disorienting at a visceral level—as when we mistakenly think there is one stair left going into the basement.

Thrill rides mess with these well-designed internal systems, violating our expectations and thumbing their nose at the work of evolution. They take us to speeds we could never run, launch us in the air as though we could fly, take us around turns faster than we could ever survive on our own, and basically confuse the hell out of our bodies. There are very, very few ways we can achieve these sensations naturally—or without some sort of mechanical manipulation. Prior to the innovative and creative thrill rides of the twentieth century, the only ways to feel the sensations caused by acceleration and direction manipulation were accidental, to say the least: being swung back and forth in the mouth of a lion, for instance, or falling down a steep hill, neither of which bodes especially well for our survival. Yet today we've built machines that allow us to experience physical sensations our ancestors couldn't even imagine, just to see what it feels like. The outcome—it can feel great, but it can also leave you begging for the comfort of your safe, warm bed or, worse, dead.

Thanks in part to the research of a former US Air Force officer named John Stapp, we know that the body's ability to tolerate changes in g-force (which is essentially the measure of gravity

---

*Fun fact: this is also why we can't tickle ourselves. Our brain knows what our hands are doing, so there is no surprise. See Sarah-Jayne Blakemore, Daniel Wolpert, and Chris Frith, "Why You Can't Tickle Yourself," *NeuroReport Review* 2 (August 2000).

acting on your body: 1 g being normal, 3 g being the force you'd feel if you were three times as heavy) depends on time, direction, and rate of acceleration. You may be able to take a 100 g punch to the gut that's over in a second, but the longer the duration, the smaller the g-force we can tolerate. Most people start to get uncomfortable past 5 g, which is when some of the real danger kicks in. During rapid changes in acceleration and direction, our blood pressure is significantly affected, which can cause everything from lightheadedness to a "gray-out," where we lose some visual acuity, to blacking out and losing consciousness completely, or even dying. Over the course of Stapp's experimental rides (he took several extreme ones in the name of science, peaking at 46 g), he experienced broken bones, a detached retina, burst blood vessels, and permanently impaired vision.

Human beings were simply not designed for these unnatural experiences, which is why our body essentially freaks out. Moreover, everyone has different levels of tolerance. For some a Ferris wheel is enough to cause nausea, while others leave the 6.3 g Tower of Terror begging for more. The key for designers is to hit that sweet spot between 4 and 6 g with just the right path, height, speed, and time to trigger the sensations without giving us whiplash, making us sick, or putting us in real danger.

> > >

These are the sensations that people talk about the most when they discuss thrill rides: the "dizzy feeling," the "airtime" or "weightlessness," and the "stomach drop." The rides best known for the "dizzy feeling" are the antigravity spinners that confuse our bodies by upsetting our semicircular canal system (part of the vestibular system, it is the intricate and sensitive labyrinth of canals that comprise our inner ear), which is responsible for reporting on our rotational movement. And of course our visual cues are completely disrupted (it's hard to focus when you're spinning). A lot of people really love the dizzy feeling—especially kids who are just beginning to understand how their bodies work. For them it's novel at this time of self-discovery. Who doesn't remember spinning as a child until collapsing on the grass, giggling as the sky spun above you? As we age, however, so does our vestibular system, making it harder to find our balance and thus making that dizzy feeling not so much fun anymore. The loss of control and disorientation can also be hard to tolerate in adulthood. You have to choose to relax and embrace the dizziness, and then maybe you can recapture some of that childhood delight.

I don't hate spinning rides, but the residual feeling of dizziness leaves me feeling unsteady and drunk for a half hour afterwards—it's sometimes just impractical. Turns out that I and those who have poor postural control or balance are more sensitive to dizziness—as I would be reminded more than once during my adventures. I felt this intensely after riding the Eejanaika, which has over fourteen inversions and rotating seats—after that I wasn't sure which way was up for a good five minutes.

Next, there is my favorite thrill ride sensation: the feeling of weightlessness. This happens in those brief but treasured seconds when a ride tips over the apex of a steep hill or begins its decent back down to the ground. In that second we feel weightless—though we're not, of course, since zero g-force is different from zero gravity. On Earth gravity is constant, so it's only through manipulating downward acceleration that we can approximate the feeling of zero gravity. Thrill rides give us a few seconds at best. The Zero G: Weightless Experience Flight gives you a total of 7.5 minutes (in 30-second intervals) for "just" five thousand dollars.

Right before and after the far too fleeting feeling of weightlessness, we experience what everyone calls the "stomach drop" sensation. This is not really a metaphor—it's the literal feeling of gravity acting on your stomach, which sits loosely inside your body. When you are accelerating toward the ground faster than 1 g—for example, when you are dropped 415 feet at 90 miles per hour from the Zumanjaro: Drop of Doom at Six Flags Great Adventure—your stomach is going to feel as if it's in your chest (another common description). When you're being launched forward at 106.9 miles per hour in 1.8 seconds, as on the Dodonpa, it's going to feel as if you left your stomach at the station. The Dodonpa is especially cruel to our systems of prediction and balance, as I learned later that day. There, I waited in the car as the loudspeaker began the countdown, and with each beat my body tensed up, preparing for takeoff. Finally the clock reached zero. Only, nothing happened except for me lurching forward in anticipation. The designers wisely built in a "false start" and an "accidental start," leaving me feeling as if I just threw open a door I thought would weigh a hundred pounds but was instead light as a feather. Since gravity is acting on us all the time, our bodies are calibrated to expect to be constantly pulled to the earth at a steady rate. When that rate is radically adjusted, or not what we predicted or prepared for, our system gets confused and sounds the alarm.

Getting on a ride that shoots you straight up literally results in your insides "dropping" to the floor, or at least as low as they can get. This leaves you feeling all kinds of sensations, some caused by a drop in blood pressure, but mostly because of the signals being sent to your brain via the vagus nerve. The vagus nerve is a mixed bundle of both afferent nerves (they send messages *to* the brain) and efferent nerves (they receive messages *from* the brain) that stretch from your brain all the way to the bottom of your stomach, or lower viscera. The vagus nerve plays a big role in our threat response: it's an umbrella of nerves that alert us that something is wrong by collecting information—for example, the fact that your organs are "floating" around inside your torso, which they are if you're riding the Drop of Doom—and sending the messages to the brain's limbic region, where you process threat. Researchers in Zurich have also found that it plays a central role in our responses to innate fears; when a rat's vagus nerve is severed, it exhibits a lower level of fear of open spaces and bright lights. The human equivalent of this might be a lack of fear while standing right on the edge of the Grand Canyon.

The vagus nerve also works with the parasympathetic system (the rest and digest part of the autonomic nervous system) to lower heart rate and blood pressure. In fact, it also signals changes in the neurotransmitters responsible for making us feel *better*. (Neurotransmitters are chemicals stored inside of neurons, which process and transmit information in our brain through chemical and electronic signals; different stimuli trigger different neurotransmitter responses.) In fact, current research shows that vagus nerve stimulation through an implant that delivers electric pulses may be an effective intervention for people with treatment-resistant depression.* Needless to say, if electric stimulation of the vagus nerve through a surgical implant can help those with depression, just imagine what a roller coaster ride can do for the masses. No wonder people are standing in line four hours for a two-minute thrill.

Not everyone likes these sensations. For example, those who fear flying relate these sensations to the anxiety-inducing feelings that occur during takeoff. For others, the intense g-force can feel like a panic attack, which I can empathize with. It feels the same because it essentially is the same physiologically: panic attacks involve the same systems and symptoms of the threat response— sweating, heart racing, chest pounding, dizziness, and basically feeling you're going to die. It makes sense that someone who has only experienced these sensations in the context of a panic attack wouldn't like them. Lucky for me, I was riding roller coasters long before I started waking up at three in the morning feeling as if I were being crushed by an invisible anvil.

---

*To stimulate the vagus nerve, patients have a pacemaker-like device implanted in their left chest wall with an electrode that wraps around the nerve by the carotid artery in the neck. Electrical impulses are then sent to the electrode that stimulates the nerve, sending signals to the brain. Researchers do not quite understand how vagus nerve stimulation has antidepressant effects. One theory is that it increases activity in regions like the rostral anterior cingulate cortex, which increases emotion regulation and increases parasympathetic response, leaving us more emotionally flexible. Additionally, the stimulation is likely activating changes in neurotransmitters like serotonin, norepinephrine, GABA, and glutamate, which are associated with reducing stress. This is a breakthrough finding for those with drug-resistant depression, but the intervention is raising some eyebrows. Psychosurgery is shrouded in a dark history full of stories of misuse and abuse, most notably the tragic consequences of the thousands of needless lobotomies during the twentieth century (by 1951 twenty thousand lobotomies had been completed). Understandably, any surgical intervention for mental health purposes is met with hesitation and concern from the medical community and others. Questions of whether these measures fundamentally change a person's identity abound, along with the concern over potential manipulation and control over another individual through an artificial implant.

For me, the crushing weight and my racing heart while climbing to the top of a 141-foot hill inside a small car attached to an elaborate metal beast signal not panic but relief. I know that as soon as the car tips over the apex, I'll feel as if I'm flying, weightless and wonderful. This is just one reason I love thrill rides (we also release dopamine, the "feel good" neurotransmitter, in anticipation of doing something rewarding); I never know how long a panic attack will last, but I know when I get on a roller coaster, in two minutes I'll return to the station, feet flat on the ground, feeling good and liberated.

> > >

My screaming came to an abrupt halt after the Takabisha looped through an "inverted top hat" and over two "airtime" hills and slowed to a crawl around a 180-degree corner. I gasped as I saw the track take a 90-degree turn straight up. As the car latched into place, the chain lift began its click-click-click, and soon I was perpendicular to the ground and beginning the upward climb. Fastened tightly into my seat with my back to the ground, I felt heavy and unmovable, like a sack of potatoes (gravity works on our organs separately—we can't feel our organs the way we can our skin, but our nerves pick up different, loose sensations inside of us). The car was silent except for the click-click of the chain lift. Gazing up into the open sky in front of me, I felt the whole world drop away, and I was ready for liftoff.

The anticipation was excruciating as the car slowly climbed the steep hill to the top—where it paused. And the view was incredible: Mount Fuji in the distance against a clear sky, looking back at me with royal wisdom. But that moment didn't last long. My attention was quickly diverted back to the disappearing track in front of me. Because the angle is 121 degrees, you cannot see the track as it curves back against itself. This is terrifying; it looks as though the car will unlatch from the track and go plummeting to the ground, scattering its passengers into the air like the sacks of potatoes we were.

As the car inched forward over the peak, my legs started shaking uncontrollably, and I kept repeating, "Oh my God. Oh my God. Oh my God." Suspended in midair, 141 feet high, I could feel every muscle in my body wrap forcefully around my bones as I braced against the restraints, preparing for the eventual drop. Even my teeth were clenched. I forced my tightly curled fists over my head and extended my arms as far as I could (it really does make it more intense!). Finally, the car tipped over the apex and dove toward the ground. I started screaming louder than I ever have before, as tears streamed down my face.

> > >

There's something freeing, and even a little bit dangerous, in screaming as loud as you want. Screaming is part of our evolved survivor tool kit, protecting us by scaring away predators and alerting others of danger nearby. Pulling our face into a scream is also believed to make us more alert, intensifying our threat response (just as squinching our nose in disgust blocks foul odors from going into our nostrils). Adam Anderson at the University of Toronto found that when people make a frightened expression, they increase their range of vision and have faster eye movements and a heightened sense of smell from breathing more rapidly through their nostrils. Not to mention, when we scream, our eyes widen, and we show our teeth, making us appear all the more intimidating and frightening to any predators.

Screaming, whether it be a small shriek or a loud long wail, happens instinctually when we're stressed, but it's hardly a socially acceptable response outside of the proper context—on a thrill ride, in a haunted house, or when we're in real danger. As a controlled or policed behavior, screaming (while safe) can make you feel a little rebellious. How many of us have thought about unleashing a rebel yell in the middle of church, class, or a never-ending business meeting? For those of us who resist that impulse on a daily basis, the opportunity to really let loose can be cathartic, especially for people with impulse control problems like attention deficit hyperactivity disorder (ADHD). The anxiety, attention, and focus required in trying *not* to do something can feel exhausting. Thrilling activities provide a safe space to give our internal impulse-control police a break (and for those who believe screaming and being scared are signs of weakness, being in a situation in which it is OK to express fear can feel pretty good).

Others describe it as a way to release "bottled-up emotions." The concept of bottled-up emotions is standard in Western societies: whether people talk about going out to "blow off some steam" or "unlatch the floodgates," the idea that our bodies somehow store emotions is widely popular. While it's tempting to think there is some reservoir inside us full of pain, or sadness, or happiness, it's just not the case. Rather, we experience emotions in the moments following different chemical responses triggered by stimuli (which can be anything from a memory to a real live bear). In this case, the tears streaming down my face as I turned the apex were a result of irritation and dryness from the wind, triggering my reflex and basal tears, and a result of a high arousal response, triggering what are called the "psychic" tears associated with strong emotion. (Yes, there are three types of tears.) But even though bottled emotions are not a physiological reality, the concept can be meaningful. Perception and meaning making are everything—so if you *believe* that by screaming your head off or crying your eyes out you'll release some bottled-up emotions, you'll feel better.*

> ▸ ▸ ▸

As I flipped and twisted through the final loops of the Takabisha, I let myself scream and laugh with abandon, no self-policing needed. All feelings of sadness, self-consciousness, and embarrassment were gone. My body was tingling all over as I came to a stop in the station, but I felt as if I were still moving. All I wanted was to stay in my seat and ride again. I also wasn't sure I could stand; my legs had already started to relax—this sack of potatoes was now mashed. But I still felt full of energy, slightly flushed, and excited.

All too quickly, the friendly attendants were escorting me to the exit. I let out a large sigh and looked back at the coaster

---

*Important side note: Primal scream therapy, which is screaming loudly while reliving traumatic experiences, has been discredited by psychologists and is *not* an effective or recommended treatment for trauma or mental health. In fact it can do more harm through further associating high arousal states with negative memories.

stretching into the sky in awe of the intelligence, time, energy, labor, and $32 million that went into building a two-minute ride that people will wait in line for four hours to experience.

The rest of the day I ran from ride to ride and even went through the longest haunt in Japan (and second longest in the world in 2014), the Super Scary Labyrinth of Fear, aka the Haunted Hospital. Admittedly my enthusiasm waned each time I turned around to share an "Oh my God, that was so cool" moment, only to remember I was there alone. It wasn't that I felt sorry for myself; I was constantly reflecting on how lucky and privileged I was to be there. And I'm not one to shy away from doing things on my own—quite the opposite. What I was feeling was a longing to share, a desire to express the thrill I was feeling to someone I cared about. Sharing feels good (literally: dopamine is released in our brain when we share), and as mentioned above, our emotions are intensified when they are experienced in the presence of others, especially close friends. James Coan, director of the Virginia Affective Neuroscience Laboratory and author of *The Handbook of Emotion Elicitation and Assessment*, offers an explanation for my sad state; basically when we do evolutionarily salient activities (things that activate fight or flight, or that influence our survival) by ourselves we find them less rewarding. We have evolved to be together, especially in times of stress. But, I tried to focus on the upside: I had never spent a full day on thrill rides by myself, so now I could compare it to the many experiences of going with friends. I'm confident to say now, while I felt the most intense thrilling sensations ever at Fuji-Q, I know it would have been even more fun with friends. Still, I left the park that day on an incredible high.

It was a pretty remarkable thing to have my day so profoundly altered by actions that took no more than a couple of minutes. What would life be like if I could start every day riding a thrill ride? And I had to wonder what it would be like to experience the same sensations, but for a longer period—an hour, say, or more. Could a thrill like that elevate your mood for longer? A week? A month? The next stop on my journey would help answer that very question.

2

ACROPHOBIA

CN Tower EdgeWalk. Photo courtesy of CN Tower.

The CN Tower EdgeWalk in Toronto is perhaps the single worst place on Earth if you are scared of heights. I say "perhaps" only because the description "on Earth" is debatable: only a few thousand square feet of this communications tower are actually physically attached to planet Earth; the rest is a thin spire extending more than a thousand feet into the air. The EdgeWalk, billed by the Guinness World Records as the world's highest external walk on a building, takes guests outside of the observation deck so they can walk the circumference of the Tower on a five-foot-wide, metal-grate walkway. Guests are strapped to the side of the Tower with a harness and trolley system so they can walk and lean over the side, hands free. There is no guardrail.

The solid concrete 1,815.4-foot-tall CN Tower opened its doors in 1976. From a distance it looks like a cross between the Seattle Space Needle and a giant light saber, especially at night, when it is fully lit. It has broken numerous world records and received many notable awards: it held the title for tallest free-standing structure in the world from 1976 to 2010, when it was surpassed by Dubai's Burj Khalifa skyscraper and China's Canton Tower. Today it remains the tallest in the Western Hemisphere. The CN Tower is also listed as one of the Seven Wonders of the World by the American Society of Civil Engineers and quickly became a symbol of pride for Canada. Today it is primarily known as a tourist attraction, with over two million visitors a year, but the tower continues to broadcast over thirty regional television stations and FM radio stations, and to act as a wireless paging and cellular tower. The EdgeWalk, which is 1,168 feet high (116 stories), opened in 2011 in celebration of the tower's thirty-fifth anniversary.

Today, standing on a tiny catwalk in the middle of the sky is just one of many atypical vacation ideas available to tourists. There is also volcano boarding, train surfing (running on top of a moving train), AirKicking (being launched from a human catapult), Zorbing (throwing yourself down a hill in a giant ball), and slacklining (walking a tightrope that is not actually tight). Lately it seems that thrilling experiences have become a major component of attracting tourists to otherwise tame destinations. Yes, luxurious hotels, all-you-can-eat buffets, and clear blue water still have their appeal, but people in the twenty-first century want a hands-on experience. Museums, historical sites, and national landmarks are increasingly incorporating activities that turn a passive observer into an active participant. These days you don't just observe from the edge of the Grand Canyon. You stand over the middle of the Colorado River on a transparent bridge and stare it down.* How did we become so daring in the face of a threat that will surely kill us?

---

*In October 2014 the Eiffel Tower opened its own glass floor at 187 feet up.

> > >

A full 100 percent of humans experience height-related physical symptoms. We are, after all, humans and not birds. Even Greek, Roman, and Chinese antiquity is full of descriptions of the consequences of heights like poor eyesight, dizziness, and, as the Greek Corpus Hippocraticum of the fifth century BCE describes it, "a slackening of the muscles of the entire body." A healthy fear of heights is normal—we can't fly! But that hasn't stopped us from finding inventive ways to challenge our fear and for a moment feel what it's like to soar through the clouds like an eagle.

People have been jumping out and hanging off tall structures for thousands of years. In fact the use of parachutes dates back to twelfth-century China. For as long as the villagers can remember ("many, many centuries"), men on the Pentecost Island in Vanuatu would jump headfirst from tall wooden platforms with vines tied around their ankles.* The Aztecs similarly practiced the Danza de los Voladores (Dance of the Flyers), or Palo Volador (Pole Flying), which involves climbing to the top of a pole and carrying out a ritual of song and dance.

In the United States the general popultion first became aware of the thrill of playing with heights while watching "barnstormers," who would parachute into the crowd during air shows beginning in the 1920s. By the late 1960s skydiving, a term coined by Raymond Young in the '50s, was a commercial business in which citizens could get trained and certified and jump out of planes for fun. Today millions of successful free-fall jumps have been completed—from base jumping off of tall buildings and cliffs to Felix Baumgartner's record-breaking highest and fastest jump from 128,000 feet on October 14, 2012.

Despite the perception that skydiving is one of the most dangerous and reckless activities a person can do, the truth is that it is incredibly safe, as long as you're working with professionals, of

---

*This practice stems from a legend passed down for many centuries and is the forerunner of bungee jumping. The practice is still popular today and has now become a tourist attraction.

course. There were 3.2 million jumps in 2013 and 24 fatalities. That's about .00075 fatalities per 1,000 jumps, and for tandem jumps it is .003 per 1,000. We're more likely to die from suicide, drowning, electrocution, asteroid impact, lightning strike, or legal execution.

Then there is bungee jumping, another outgrowth of ancient traditions turned into thrills. Modern-day bungee jumping began in 1979 at the Clifton Suspension Bridge in Bristol, England. The jump was carried out by members of the Oxford University Dangerous Sports Club.* Their jumps caught the attention of the media, which televised their dangerous sports and exposed an entire population to a brand-new thrilling experience. Soon bungee jumping, paragliding, zip lines, rope swings, and other fear-inducing height challenges were popping up around the globe.† Since the first modern jump in 1979, the public has completed several *million* successful jumps in lots of new inventive ways—including the new popular practice of bungee jumping from a hot air balloon and then skydiving down to the ground. Some even further combine this with snowboarding down the mountain on which they landed.

❯ ❯ ❯

I thought that the EdgeWalk would be one of my least challenging adventures. After all I'm not acrophobic, which is having a pathological fear of heights (meaning the fear is such that it significantly disrupts a person's ability to function) and affects about 3 to 5 percent of the population. I'm not even among the 28 percent of the population that experiences what psychologists call a "visual height intolerance," meaning the image of tall buildings, bridges, or cliffs leaves them with a feeling of uneasiness and distress. They might avoid heights, but it's not interrupting their ability to function. I had been rappelling, rock climbing both indoors

*The jumpers were arrested but continued to jump from iconic bridges and locations across the globe, including the Golden Gate Bridge and the Royal Gorge Bridges.

†The most successful commercial height-defeating enterprise was opened by A. J. Hackett in Queenstown, New Zealand, in the 1980s. He has locations around the globe.

and out, and done my fair share of climbing trees as a child, so I felt confident about my resolve in the face of heights. I was far more nervous about my skydiving adventure happening later in the year. Surprisingly, that adventure turned out to be nothing but pure joy and bliss—there was no fear whatsoever—which is why this chapter is about the CN Tower. As it turns out, it is one thing to be calm in the limbs of a tall tree and another thing entirely to hang by a harness off the side of a 116-story building.

> > >

Upon arriving, I stopped at the base of the tower and stared straight up to try to appreciate its enormity, which immediately made me dizzy (the first of many unexpected physical sensations). Even as I held on to a bench to steady myself, I couldn't stop looking up. This was a transfixing experience, but my reverie was soon interrupted by something I hadn't anticipated: the bustle of dozens of little kids around my legs. The entrance to the tower was a madhouse, and there were families with strollers and rowdy kids everywhere I went. I don't have any social phobias, and big crowds do not generally bother me, but there was something about the juxtaposition of this enormous, grand tower with the sound of kids crying and screaming (I'm sure they were laughing too, but I didn't hear it) that made me release an involuntary and very audible "UGH."

Usually experiencing a sensation of awe, as most people do while standing at the base of a massive structure or, say, a mountain, leads to more prosocial behavior. Dachner Keltner, codirector of the Greater Good Science Center at the University of California, Berkeley, has found that awe-inspiring moments lead to people reporting more feelings of modesty and humbleness, and even result in helping others. This was not my experience; instead I was frustrated and anxious and in no shape to deal with crying kids. In context, this makes sense: my brain was shifting focus to the thing that I was afraid of, so emotional regulation became a big challenge. Psychologist Candace Raio and colleagues recently confirmed that even after lots of practice with successful emotional regulation in the lab, most people are unable to bring those skills of acceptance and reappraisal, or telling yourself that something stressful actually isn't, to real-life fear-inducing situations (but it's not impossible). The next time someone tells you they are stressed out and it's not a good time to talk, listen to them.

I hastily searched out the EdgeWalk entrance and retreated into a cozy locker room protected from the crowds behind floor-to-ceiling glass walls. There I met the group of five I would be joining on the walk—all speaking French and talking among themselves.

At this point, our tour group was joined by two guides—Margot, who would be our guide on the edge, and Chris, who would run the prewalk orientation. They had control of the room from the moment they entered. They used a number of subtle but effective little tricks that are taught to many public authorities, like doctors, police, and flight attendants: for example, walking in tall, with assertive body posture; using a loud but friendly tone of voice; and even adjusting sentence structure. The guides were obviously trained in these methods as well. They didn't ask everyone to gather round in a circle to listen but rather stated loudly and cheerfully, "Everyone gather round. We're going to tell you how this works." They didn't ask, "Would you mind stepping over here?" but instead placed their hands on our shoulders and said, "Now stand over here." Their instructions were not invitations but commands couched in a smile. I had agreed to this experience (after reading and signing a very long waiver) and turned my safety, indeed my life, over to their hands. I would see this approach again in a few months when I went skydiving—a perfect balance of authority and congeniality that was essential for any situation that requires unwavering compliance.* If someone

---

*Over the course of my adventures I'd been pushed, pulled, and manhandled in just about every way imaginable (and signed at least seven waivers excusing businesses in the case of death). By the CN Tower guides, thrill ride attendants, and haunted house actors I'd basically been treated like a ventriloquist doll. Getting over this loss of personal control was an adventure in and of itself, and taught me a powerful lesson about the importance of control and consent. But I wanted to challenge myself and do all the things I had planned. So by the time my skydiving tandem jump partner grabbed me, lifted me onto his lap, and wrapped his arms around me in front of an open door at three thousand feet in the air, well, let's just say my anxiety around stranger danger was the last thing on my mind.

doesn't follow instructions on the ground, they're not going to follow them in the sky, and it's better to find that out sooner rather than later. No matter how strong your cables and harnesses are, you have to know whom you're dealing with. People do irrational things when they're scared.

> > >

The first safety check, while unexpected, confirmed that irrational behavior was a concern: we all had to pass a breathalyzer test. And the next check was a complete surprise: they swabbed our clothes for explosives. I wanted to ask if this protocol was reactive. Had someone tried to strap themselves with explosives and blow up the CN Tower? But I didn't want to raise suspicion just by asking: these guides had a grip on me just like cops or border security. Next we had to take off nearly everything except our pants and shirts and stand feet and arms apart while they scanned us with a handheld metal detector.

Standing there in a circle feeling vulnerable and exposed with strangers, I started imagining all sorts of awful things, like people going up with knives in their pockets with murderous or suicidal intentions. I couldn't tell if it was on purpose or not, but my guides were confirming the fact that we were about to do something seriously dangerous and very scary. My stress level was rising.

We stepped into orange jumpsuits, clicked on our harnesses, and then loaded into a tiny elevator packed to the gills. Being in an elevator in a fifteen-story office building is a breeze, one of those modern inventions we now take for granted. Taking an 1,100-foot ride in a tin can full of French-speaking strangers all dressed like prisoners: that is different. The suits were hot, the space was tight, and my ears kept popping. I tried to stare down through the scuffed glass on the bottom of the elevator at the quickly disappearing ground and felt my stomach turn. I decided it was best to just close my eyes and *not* think about getting stuck, which of course didn't work thanks to a very efficient part of our brain called the hippocampus.

One of the ways our brain determines if a situation is really threatening is by retrieving information via our hippocampus of every previous experience we've had with similar conditions. We remember scary and exciting events, often called "flashbulb memories," really well because the chemicals and hormones that are released when we're aroused, as during fight or flight, work to make the moment stick in our brains. That way we'll remember who and what we're supposed to fear (or love), so we know to avoid (or get closer) next time. The hippocampus is amazing. Imagine a never-ending, multicompartment, U-shaped filing cabinet with a very smart filing clerk who knows how to store memories and when to retrieve them. The hippocampus can, within milliseconds and outside our conscious awareness, begin calling up memories triggered by a sight, sound, smell, location, or action associated with a previous experience. The hippocampus has a strong connection to our amygdala, and together they create a feedback loop of memory, sparking a feeling that brings up another memory, and on and on. Maybe you get the shivers every time you walk by the alley where your friend was mugged, or you tense at the smell of gasoline, knowing the chainsaw-wielding maniac is on his way. Or maybe, like me, you tense up the moment you walk into an elevator, anticipating the worst.

When I closed my eyes on the CN Tower elevator, I was transported back to the time I was once trapped between floors of the Veterans Hospital in Pittsburgh. It had never been something I'd expected to fear, but the reality of being inside a sterile steel box for an indefinite period of time triggered serious panicking. I did some pacing as my breaths became short and rapid—even a few minutes is a long time if you don't know when it will end. After pushing the "Emergency Call" button for the tenth time with no response, I stopped myself, took deep breaths, and told myself to relax. I was on an unplanned break, so I might as well have a seat and put my feet up. This worked—until I was actually rescued. Ironically it was as the doors were pried open that debilitating fear overpowered my sly mental manipulation.

The maintenance men had wedged open a two-foot gap, revealing that I was four feet below the nearest floor, meaning I had to jump up to crawl out of the elevator. The man held out his hand and said, "Come on," but all I could see was his arm being severed at the shoulder as the elevator crashed to the ground floor. I hadn't thought much about the elevator cable snapping until that moment—after that, visions of dismemberment, decapitation, and death froze me in my place. After lots of self-talk and friendly coaxing that turned to stern requests from my rescuer, I made the jump. Still today I imagine what it would be like to be stuck on every elevator I ride. With the EdgeWalk being 116 stories up, I had a lot of time to think.

⸭ ⸭ ⸭

When the doors finally opened, I walked onto what seemed like a sci-fi movie set: white metal grating for a floor; ropes, chains, and harnesses hanging from the ceiling; multiple computers with large flat-screen monitors against the wall; and an opening at the top of a metal ramp through which nothing was visible but endless blue sky. I kept expecting to see a UFO or at least Harrison Ford. We stood in line against the wall and were hooked up to ropes and harnesses and carabiners, like the human puppets we more or less were. *What if the trolley track cracks?* I wondered. *What if the harness breaks?* I walked myself through every potential fail point, which was meaningless—either I was going to walk out there, or I wasn't; either I trusted the guides, or I didn't. I decided I did, and then we stepped out of the building and entered the sky.

Good-bye, detached analytical sociologist, who is writing a book about fear. Hello, primal self. I could see straight through the five-foot-wide metal grate beneath my feet, and the square gaps in it must have been at least six by four inches—definitely big enough for a child's foot to slip through. I—well, my body—decided to stop moving, permanently. I couldn't stop staring down at what looked like flecks of pepper moving around below me: people on the sidewalk. "Oh my God," I said in a whisper. I stopped breathing. Margot was talking about something, but I had no idea what. I felt altitude pressure on my temples, and I could hear and feel my blood rushing and my heart beating—the way it does after a thirty-second, all-out sprint. Everything outside my body sounded muted, as though I were under water.

The wind was blowing hard, and I had to squint my eyes, but I couldn't focus on anything anyway. I wanted to move my hands to protect my face, but I was too scared to take them off the lead rope. I felt dizzy and disoriented, but I wasn't flipping and flying around the tracks of a roller coaster. I was frozen in place.

These are all symptoms related to the fight or flight response, but also vertigo—which can happen when the distance between the observer and the closest stationary object is too far away to use as a reference point to maintain balance. (I'd actually experienced it in miniature when I'd been on the ground while looking up.) Vertigo occurs more often with people who have poor postural control, which is basically our ability to keep our balance and synch up information about the environment with our internal systems. If you have poor postural control (as I evidently do, at least when I'm standing on a metal donut 1,168 feet off the ground), you rely more on visual cues to determine balance, so when a visual cue is not available, your internal system gets confused, to say the least. This is why I was fine 30 feet up in a tree as a child but totally out of my mind (and there is a good reason for that expression) at 1,168 feet in the air.

I stood unmoving on the grate, feeling as if I had forgotten how to walk while at the same time fighting a strong urge to start running. My fight or flight response was in full "go" mode. When the body goes into fight or flight, the sympathetic branch of the automatic nervous system—which controls all of our essential living systems, like breathing, heart rate, digestion, and even sexual arousal—reacts by releasing a cascade of chemicals. The sympathetic nervous system responds immediately, sometimes without our conscious awareness of what we're responding to, and releases the "go" hormones in the fight or flight, including adrenaline, or epinephrine and norepinephrine, which are secreted by the adrenal gland (norepinephrine is also released into the spinal cord to decrease any pain). The result is our body going into overdrive. Cortisol, another stress hormone, is released in the body to turn fatty acids into energy and deliver it to our muscles, making them ready for any kind of immediate action. Our blood pressure increases so that oxygen and glucose can be distributed through the body. Other effects are a temporary loss of hearing and tunnel vision. All of this happens in an effort to focus attention on survival, turning our bodies into a ready-to-go strong and powerful machine.

I definitely felt that my body was in "go" mode, but I was not feeling like a powerful machine. My legs were shaking uncontrollably; usually when this happens, I'm strapped into a thrill ride and don't need to worry about supporting myself, especially since those rides normally last about two minutes. This was totally new. I tried to get myself together, but I couldn't pay attention to what Margot was saying. My thought processing had stopped, which is also part of our body's attempt to focus our attention on survival. Our executive functioning, namely our prefrontal cortex, which is responsible for rational and logical decision making, takes a backseat to the lower, more primal, "older" animal part of our brain. It's hard to think when we're scared (a lesson I would learn all too well over and over again). I felt very strange sensations through my body, like waves of heat passing through me.

Then I noticed something quite unexpected: I had peed my pants. Or, at least, I thought I had. I know lots of people pee themselves when they are scared, but the reason this happens has been the subject of much debate. The sympathetic nervous system does inhibit or shut down digestion to redirect blood flow to our muscles, but that doesn't necessarily result in relaxing our bladders. The parasympathetic system, which comes in to counterbalance the sympathetic, does regulate the rest and digest; however, that also doesn't necessarily result in peeing yourself. What is likely happening is that we're simply too scared to remember that we should "hold it." Our prefrontal cortex is responsible for sending signals that allow us to control when we urinate, but as mentioned above, when we're scared, communication from our thinking brain doesn't always get through.

I had seen the consequences of this many times at the haunted house, when people would come out with wet pants, and I would say, "That would never happen to me. How embarrassing." Now it appeared that it was my turn, but as I stood frozen in fear on the EdgeWalk, it was hard to know if I really had peed myself: I could not distinguish wet from dry, hot from cold, and, at that point, up from down. My whole body was on fire with the overwhelming rush of blood that felt even more intense against the blustering wind. I wanted to reach down and check for a wet spot, but no way on earth was I letting go of that harness. And every time I tried to look at my jumpsuit I looked straight past my own legs and stared at the ground.

The humiliation and frustration of the situation suddenly became the only thing I could think about. This is actually an amazing bit of human psychology—the psychological and chemical responses associated with different emotional states can work against each other, but usually in an adaptive way. Emotional responses recruit, or use, the same brain structures—and sometimes in opposite directions. For example, Peter de Jong and colleagues found arousal can cancel out or diminish a feeling of disgust (just take a second to think about that in the context of sex—yeah). The "warm glow" of compassion (connected to dopamine and serotonin) is diminished by the feeling of hopelessness and helplessness. And when I was stuck on the elevator at the VA, it was the thought of distressing and frustrating the very person who came to save me that finally pushed me to "get over myself."

Paul Slovic recently observed this phenomenon in a study: he showed that people are willing to give money for one child suffering, but not hundreds of children. One child makes us feel good, as if we're making a difference, but when we find out the need is great, that makes us feel helpless. The winner of this emotional battle should be whichever reaction aids in our survival and is most efficient. Today, when our survival depends more on social connections than on our ability to survive a bear attack, it is no wonder that public shame and social phobias, more than precipitous falls to our death, take the lead in most fear-provoking situations.* Believing I had peed my pants made me feel embarrassed, and that became my number one focus that helped bring my thinking brain back online. Eventually, I was able to look down

---

*Generalized anxiety disorder and social phobias are the most prevalent in the United States, according to the National Institute of Mental Health.

to see blessedly dry pants. As I said, people act irrationally when they're scared.

At the urging of Margot, I turned around, my back to the open air, and focused on my own harness and the building right in front of me. I took a couple of deep breaths and told myself to be brave and not to look down. As I turned around, the reward was a breathtaking view. We had come out on the southeast side of the tower, and in front of me I saw the green water of Lake Ontario against the perfectly clear blue sky, lots of big fluffy clouds, and—I swear—the curve of the Earth.

But back to work. Margot instructed us that it was time to circle the tower and do what she called "stunts." The first one involved turning around with my back to the sky (this word seemed less scary to me than "ground," but that's all a matter of opinion, I suppose) and squatting down until the rope and harness were fully supporting my weight. Basically I would be sitting over the side of the tower. I put my legs hip-width apart and took a seat into my harness—still on top of the catwalk—but quickly stopped, since it felt as if I were slipping out. (Margot promised this was normal, which allowed me to relax very, very, very slightly and then press on with the stunt.) I took tiny steps backwards on my shaking legs, stopping to close my eyes and trying not to faint. Next I pushed myself backwards until my heels were over the edge and the arches of my feet were against the metal grate. Everything in my body was telling me this was a bad idea. "Oh my God," I muttered.

I looked down and took a breath and kept pushing out until my entire body was hanging by a rope 116 stories off the ground. I slowly straightened my legs until they were at a 90-degree angle to my torso and momentarily took my hands off the rope, before hurriedly putting them back—I wasn't ready for that yet.

This was truly the most terrifying experience I had ever had (and still is to date when it comes to physical thrills), yet when Margot asked if I wanted to stay out over the edge, I heard the word "yes" come out of my mouth, but I don't remember saying it. Later, watching video of this moment, I saw that I had a huge smile on my face.

I hazarded another look down. There was the Steam Whistle Brewing Company, located inside a very large old train station. An antique train was set up on an old set of tracks in the oval-shaped yard, which from the distance looked like a child's toy. I moved my gaze down farther and focused on the Rodgers Center, an 11.5-acre baseball stadium and home to the world's first fully retractable roof. The roof itself rises to 282 feet (thirty-one stories), and yet from the top of the tower it looked like a small, round marshmallow. I shifted my gaze to the right and looked down over Ripley's Aquarium of Canada, which has a large shark painted on the roof. As soon as I saw it, I thought of my rope snapping and falling into the mouth of the shark and felt a wave of heat rush through my body again. I've never been that afraid of sharks in my life.*

We stepped a quarter of the way around the tower and performed our next stunt: leaning out from the tower, face first. About fifteen minutes had passed, and I was beginning to feel comfortable on the edge, but just thinking about leaning face first made me regress right back into lizard brain mode. Each of our group members approached this task a little bit differently. Some took tiny baby steps, refusing to look beyond their feet. Others confidently walked to the edge, then stopped, and slowly lowered themselves. I wanted to run to the edge and throw myself over just as the woman beside me had, but I found myself taking baby steps again in a waddling fashion, as though I couldn't bend my knees. I forced my feet about four inches away from the edge, but that was as far as I could go. I desperately tried to remember the instructions, my hands gripping the rope tightly as I pushed it in front of me. I kept reminding myself that the harness could hold hundreds of pounds and the cables over fifteen thousand pounds, so there was no way I was going anywhere. Finally I was able to

---

*Another fun fact: our amygdala responds strongly to images of upside-down triangles—in other words, shark teeth. Christine Larson, Joel Aronoff, Issidoros Sarinopoulous, and David C. Zhu reported in their study "Recognizing Threat: A Simple Geometric Shape Activates Neural Circuitry for Threat Detection" (*Journal of Cognitive Neuroscience* 21, 8 [2008]: 1523–1535) that even a simple, context-free, downward-pointing V can trigger the threat centers in our brain.

fully lean out over the edge and allow the rope to hold me for more than two seconds. Leaning out, I slowly raised my heels so only my toes were gripping the metal grate. Margot was impressed when I tried this, but it wasn't an act of bravery; I just wanted to try to follow the directions exactly so I wouldn't die. I had missed the part about the tiptoes being for the "extra adventurous."

I looked down and let myself relax into the harness, which turned out to be a terrible idea. I immediately lost my footing on the grate and felt myself falling forward. Just like my visions of decapitation in the elevator, I saw myself hitting the metal ledge, which (obviously) would cut the rope and send me hurtling toward downtown Toronto. I felt my stomach drop as though I were on a roller coaster and then a hot wave pass through me as I jumped back. This same progression happened every time I thought of falling. I told myself to stop it. Thinking about falling made me feel as if I were actually falling, and as long as I didn't imagine falling, I felt safe (the brain is incredible). I walked to the edge again, leaned out, and looked down. I watched all the tiny pepper spots walking around; I looked up and out at the buildings in front of me; I held my arm out in my best Supergirl pose. I wasn't falling; I was flying, and I felt powerful.

We walked another quarter turn around the tower to the north side. All of Toronto was at my feet. I felt as if I were hovering over a map of the city. We could see the bustling streets of Chinatown and some very large and impressive buildings I completely forgot the names of, but they were beautiful. This time we would do the same stunt as before, but instead of facing out we would have to turn our backs against the ground and lean straight back, rather than bending at the waist like the first stunt. It was a bit like a trust fall, though with a *lot* more trust and, one hopes, a lot less fall. I was getting more comfortable, but it was still a challenge to look down and walk backwards to the edge and hang my heels over the side. It felt like a constant battle between my thinking brain and some primal animal self hiding inside me. But once I looked up and leaned back, it was easy enough to pretend I was only five feet above the ground. I fully extended my arms and legs, leaned all the way back, and looked up at the sky. The whole group did this at the same time, and we let out a big "YEAH!" It was pure exhilaration, and today when I'm feeling stressed or vulnerable, I remember that moment.

By the time we reached the south side of the tower, about forty minutes since that first step, I felt at ease. I leaned forward over the edge and stared out into the distance, listening to the blowing wind. I closed my eyes. Epinephrine and norepinephrine (aka adrenaline) have a reputation for being a part of moments like this: the feeling of energy and thrill. But those are not the chemicals responsible for what I was feeling at that moment (also any adrenaline in the blood and body is not going to affect our mood, since the blood is toxic to neurons in the brain). I was in a calm, almost trancelike state thanks to my parasympathetic system and the other chemicals involved in fight or flight—namely, cortisol, which works to decrease stress; endorphins dopamine, serotonin, and endocannabinoid; and what's known as the love hormone, oxytocin.

These are just some of the chemicals researchers have identified in creating a general sense of well-being that I'll come back to over the course of my adventures. But our brain is complex: it would be nice to say that chemical x = feeling y, except it is so much more complicated than that. Here are the basics: Dopamine contributes to the warm fuzzy feeling we get when we know we're about to do something we enjoy, like eating good food or having pleasurable sex. Researchers like David Zald and colleagues have found those who have especially efficient dopamine systems tend to be more thrill seeking—they get an extra feel-good kick. Oxytocin is the hormone that bonds mother and child after birth, but it also plays a role in the fight or flight response by making us feel closer to those we consider safe and stay farther away from those we consider a threat. Serotonin is the neurotransmitter researchers have linked to mood, social behavior, appetite, and sleep. Similar to the hype around mirror neurons, serotonin was celebrated as the key to happiness in the '80s, and selective serotonin reuptake inhibitors (such as Prozac, which works by increasing the amount of serotonin available in the brain) were believed to be the miracle happy pill. With over two decades of research behind us, and lots of evidence showing SSRIs do not in fact make everyone happy, scientists now have more questions than ever (which is always a good thing in science). As Judy Cameron, a professor in the Psychiatry Department at the University of Pittsburgh, told me in jest, "We knew more about serotonin twenty years ago than we do today."

And then there are endorphins. The name "endorphin" comes from "endo," meaning endogenous or originating inside the body, and "orphin," meaning "like morphine"—literally a morphine-like substance originating from within the body. These endogenous opioids are released during times of pain and pleasure, and they work similar to opioid drugs like codeine, hydrocodone, and opium, in that they can produce a feeling of well-being.

The story on endorphins is actually a lot more complicated than most people think, and worthy of a bit more attention simply to clear up the misconceptions. For one thing, there are about forty types of endorphins, just as there are many types of dopamine, serotonin, and so forth. They are organized into three different categories: endorphins, enkephalins (these are found in our tears), and dynorphins. All three bind to opioid receptors in the brain and work to decrease our pain by blocking our cells from sending pain signals (that's one of the reasons why you're begging your coach to return to play while your knee continues to swell). But only endorphins and enkephalins bind to certain opioid receptors (mu and delta) that produce the sense of euphoria everyone craves. Another system that works to make us feel relaxed and at ease is our endocannabinoid system—basically our body's version of tetrahydrocannabinol, the main psychoactive component in cannabis. Science is finally taking a closer look and showing what pot smokers across the world have known for years, namely that cannabinoids help produce a relaxed state by decreasing our experience of pain through binding to our nociceptors (pain-processing receptors). But, as with all systems, individuals vary in how efficiently their bodies produce and use these chemicals.

Leaning over the edge, I opened my eyes, looked out over the water, and felt a comforting warmth (not like the warmth I felt when I thought I'd peed my pants). All the mental chatter in my brain had stopped, and I felt an overwhelming sense of peace and calm. I was so completely relaxed I didn't hear Margot say it was time to go back in.

❧ ❧ ❧

The ride back down in the elevator wasn't so bad this time. My ears were popping, but I didn't care. I felt euphoric, and I could tell everyone from my group did as well, as they screamed and laughed.

The EdgeWalk was an experience like no other. If you can imagine a roller coaster that is forty minutes long, that may come close to the thrill, but that's just one part of it. The walk took my body to the high arousal state of the threat response, just like a roller coaster, but instead of having only two minutes, I had forty unforgettable minutes to turn my attention inward and experience the physical sensations. I was able to push through the overwhelming messages coming from my limbic system and have a conversation with my body, to see how it responded when I had various thoughts or attempted different stunts. I was able to engage in what is called "focused interoception," which is an awareness of how our body *feels* physiologically. The brain structure largely responsible for this awareness is the insular cortex, which is involved in maintaining internal homeostasis; it allows us to be aware of sensations like pain, itches, temperature, sensual touch, muscular and visceral sensations, hunger, thirst, and even air. It is what allows us to experience a sense of self, to know that we are in fact a person with a whole internal life. The anterior insular cortex is so strongly connected to what is happening in our body, via direct reciprocal connections to our amygdala and thalamus, that it is central to our emotional experiences. In fact, as Bud Craig points out, the anterior insular cortex is implicated in everything from orgasms to decision making and those "eureka" moments of sudden insight.

People who meditate are familiar with this practice of "bringing awareness to the body," when you pay attention to your heart rate, your breathing, and your physical sensations. But because most thrilling experiences happen so quickly, there isn't a lot of time to stop and think about how your body is feeling in such a high arousal state (or in the case of a legitimately threatening situation, this is not a priority). The CN Tower offered a unique opportunity to do just that. I became aware of my own threat response, got in touch with my body, and was then able to challenge myself, making the payoff of confidence all the more rewarding. I wasn't strapped into a coaster car and along for the ride, and while Margot encouraged me, I was the one who had to move my body to the edge.

I was literally and figuratively on top of the world and feeling like Wonder Woman, so when a friend asked me afterwards, "OK, now what?" I said, "Anything. I can do absolutely anything." As soon as I said that, I knew what I had to do next. It was time to give my body a break from the physical thrills and start to scare myself from the inside out.

PART II
PSYCHOLOGICAL CHILLS

After this I call to mind flatness and dampness; and then all is madness—the madness of a memory which busies itself among forbidden things.

—Edgar Allan Poe

3

ALONE IN THE DARK

Eastern State Penitentiary. Photo by the author.

Some places are scarier than others, and it's not hard to agree on which are which. When I ask my students to name scary places, they rattle off a predictable list: prisons, asylums, old places, abandoned places, places with a history of crime and murder. But one common factor stands out among the locales where many horror movies, TV shows, and paranormal investigations are set: confinement. Places you can't leave are the sites of countless episodes of *Ghost Hunters* and *Fear Factor*, as well as major motion pictures like *Twelve Monkeys*, *Session 9*, *Hellraiser II*, and *Shutter Island*. Apart from providing a convenient way to keep a story's main characters from fleeing, these places are also what sociologists call "total institutions," places that isolate people, usually without their consent. There are several types of total institutions, categorized by famed sociologist Erving Goffman: places that care for those who can't care for themselves or are a danger to themselves and others, like nursing homes and psychiatric hospitals; places that confine criminals, like jails and penitentiaries; and voluntary total institutions, like schools, abbeys, and monasteries. Though they are not inherently "evil," these places are the sites of many of history's most tragic and horrendous crimes against humanity, making them the scariest places in the world and among the most popular "dark tourism" destinations.* And they are not just scary: these places often evoke sadness or nostalgia, a feeling that being in their presence gets us closer to the stories witnessed and recorded in their walls over the passage of time. They evoke a sense of awe by reminding us that there are many things bigger and older than ourselves.

Total institutions, particularly those that hold people against their will, are frightening yet intriguing—creating a kind of attraction/repulsion dynamic. We've evolved to be drawn to the novel, which includes the grotesque; in fact our brain gets more excited and pays more attention to the new and unusual (some brains more than others). After all, we are the descendants of those who had the right balance of curiosity to find new food sources and mates, but the right amount of caution to pick our battles. But there are other, deeper, and more psychological reasons these places attract and repel us at the same time.

They are the places that keep the scary and repulsive "monsters" locked up, hidden from upright, moral, and law-abiding citizens. Yet we are attracted to what they remind us of: in the public

---

*Dark tourism is the practice of going to places that have a history of death or tragedy like war zones, terrorist sites, mass graves, and total institutions. For an overview see Debra Kamin, "The Rise of Dark Tourism," *Atlantic*, July 15, 2014.

act of confining the criminal, or the "abnormal" other, societies reaffirm their shared values, the differences between "us" and "them" become visible, and the dividing lines are fortified. Serial killers, rapists, terrorists, insider-trading hedge fund managers, child abusers—those who threaten society are imprisoned behind the walls of total institutions, away from us. Total institutions take us close to evil and in doing so allow us to celebrate our own righteousness.

I witnessed this perhaps most explicitly while touring West Virginia Penitentiary. There, an engaging tour guide told jokes and made witty quips in between sensationalized and brutal stories of inmates "getting what they deserved" because, as she put it, "if you gonna act like an animal, you gonna get treated like one." (We know, thanks to Goffman and pretty much every behavior study out there, that it often works the other way around.) The final story took place at the foot of Old Sparky, the chair responsible for nine electrocutions, including that of Elmer Brunner, the last West Virginian killed there. Brunner was convicted of first-degree murder after brutally killing Ruby Miller with a hammer during a home invasion. Huddled together at the foot of the chair, we were captivated listening to this tragic story. And that's when I saw it—the tour group that started out as a collection of strangers had become a tiny community. The story closed with Brunner getting "the chair," and there was a collective "Yeah!" and a few high fives. I think someone even screamed "AMERICA!" Thanks to our justice system, society is safe from harm, and we can rest at ease, free from fear. At least, that's what we like to think.

The fear surrounding total institutions is not all about the people inside, at least not just the people behind the bars. It's about the structure, purpose, and influence of the institution itself. Not only can the employees (and potentially the residents) kill you, sometimes without even breaking the law, but they also by definition take away your freedom and strip away your identity. Whether you enter as a patient, a prisoner, or a student, you go through a rigid resocialization process, which can leave you demoralized, pathologized, and lacking any sense of self. (Think of *A Clockwork Orange*.) Even the employees of total institutions leave their identities at the door in exchange for new and often depersonalized selves that leave them disconnected from their emotions and less sensitive to others.

The monsters inside total institutions are not necessarily the ones behind bars. Philip Zimbardo's famous prison experiment illustrated both dimensions of this problem: he assigned students to the roles of guards and prisoners in a simulated prison, but ultimately had to call off the experiments because the student guards began to abuse their power, making the student prisoners complete increasingly cruel and humiliating tasks. And even Zimbardo acknowledged years later that he had unintentionally assumed the role of the prison superintendent rather than objective researcher. Despite Zimbardo's study being less than perfect (and less than ethical), research shows any form of long-term association with an involuntary total institution can leave you feeling less than human, which is, for many, a fate worse than death. To paraphrase Michel Foucault: the executioner has power only over your death; an institution has power over everything else.

The scariest, most notorious total institution in the history of America—and maybe the world—is Pennsylvania's Eastern State Penitentiary, which opened in 1829. It was the first penitentiary in the United States and the model for over three hundred penitentiaries worldwide. There are several levels to why ESP is one of the scariest places on Earth—it's a massive, old prison some say is haunted, and it was home to Pennsylvania's most troubled people and some of the country's most notorious criminals, like Al Capone and Willie Sutton. But first it was a pioneer in the development of a new form of institutionalized torture in the United States and one of our biggest fears: solitary confinement. Over my years of reading and coding responses to the question "What's your biggest fear?" the answer "Being trapped alone" is always in the top five (along with death, the dark, drowning, and loss of a loved one). But why? Why are we so terrified of being alone?

There was a lot to explore in total institutions, but I wasn't about to go out and get arrested, or check myself into a mental institution to investigate these fears, and not just because I'm not that stupid. I wanted to tap into the attraction yet repulsion to these *old* monuments symbolizing the dark side, or at least the hidden side of human behavior. I visited a number of historic institutions to explore this phenomenon, and learned a lot along the way, but when it came to confinement, I wanted to go to the place that perfected it, and then spend the night. Alone.

> . > . >

How exactly does one figure out a way to be left alone in the dark in America's scariest historic penitentiary? I didn't imagine the staff of the Eastern State Penitentiary Historic Site (the nonprofit that runs the site as a museum today) would be open to having a sociologist wander about the grounds unsupervised in the middle of the night to see what it feels like to be trapped in a dark prison. I contemplated trying to hide in one of the cells until they closed, but criminal trespassing would end in confinement in a different prison. Thankfully, I had an in—and like a lot of my favorite stories, it starts with a trip through a haunted house.

ESP's biggest fundraiser for their nonprofit is their seasonal haunted house—Terror Behind the Walls (TBTW). It's the most popular haunted attraction outside of an amusement park in the United States (seriously, it sees over a hundred thousand visitors a season), and luckily the people who run it are fans of ScareHouse. On the last night of the 2013 ScareHouse season, Brett Bertolino, director of operations at ESP, and Amy Hollaman, creative director for TBTW, came to check out ScareHouse. I had been debating and delaying how to reach out for months, but when they came out of the haunt smiling and excited, I saw my chance. It's always better to ask for things when people are happy. I casually asked Brett if I could "you know, come hang out at ESP for a while." Brett said, "Sure," and that I should follow up with Amy to make arrangements. Little did he know I meant a whole night, and little did I know that would be the first of many, many days and nights at ESP and many more adventures with a new partner in fear.

Amy and I hit it off from the very beginning, which was great because I hadn't met many women I connected to in the haunted attraction industry outside of ScareHouse.* She's a natural leader—charismatic and magnetic—but she's also the creative director for a haunted house, so she has a bit of a dark side. She's the type of person who would be a really good cult leader (I told her this, and she took it as a compliment). When Amy said yes to me spending the night at ESP, I'm pretty sure it was because she didn't think I would actually go through with it, but as she would learn, I don't tend to chicken out.

⋟ ⋟ ⋟

It is hard to describe how small I felt when I arrived at the penitentiary just before closing on a warm May evening. From the outside, it looks like a massive fortress, with forty-foot-high walls encircling ten acres of land and watchtowers on each corner. Its thick stone edifice is both oppressive and awe-inspiring, as it's supposed to be. Architect John Haviland had intentionally chosen the intimidating neo-Gothic aesthetic to instill fear in those who would enter, and any who passed through Philadelphia's Fairmount District. It's the building that haunts you in your dreams and the setting of your worst nightmares—an irony, because ESP was founded on the humanitarian belief that all criminals could be rehabilitated.

ESP was meant to put an end to some of the worst elements of seventeenth-century prisons, such as torture, beatings, public executions, and unsanitary living conditions. Old World prisons

---

*The haunt world is still a very white, male-dominated industry that tends to lean to the right of the political spectrum. There aren't many women owners or creative directors, and attraction sets and props are often designed to be exploitative, pointing to sexism within the industry. ScareHouse is one of the few haunts that explicitly state they do not have scenes depicting violence against women, and it has a balance of men and women in leadership positions. So as a liberal feminist sociologist, I found it refreshing to meet another like-minded haunter.

were something more like dungeons or holding cells for criminals and the insane awaiting their real punishment—which was usually death by hanging, flaying, or impaling, or torture in the form of dismemberment, stocks, or castration. One particularly terrifying such device was the "scolds bridle," used in Scotland in the sixteenth century, mainly on women. It was an iron muzzle that encased the prisoner's head and prevented her from moving her mouth to talk. Some versions included an iron plate, covered in spikes, that went into the prisoner's mouth to punish anyone who dared move their tongue. Perhaps even more disturbing than the device itself, and the fact that it was a socially accepted form of punishment, is that it would ironically serve as inspiration for a similar form of punishment used at ESP, with slightly more torturous modifications.

The visionaries of the penitentiary, including one of the US founding fathers, Dr. Benjamin Rush, believed in a different path. They insisted that criminals could achieve moral rehabilitation and spiritual salvation through confinement in a small cell with no human interaction whatsoever. This new "Pennsylvania System" would give criminals time to reflect on their behavior and offer penance. Despite their best intentions, what was meant to be a place of salvation turned into a place many would refer to simply as "hell."

> > >

I shuddered and felt goose bumps while standing outside the wrought-iron entry gate, just inside the main entrance. The heavy gate is a good twenty feet tall, as though it had to make room for the mounds of crime, guilt, and shame piled high on the backs of inmates. (Really, it was just to allow large carts and later trucks to pass through, but it's hard not to get incredibly ominous at ESP.) Amy met me at the gates and let me in; watching her open the padlock and remove the chains (employees have to do this every day), I thought about how many people before me had wished to be on the side I was standing, and here I was asking to be let in.

Through the gates are massive stone cellblocks arranged in a wagon-wheel design around a central rotunda.* While the outside is beyond threatening, the inside of this building is, surprisingly, designed to be inspiring. The original cellblocks and rotunda resembled those of a majestic church: vaulted ceilings, skylights, and spacious hallways. Guiltily I acknowledged that it was beautiful. Haviland had designed the exterior to be intimidating, warning free citizens away from a life of crime. But he wanted the space inside to feel like a monastery, albeit an involuntary one. Even the cells, which in the original cellblock were spacious even by today's standards, at eight by twelve feet, had a single skylight at the top of the ten-foot vaulted ceiling symbolically called "the Eye of God." Haviland included flush toilets, central heating, and a private outdoor yard eighteen feet long. Put a "Vacancy" sign out front, wire it up for cable TV, and you could charge $100 a night.

Well, not quite. Very quickly the prison design revealed its flaws: the central heating rarely worked, leaving the prisoners shivering on solid cement floors (later to be overlaid with wood), the flush toilets weren't quite as effective as hoped, and the stench was overwhelming and nauseating. Perhaps worst of all, the windowless cells and wagon-wheel design inside forty-foot walls made airflow virtually impossible. The lack of ventilation left cells damp and cold in the winter, humid and stale in the summer. The environmental conditions were among the top causes of illness and death according to the physicians' reports, second perhaps only to the grim consequences of solitary confinement.

Inmates, referred to strictly by their number from the moment they stepped inside the gates, spent twenty-three hours

---

*This radial design is similar to the Panopticon (which philosopher Michel Foucault famously used as a metaphor to describe our disciplinary and controlled society), designed by English philosopher Jeremy Bentham in the late eighteenth century, but only in terms of its function of surveillance. The Panopticon also places the guard at the center encircled by inmate cells, with openings facing the middle. This meant the guard could see into the cell at any given time from his central location. The radial design limits the surveillance from the center to just along cellblock aisles.

a day inside their cell, with one hour of exercise in their private yard. Interacting with fellow inmates, friends, and family was prohibited; they even had to wear hoods when moving through the hallways. Nevertheless, keeping the inmates separated proved to be harder than expected. The desire—really, the need—of inmates to communicate and interact was too strong to suppress. Inmates would send messages through the plumbing with the "rapping alphabet," throw notes tied to stones over their exercise walls, burrow tiny holes through to their cellmates, and shout through their skylights. To each inventive attempt to communicate, the prison warden responded with further confinement; skylights were nailed shut, privileges were restricted, and punishments were introduced. Physical punishment was not part of the Pennsylvania System; even flogging had been banned. But an 1835 investigation by the state legislature revealed that warden Samuel Wood had been using various forms of torture, including the "tranquilizing chair," which so violently restricted inmates that it cut off circulation, leading in some cases to the need to amputate; forcing inmates to take a bath in cold water and then leaving them in the winter air so long that icicles formed on their skin; and the iron gag—similar to the scolds bridle, but with the addition of chains connecting the gag to the inmates' wrists. The penitentiary was investigated three times (1834, 1897, 1903) in its first seventy-five years, and the investigations found guards and inmates involved in "licentious and immoral practices," embezzlement, "cruel and unusual punishment inflicted by order of the Warden upon refractory convicts," and "substituting [the Warden's] individual caprice or discretion for the decisions of the law." The ideals of the Philadelphia Society for Alleviating the Miseries of Public Prisons were quickly slipping away.

> > >

I had arrived about an hour before the site closed, and I took advantage of the time before the sun set to see as much as I could, thinking maybe if I knew what the space looked like in the daylight, it wouldn't be as frightening once it was dark. Staring into one of the original cells in cellblock 1, I imagined what it must have been like, sleeping on a small, wire-frame bed, isolated in a monster of a building. I felt a deep sense of sympathy for those confined, but I also knew they'd been imprisoned for a reason—at least according to the political and religious authorities of the time. Those who'd committed petty crimes like theft or public drunkenness, or who were here because of "association" or "moral weakness": Did they deserve to be here? Did anyone?

Human interaction is fundamental to well-being. Period. We need each other; study after study shows the damaging effects of neglect and isolation at every stage in life. Babies across species will die if they do not have skin-to-skin (or fur-to-fur) contact, and studies of institutionalized children who were severely neglected show behavioral, cognitive, and physical disabilities. We know people recover from illness more quickly, handle sad news better, and even perceive challenges as less threatening when they have the support of other people. Solitary confinement takes the lifeline of human interaction away—the very thing needed for rehabilitation. Even at the time ESP was in operation, people realized such isolation was not a good idea, and a number of activists began to denounce it, among them Charles Dickens:

> In its intention I am well convinced that it is kind, humane, and meant for reformation; but I am persuaded that those who designed this system of Prison Discipline, and those benevolent gentlemen who carry it into execution, do not know what it is that they are doing. . . . I hold this slow and daily tampering with the mysteries of the brain to be immeasurably worse than any torture of the body; and because its ghastly signs and tokens are not so palpable to the eye, . . . and it extorts few cries that human ears can hear; therefore I the more denounce it, as a secret punishment in which slumbering humanity is not roused up to stay.

Eventually solitary confinement was phased out, not because of Dickens's objections but simply as a result of overcrowding. In

1867 there were 569 inmates for 540 cells, and only thirty years later there were 1,200 inmates and 765 cells. Yet officials still maintained they were operating under the superior separate system until 1913, when it was officially recognized that it was not sustainable or more effective than the congregate system.

Expansion continued all the way up to 1959, but each new cellblock moved further and further away from Haviland's spacious design and the founding principle that all are capable of redemption. New cellblocks had low ceilings, individual cells were smaller with no skylights or exercise yards, and a new physical punishment was introduced with cellblock 14, which was underground and full of windowless cells, appropriately renamed the Klondike for reasons I would soon learn. The final nail in the coffin of the reformers' ideals was the construction of cellblock 15 in 1956: Death Row. There could hardly be a more explicit move away from the founding principle of rehabilitation.

The prison was active until 1971, when the extent of needed repairs was way out of budget for Pennsylvania. The inmates were all relocated, and the abandoned site quickly began to deteriorate as politicians, developers, and community groups argued over its future. After years of conflict the Pennsylvania Prison Society took over the property and opened the doors to the public for the first time in 1991. To pay for the repairs and at the very least stop the deterioration the prison would need to raise money—a lot of it. Inspired by the popularity of charity haunted houses, the prison opened Terror Behind the Walls in 1991. With the funds raised from the haunted house, ESP was able to stop some of the worst deterioration and make essential repairs. Now it's considered a stable ruin. But they didn't stop there; today they offer educational programs, lecture series, interpretive artist installations, and they have a library of information curated by their full-time researcher and archivist. It's not just a scary old historic site making money off of curious tourists.

Over the course of my adventuring I have come to appreciate the critical importance of forethought and respect when it comes to creating any experience inside a former total institution, or really *any* intensely emotional experience. Much like a roller coaster, curated or manufactured intense emotional experiences like haunted houses, scary historical sites, and even things like sweat lodges and physical challenges need to start from a place of safety, take you on an out-of-control ride in which you push yourself beyond your boundaries, and return you safely, feeling better and a little wiser. One of my biggest pet peeves is places that do not do this—that take you to the top, where you push past your boundaries, but then leave you there or drop you, leaving you feeling the opposite of confident and inspired. ESP offers an example of how *not* to do this. The staff knows the content you're engaging with is *scary* and makes sure that the dark and scary is balanced with messages of hope and stories of resilience. Most importantly, though, the nonprofit that runs the site does not sensationalize, exaggerate, or exploit the history of the building and the people inside for profit. You tour the space, you learn the history, and you get scared, but through its messaging, its sculptures,* and its commitment to helping people learning from history so as not to repeat it, ESP makes sure you leave with a feeling of deep understanding, not sensationalized atrocity. Even the haunted house is thoughtfully designed so as not to sensationalize ESP's tragic history or make light of the serious issues surrounding crime and prisons today. This, I have learned far too many times, is not the case for many other historical total institutions turned tourist attractions.

Using the same tactics employed by P. T. Barnum—exaggerating the "freakish" and "abnormal"—some former total institutions sensationalize the history of vulnerable or marginalized populations to tap into our attraction to the unusual and novel. One of the more high-profile examples of this (though not the worst offender) is found at Pennhurst Haunted House, the site of

---

*Throughout the site ESP connects the injustices of the past to concerns around criminal justice today. In some places it is a simple statistic or fact at the end of a historical plaque pointing out the rates of or reasons for incarceration. In other places it's more explicit. In 2013 ESP erected the Big Graph, a sixteen-foot, 3,500-pound, plate-steel bar graph that offers a powerful visual representation of the growing prison population.

the former Pennhurst Asylum, also located in eastern Pennsylvania, which was open from 1908 until 1987. The Asylum finally closed its doors after years of reports from family members, staff, and residents of ill treatment, horrendous abuse, and neglect. Malnourishment was rampant, and patients were tied to beds or kept in cages, often in their own filth. These issues were exposed by Bill Baldini in 1968, but even after his scathing report and documentary titled *Suffer the Little Children*, the asylum remained open. Lawsuit after lawsuit was filed against the institution until the courts ruled that forced institutionalization of those with disabilities is unconstitutional. The final agreement forced Pennhurst to close. Pennhurst is another tragic example of the destructive conditions created in total institutions that deny personal freedoms. Unlike Eastern State, however, the commercial business that moved into Pennhurst emphasizes and sensationalizes the dark side of its history. It takes guests to a very dark place and then leaves them there.

In 2010 Pennhurst Haunted House, which was met with criticism and condemnation from mental health advocates who felt a haunted house on the grounds was insensitive, opened with the promise that they would not incorporate the history of the asylum in the attraction or exploit its former residents. Nevertheless, today the haunted house not only highlights its use of artifacts found on-site but also re-creates or reimagines scenes from the asylum's awful history in which "insane" patients are unapologetically portrayed as weak, damaged, and childlike, or on the other hand murderous, evil, and "demented"—basically the stereotypes mental health advocates have been working so hard to combat. The Pennhurst Memorial and Preservation Alliance, which seeks to "promote an understanding of the struggle for dignity and full civil rights for persons with disabilities," is adamantly opposed to the haunted house and would like the property to follow a similar path of other Sites of Conscience, which work to engage the public with tragic histories to teach and inform future generations (ESP is also an SoC). In 2010 PMPA issued a statement that remains posted on its website:

PMPA is completely opposed to the operation of a haunted attraction at Pennhurst that portrays people with disabilities in a demeaning and degrading fashion. Demonizing people with disabilities as a profit-making "entertainment" is (and should be) offensive to everyone. We urge everyone who shares our disgust to speak out against the "haunted asylum" and boycott this travesty.

While Pennhurst is still privately owned and run as a commercial business, PMPA continues work to get the "real" history out to the public with traveling displays. Hope persists for preserving and converting the institution into a space to educate and remember.

Re-creating scenes that mirror a site's terrifying history is not necessarily problematic, as long as it is done with respect and purpose, as in showing the true terror that is a history of violence and abuse, not reinforcing stereotypes. This requires thinking about the historical context, power dynamics, and respect. For example, rather than having tour guides gossip with guests about salacious stories, exaggerated and stretched to the point of fiction, have them share the truth. After all, reality is often scarier.

Trans Allegheny Lunatic Asylum is another former "haunted" asylum opened before the Civil War; the organization in charge also runs a haunted house. The staff did a good job of not reinforcing stereotypes with their daytime tour (I haven't been through the haunted house). The tour was intriguing and frightening (the tour guides dressed as medical staff were a little over the top), but they made sure everyone left with a better understanding of history and of those who struggle with mental illness. After touring buildings where mentally ill people were confined to rooms and chained to walls, the tour ends in an art gallery, which features artwork from those who have or had mental illness. On display are over forty masks painted outside and inside—to represent how the artists feel the world sees them and how they see themselves, respectively. These masks put a human face on mental illness, and while there is sadness, there is also

love, confidence, and hope. Stories of atrocious histories are titillating and scary, but they are only one side of the mask, so to
speak. Touring or re-creating scenes of tragedy offers opportunities to put a human face on those who have been invisible or
ostracized, or considered monsters. It's an opportunity to expose
and flip the power dynamics, and when done well, it can leave
a powerful impression on guests. When done poorly, it's down-
right offensive.

> > >

I had been touring ESP for at least an hour by myself, but I noticed
even those who were with larger groups and families toured the
cellblocks alone. And while there were no irritating museum
attendants shushing guests, no one was talking. The constrict-
ing, silencing power of the institution is inherent; it doesn't need
anyone to enforce control. I watched everyone leaving as the tour
guides announced they were closing. Guests walked slowly and
deliberately, fearing the slightest misstep would disturb the spirits
or awaken some sleeping evil. At least that's what I felt. The sun
was setting, and as I walked through the last cellblock, I sensed
the presence of every prisoner and guard following behind me.
It's no surprise I jumped a foot in the air when Amy came up and
tapped on my shoulder. After a good laugh at my expense (the first
of many), she asked me, in the most dramatic and scary voice possible, "Are you ready to venture into the dark?" I laughed, but only
to hide the fact that I actually was starting to grow a little anxious.

Amy would be taking me to explore parts of the prison not
open to the general public. I jokingly asked if I needed a hard
hat and respirator and was surprised to hear "No, not where we're
going," implying that there are places where you would need a
full hazmat suit—those that are underground. Apparently sub-
terranean tunnels were built beneath the cellblocks to move air,
water, heat, and gas throughout the prison. There is also suspicion that underground punishment cells existed in addition to
the Klondike, but most of the tunnels are simply too dangerous

to thoroughly investigate. After all, ESP is in a state of ruin; it's dangerous and full of lots of things that can kill you, and not just the things that were built to do so. Crumbling ceilings and deteriorating stairs and handrails make the nonpreserved areas literally a death trap.

"Sociologist Dies Exploring Abandoned Prison" and other headlines were running through my head as Amy unlocked the gate to cellblock 12, pointed her flashlight at a steep staircase against the wall, and said, "Ready?" This cellblock was built eighty-two years after opening, with three stories of cells, accessible via a narrow catwalk. After 1900, new construction was generally not the same quality, with thinner walls, smaller stones, and poor masonry and concrete—all built by prisoners themselves. I wondered if an abused prison laborer really cared about things like craftsmanship and quality. From the ground I could see all the way up through the debris and to the night sky—at least two-thirds of the roof had fallen in. The cellblock looked like a giant ogre had torn the place apart. There's no way I was going up there; the narrow metal steps were barely wide enough for my whole foot, and the rusted handrails looked as if they would disintegrate beneath my grip. I looked up at the collapsing ceiling—the floor that would be supporting my weight should I risk the flight. The cracked paint was hanging from a mixture of wire, wood, and concrete that formed the foundation of the catwalk. I shook my head and said, "Nope." I am all for going into off-limits places, but the entire cellblock looked as if it would crumble like ash at the smallest movement.

Amy wasn't helping—instead of reassuring me it would be fine, or even playing the part of instigator, she kept telling me how to be safe, where to step and what to hold and how not to die. This wasn't the CN Tower; there were no safety harnesses. This was for real. I was stalling—I investigated every nook and cranny of the stairs with my flashlight. Finally, Amy told me to just wait there, since she had to go up and check something out anyway. As she began to climb, my curiosity got the best of me, and I followed her. My competitive nature had kicked in, telling me that if she could do it, I could do it. But I had to force myself to take that last step off the stairs and onto the two-foot-wide path that stretches the length of the cellblock. The floor was covered with chipped paint, dust, stones, and rubble that crunched beneath my feet, and with every crunch I could feel the floor give way and see myself tumbling to the cement below.

I couldn't believe what I was seeing: the tall vaulted ceiling flanked by two narrow pathways with a simple metal railing that would protect no one from falling three stories down. The walls, a mix of cracked and shedding green, gray, and blue paint, appeared slashed and burned. It was frightening to look at, and I anticipated that at any minute whatever monsters destroyed the space would return and do the same to me or, worse, lock me in one of the cells forever. Perhaps the most eerie sight from my platform view: every eight feet was a small, dark, rectangular hole in the wall. All 120 dark holes stared back at me, each one witness to countless stories. Even in the best conditions, without the ruin and rubble, this image of total mechanical confinement of human beings is frightening.

Next to cellblock 12, the medical ward is the scariest place in the prison, and not open to the public because of its extreme state of ruin. Smallpox, tuberculosis, and other infectious diseases claimed the lives of hundreds at the turn of the century. Sick prisoners were treated in individual cells until a modern hospital was built in the old steam and electric room in cellblock 3. During its years of abandonment, scavengers and vandals stripped the building of any and all copper and scrap metal, leaving behind what they couldn't carry. Evidence of their looting remains throughout cellblock 3, where X-ray machines, gurneys, surgical equipment, and machines beyond recognition were scattered through the corridor, torn to shreds like gutted animals with their intestines pulled out—a kind of mechanical carnage. The archaic equipment looked more like devices of torture than health care instruments.

Standing beneath the giant surgical lamp, I felt the collective weight of prisoners' fears as they were forced onto a surgical table and placed into restraints, while doctors prepared syringes full of unknown drugs. I'm unsure of which would have been scarier, being unconscious or awake for what was about to happen. And anything could happen. Whether or not someone was guilty of a crime, that kind of loss of control in the face of total authority is utterly terrifying, and something difficult to feel the true force of without experiencing it directly. We don't have this kind of access to active prisons, but touring ESP allows us to get closer to what it must be like to have so little control.

The medical ward was especially damp; there was moss growing on the walls and ground. I could hear water dripping and turned to see a room full of thin, white stalagmites, which looked almost like icicles except for the fact that they were surrounded by rusty instruments and patches of bright green mold. I passed my flashlight over a gigantic centipede making its way across the floor and screamed—which surprised me. I'm not generally afraid of bugs, but in my sensitized state I was right on the edge. I also hadn't noticed any bugs in the other cellblocks; here they were everywhere. Big beetles, centipedes, spiders, and, of course, spiderwebs were all around me. I couldn't shake the feeling that insects were crawling all over me.

I slowly inched down the corridor, peeking into cells. Amy cautioned me not to move any of the doors or touch anything—the protective netting covering the deteriorating roof in the public spaces didn't exist here, and if I should hear something like crumbling, I was to run to the center rotunda. I tried to pay attention, but I was distracted; there was a beauty to the deterioration, especially in the rooms that hadn't been touched since the prison closed. They were frozen in time, a snapshot from the moment of mass exodus. It was the closest thing to time travel I could imagine: a piece of paper on the ground, a pile of clothes, a solo shoe.

Tiptoeing further down the ward, I caught what I thought surely must be an illusion out of the corner of my eye. I turned, let out an audible gasp, and then felt a hand on my arm pulling me back as I instinctively tried to duck into a cell. "Margee, you can't go in there!" I stopped and listened to Amy lecture me about safety (again). I was quickly learning the difference between reckless and brave and was not about to push my luck in a building in a state of sustained ruin.

Turning back to look into the cell, I saw a wire-frame bed tilted precariously on its side against a wall with peeling white paint, surrounded by broken bricks and crumbling stone. But beyond the piles of pink and gray rubble were green leaves, moss, and branches all stretching from a tree that had refused to accept the restrictive borders of the penitentiary. The image was captivating: the unmoving staleness of the cell was such a sharp contrast to the signs of nature fighting to reclaim the space. In fact, the whole place was filled with little conflicts like this: beautiful next to disgusting, free next to confined, compassion next to torture, death next to life.

Cellblock 3 also had held a number of the mentally ill prisoners, many of whom were not criminals but just sick. It has been suspected that the prison was underreporting the number of inmates who were mentally ill or driven insane by the conditions in which they were kept. An ESP warden's report from 1831 reads: "use of dark cell and straight jacket for 3 days for suspected insane prisoner, No. 10, w/o food or drink." These types of reports prompted the 1897 investigation, which found that the "cells of the prison were in a filthy condition, that the diet was of inferior grade, and that there existed an attitude of indifference if not cruelty toward some of the inmates, especially those who were insane." The result of the investigation left Judge Gordon unapologetic in his charges against Eastern State:

> I wish now to charge the Inspectors of the Eastern Penitentiary with falsehood in their official reports; with conscious and deliberate misstatements before this Committee under oath. I wish to charge them with cruelty and inhumanity in the discharge of their duties, with neglect, with incompetence. I wish to charge them with secreting evidence, with fabricating evidence. I wish to charge them with intimidating witnesses. I want to present the proof seriatim against every one of them; and I am glad they are all here.

Housing the mentally ill alongside criminals was not unusual (in fact it still isn't).* Before modern medicine, anyone who was physically or mentally different was seen as an abomination. They were bad signs from God(s), evidence of sin, or possessed by the devil and consequently shackled out of sight. This often led to brutal treatment of those who were different, including death. The 1896 case of Archibald White, a mentally ill inmate at ESP kept in his own filth, naked, with a broken nose, and unable to speak, became a rallying cry for reform. Judge Gorden recounted his visit with White:

> I went down and I found lying upon his cell floor, in an absolutely empty cell—an emaciated man, filthy in his person, filthy in all his surroundings, unable to rise; who, when spoken to by me, raised his head up but could not get upon his feet. Mr. Cassidy dominatingly commanded him to rise, but it was futile. He could not.

Just as crusaders were fighting for prison reform, activists like Dorothea Dix and Thomas Kirkbride were condemning the US practice of keeping the mentally ill in prisons and basements, and they called for the adoption of a "moral therapy." Based on

---

*Today's prisons have largely replaced mental institutions: there are ten times more mentally ill patients behind bars than in hospitals. The Treatment Advocacy Center recently called attention to the wholly inefficient and indeed eighteenth-century approach to addressing mental illness. It reports that in 2012 35,000 patients with severe mental illness lived in state psychiatric hospitals, compared to 356,268 with similar severe mental illness in prison. TAC also reports that severely mentally ill prisoners are more likely to be victims of assault, rape, and abuse while behind bars. They are more likely to commit suicide and to be sent to solitary confinement. It's hard to understand why this is happening; it certainly is *not* more cost effective. It costs taxpayers *more* money to house the mentally ill in prison than in a state hospital. But in the wake of deinstitutionalization brought about by calls for community-based care and newer effective medications, many state hospitals closed. So mentally ill people are arrested, sometimes for violent offenses but often for minor ones, and sent to prison, where they get no treatment or medication. They are released, and the cycle repeats. Prisons are the new asylums, once again putting our "monsters" into cages.

the ideas of French physician Philippe Pinel and English mental health reformer Samuel Tuke in the late 1700s, moral therapy included treatment based on certain Christian values and a rigorous schedule of work, rest, prayer, and sleep. But the new asylums were still an involuntary total institution—surveillance, control, and dehumanization were built into the design. The power of the involuntary total institution eclipses even the most humane intentions; just as the best attempts at prison reform devolved into abuse and punishment, so did insane asylums, which became places of torture, neglect, and confinement, like Pennhurst. Threat of punishment and actual punishment were still used to assert control. Prisons actually adopted some of the most violent punishments from mental institutions, like the straightjacket and the "cold shower," a euphemism for water torture.

I thought of Archibald White, dismissed as a "malingerer" by the warden and kept in a cell on the cold floor, probably shackled to the wall at some point, unable to move farther than four feet. I tried to imagine what that would feel like, but it was impossible: my closest point of reference was when my mom would put me in a child harness at the beach. I remember the frustration in pulling against the leash when I tried to go farther into the water. Being chained to a wall would be unbearable.

The reasons for commitment to an asylum during the late 1800s reflected the values and ignorance of the time: domestic trouble, superstition, being a young lady (that was enough), parents who were cousins, nymphomania, greediness, seduction, being "menstrually" (*sic*) deranged, female disease, hysteria, fear, immoral life, political excitement, masturbation, business nerves, imaginary female trouble, and bad company. It was frightening to see how many reasons were connected to simply being a woman. This was before the *Diagnostic and Statistical Manual of Mental Disorders* (aka the DSM) and medical coding, when a judge didn't need a diagnosis to commit somebody. If he, your family, your priest, or your husband thought you should be committed, you were. It's likely that had I been born a hundred years earlier, I would have been committed, maybe even chained to the wall and stripped not only of my freedom but of my dignity and the power of my own voice. I felt the air being sucked from the cellblock, and I could feel my body pulling me out. It was suffocating.

> > >

Right around the corner from cellblock 3 are the punishment cells, aka the Klondike, or just the Hole. I wondered how intentional that was—locating the medical ward right next to the place that left hundreds malnourished and physically or mentally ill. A warden's report from 1924 describes the Klondike as an underground row of unsanitary windowless cells, where the walls and ceilings were painted black. There was no furniture—only an iron toilet and a faucet. Inmates were thrown in naked on the wet floor, with only a blanket (which was sometimes taken away), and allowed only a small ration of bread and water. The report notes that it was described as barbarous, yet the Hole was used all the way up until the prison closed, despite a 1953 bill signed by the governor recommending the abolition of the underground punishment cells.

Amy walked me over to the top of the Klondike stairwell and stopped. "Down there?" I asked. She nodded and went down to unlock the gate. I felt anxious and kept sweeping my flashlight back and forth across the stairwell. In the late 1800s reformers argued over which was a worse fate for prisoners: the physical violence and pain of the congregate system or the mental anguish and torture of the Pennsylvania System. In the Hole, the prisoner experiences the worst of both, in the dark. I couldn't stop thinking about the story of a sixteen-year-old prisoner kept in the hole for forty-two days with no food.

While the public can look into the Hole, they aren't allowed inside. As Amy left me standing there alone, I understood why. I reluctantly descended the stairs and crouched over to enter the short hallway with four cell entrances off to the right. That would be the last time I could stand up straight for the next two hours. It felt at least 10 degrees colder inside, with puddles of water a couple of inches deep pooled in spots on the cold cement floor. The name "Klondike" was fitting.

The cells were full of old steel beams and iron cell gates covered with at least an inch of rust. I moved around the gates cautiously, trying not to think of falling onto the sharp end of a rusted and broken frame. I crept into a cell and looked around. I was beginning to feel the strain from hunching low, but there was no dry place to sit. You don't think of a low ceiling as a source of discomfort, but it is an incredibly effective form of punishment. The thick, damp air made breathing unpleasant. I had only been inside for twenty minutes, and I was starting to seriously wonder how much longer I could last. An image of myself trapped in the elevator at the Veterans Hospital in Pittsburgh flashed in front of my eyes. I wanted more than anything to open them and be back on the elevator going to the top of the CN Tower.

I pushed myself to stay, or more accurately told myself I couldn't leave. Not yet. The Hole gripped me. I turned off my flashlight and tried not to move. It wasn't just dark—it was pitch black. There are few places in our well-illuminated world that dark; streetlights, digital clocks, the tiny light on your laptop as it's charging—these make even the darkest spaces discernible and give our senses of proprioception something to use to get oriented. Not here. I kept trying to focus, to see the metal grates that I knew were there in front of me, yet I couldn't. I felt frantic. It's one thing to close your eyes or to have a blindfold on—you're not really in the dark. As soon as you open your eyes or remove the blindfold, you'll be able to see, and there is a comfort in knowing that. But when your eyes are open and the space around you is completely dark, you feel a profound powerlessness, disorientation, and loss of balance. These small, effortless manipulations of sight and space inside the Hole are physically crippling. Blind, naked, confined in a total institution as a number instead of a person, you have nowhere to go except into your own mind. For many that is where even more horrors await.

＊ ＊ ＊

We do bad things in our lives that have painful consequences, but most of us don't spend every day thinking about the worst things we have done. We deal with them at the time, and our lives go on; we have opportunities to try to do better; we create new memories. But a prisoner's world can be frozen on what is likely the very worst day of their entire life, and every day after it is just a reminder of how they failed—maybe not just because they had committed a crime and feel remorseful, but because they got caught or were unfairly convicted. Whatever the perspective, if they're in prison, they failed. They are left with nothing to do but recycle the events that got them there, to ruminate endlessly. Rumination is the practice of turning over negative events in your mind again and again, usually adding layer after layer of self-blame. It is agonizing. It leads to serious negative health consequences like increased stress, depression (which it makes more severe, longer-lasting, and more difficult to treat), anxiety, negative or dysfunctional coping mechanisms, and an overwhelming feeling of being stuck.

I would hear these sentiments from prisoners themselves the next day during a question-and-answer session put together as part of Reunion Weekend at ESP. One prisoner, who was released just prior to ESP's closure in 1971, said he would replay the events of his life over and over in his mind, but it was hard to take joy in them, knowing they all ended in the same place—his prison cell. Another former inmate, who had spent time in the Hole, said he would walk through the steps of his last robbery, thinking of all the things he should've done to avoid getting caught. If punishment is the goal of a prison, then painful rumination certainly fits. But if the goal is rehabilitation, solitary confinement achieves the exact opposite.

I finally stopped trying to strain my eyes and focused on breathing. I thought inevitably about the worst things I'd done. Mainly I thought about my sister, who'd endured terrible bullying when we were young. I hadn't done anything to help her. I became overwhelmed with feelings of guilt and shame. These are thoughts I usually intentionally avoid. Typically I turn to various coping mechanisms—TV, books, a trip to the store, a rousing game of chase the laser with my cats, or (ironically) a trip to a haunted house or scary movie—to try to distract myself, but none were available in the Hole. I felt restless, anxious, heavy, and powerless underneath the weight of my own shame. My body wanted to run away, as though that would somehow leave my thoughts behind. I wanted something—anything—to look at, to take my mind off what I was thinking and feeling, but in the dark there is nothing, and I forced myself to stay in the space, both physically and mentally.

Most Americans go to great lengths to escape the monsters that are our own thoughts and imaginations. A study from the University of Virginia found that most people would rather be doing something bad—including hurting themselves by administering shocks—than sitting alone with their thoughts. This is a disconcerting finding that raises all kinds of questions about US culture and whether we've become dependent on external stimulation.* Are we incapable or ill equipped to generate a fulfilling imagination and internal dialogue? Or is it that when the external stimulation stops, our thoughts come rushing in, and we don't know how to handle it? It's likely a little bit (or in some cases *a lot*) of both. Either scenario is problematic. Suppressing thoughts and feelings is not a good form of emotional regulation or a good way to deal with stress. We have to deal with our baggage. As James Gross found in 2002, suppression (which is actively trying *not* to feel something) actually increases physiological response to the stressors, and does nothing to decrease the emotional experience, and even impairs memory. On the other hand, work on effective mood-regulation strategies by Susan Nolen-Hoeksema, who was an esteemed professor of psychology at Yale, found that for those who ruminate, distraction (which is attempting to divert attention to something else) can in fact be helpful, and even healthy.

---

*On my list to explore: Do other people around the globe also have such a hard time sitting with their own thoughts? Is it something about American life that makes us avoid our own inner processing?

And the idea of resorting to self-administered pain, fear, or anything that turns up our arousal system is certainly not a new practice when it comes to distracting the brain.

There is a long history of using physical sensation (somatosensory stimulation) to train or occupy the mind, from religious practices of self-flagellation to pinching your own skin to keep from crying. As I experienced on the CN Tower, and many times before, our thinking brain does go off-line when we're in a high arousal state. So for those who struggle with destructive rumination, high arousal (inciting fear and pain) may be just the thing that allows them to escape from their own damaging downward spiral. For example, there is evidence that administering mild shocks (not electroconvulsive therapy, which triggers a small seizure) or dunking your head in cold water can effectively interrupt a painful rumination cycle by activating the arousal system and forcing your attention to the sensation, rather than the thoughts.* In 2005 a group of Russian scientists from the city of Novosibirsk, Siberia, issued a report boasting the benefits of "whipping therapy" for those who were depressed or struggling with addiction. Their theory emphasizes the role of endorphins released during fight or flight, rather than the interruption of communication with the prefrontal cortex. Regardless, the fact that distant relatives of Old World torture methods could be therapeutic is hard to wrap my head around. It requires detaching these new methods from the negative connotations and harm done in the past.

The unraveling of the human psyche happens swiftly when involuntary isolation is coupled with sensory deprivation, like lack of visual and auditory stimulation, lack of anyone to talk to or

---

*The National Institute of Health funded a grant to run a clinical trial testing just this. Greg Siegle at the University of Pittsburgh will be testing whether shocks administered in decreasing intensity across a specific time frame will help ruminators learn how to shift their attention to physical sensation and thus out of a rumination cycle.

touch, and complete lack of control.* Our brains are built to process information and stimuli constantly. Like a mouse on an exercise wheel, we just want to run. Isolation is like pulling the wheel from the mouse, and with nothing to run on, we're left to our own thoughts and creating our own stimulation, which can lead to vivid visual and auditory hallucinations.

Starting with the 1957 study on the impact of isolation and deprivation by psychologist Donald Hebb, studies show that the consequences of isolation, like anxiety, paranoia, restlessness, and hallucinations (visual and auditory), start happening after only a couple of hours. His study was supposed to continue for several weeks, but most participants had to stop after two days, and none even made it a full week. Similar recent studies (with added layers of protection like panic buttons) have been conducted with similar findings, but now we know the damage doesn't stop when the isolation does. Even after an individual is released and in a supportive environment, the consequences from isolation continue in the form of delayed and difficult cognitive (math, science, rational thinking) and emotional processing. Recovery depends on a host of factors, including whether it is a choice (is this a voluntary wilderness retreat or a prison?), the length of time the person was in isolation, and, critically, the age at which he or she was isolated. From the time we are born we understand ourselves through our connections and communications with others; without them we are in an uncontrolled free fall, with no idea which way is up.†

---

*Context is critical—for those paying hundreds of dollars to float in sensory deprivation tanks, the isolation is relaxing and indulgent "me time." And for those choosing to take weeklong silent retreats in the woods, the experience can be transformative and inspiring. The difference is control and choice. There are instances of individuals coping with involuntary isolation; however, it usually is either after preparation and training in coping, or through communing with nature as a kind of "other," or like many sailors, turning objects and animals into people (anthropomorphizing) with whom to communicate.

†For a heart-wrenching story of what solitary confinement is like, read Sarah Shourd's story of her experience in an Iranian prison, "Tortured by Solitude," *New York Times*, November 5, 2011.

⋅ ⋅ ⋅

I wasn't sure how long I had been in the Hole. All sense of time was gone. A perceived slowing of time is another consequence of isolation. For example, sociologist Maurizio Montalbini reported that he had only been underground (in a cavern in Italy) for 219 days, when in reality he spent an entire year. The passage of time is a subjective experience; we've all sat through dry presentations that seemed to last forever, or had days at the beach that flew by far too quickly. This phenomenon in itself is fascinating: How can something as stable and fixed as time be subjective? Isn't a minute a minute? Moreover, why wouldn't we experience time accurately? What benefit could there possibly be to this subjectivity? These questions continue to confound and intrigue scientists from all disciplines; time perception is a field of research with lots of layers and contributing brain networks. We know that time perception has a lot to do with how we encode memories, particularly of novel, threatening, and thrilling events. Time perception also is influenced by the amount of attention we dedicate to a given object and its importance, or salience. And our perception of time is also highly influenced by our awareness of our physiological body, or interoception. I became intimately familiar with the concept of interoception on the CN Tower, where all systems were in overdrive: my proprioception was thrown out of whack by hanging over a thousand feet in the air in blustering wind, and I was petrified—it was a lot to be aware of. And now, in quite literally the exact opposite physical situation—a dark, cramped, cold hole underground—these same brain networks were hard at work as I was aware of every thought and sensation.

Olga Pollatos and colleagues observed the influence of interoception in a study in which participants were told either to focus on external information or to focus their attention on their internal states as they watched clips of scary, amusing, or neutral content. They found that an interoceptive focus significantly influenced the perception of the passage of time: fear-inducing clips were perceived as lasting longer, while amusing clips passed quickly. This is because we assign more attention and importance to threatening objects, which results in a perceived slowing of time. For example, we perceive objects that are moving toward us (a "looming threat") as appearing longer than static objects displayed for the same length of time. (More on that in Chapter 5, when I confront a ghost charging toward me head on.) But why?

Research from Marc Wittmann and Martin Paulus offers some answers. They show that the anterior insula (responsible for interoception) gathers and processes all the signals and sensations in the body. In times of high arousal our insula is going to have a lot more sensations to process and encode, especially if the situation is threatening or considered evolutionarily salient. The more sensations we encode, or the heavier the "load," the more likely we are to perceive time as moving slowly.

In the Hole I was not whipping through the air on a thrill ride or hanging off a building, but I was stressed. I couldn't stand up straight, and my body was giving out from the constant repositioning—I could barely crouch for thirty seconds before my thighs would start shaking. I couldn't see anything, I felt hot and cold at the same time, and I was intensely and deliberately trying to think about how I felt and confront difficult emotions. Time had all but stopped.

After overcoming numerous confrontations with my desire to leave, and almost deciding to sit in the inch-deep water, I finally succumbed to my burning muscles and turned my flashlight back on, pausing to appreciate the power of having that simple freedom. The cell lit up, along with my eyes and brain (it did feel as if a light had been turned on inside my head). I carefully stepped out until I got to the stairwell. Then I took two steps at a time to the top, where I stretched my arms into the air as high as I could, stood on my tiptoes, and let out an "Ahhhh." I looked around for Amy, anxious to hear anything except my own thoughts, but as I looked around, somewhat disoriented, I didn't see her. I felt a wave of panic: we hadn't made a plan, and the thought that I would continue to be alone was terrifying. I scanned across the never-ending walls until I saw the dim glow of a laptop and felt an instant sense of relief. I ran over and thanked her for staying close; she didn't have to, but I was glad she did. She said she was nervous something would happen and wanted to be there just in case, but then quickly changed the topic and told me a story about the filming of *Transformers 2* at ESP. Before I knew it, I was laughing. Looking back, I realize Amy did it on purpose to help me shake off the weight of the Hole. I guess when you work in a prison, you learn pretty quickly the effects it has on people.

Involuntary isolation can result in the complete obliteration of self. It is torture; even the United Nations thinks so. Yet in the United States solitary confinement is still routinely used as a form of punishment. Anywhere from twenty-five thousand to eighty thousand prisoners are in solitary today (exact numbers are difficult to determine, since not all states report them, and definitions and measurements vary). And the fact that it was not until 2014 that Pennsylvania agreed not to put inmates with serious disabilities or mental illness in solitary confinement is further testament to how far we still have to go in building institutions that do their job and also respect human rights. As philosopher and author of *Crime and Punishment* Fyodor Dostoyevsky said, "The degree of civilization in a society can be judged by entering its prisons."

> ❯ ❯ ❯

Some places are scarier than others, and sometimes we just like to go to them for a good startle or to feel the excitement of being close to fear, the taboo, or "evil" without being in real danger. But there are bigger gains to engaging with scary places; they show us the dangers of confinement, and in doing so they remind us of our freedom and reinforce our sense of self and identity. Through experiencing isolation we are reminded how much we need each other, and through touring a tragic history of abuse (by those on both sides of the bars) in a place that takes you to both sides of the mask, we are reminded of our capacity for compassion and growth.

I was no more than a tourist in solitary. Sometimes I wish I had tried to stay longer, but no matter how long I stayed, nothing would change the fact that I could turn the light back on, stand up, and walk out. I am not a prisoner; I am not trapped. I do have control over my life and my actions. I can be the person I want to be, and that is an amazing and powerful fact to celebrate.

A few days after I left ESP, it was my sister's birthday. I reached out to her for the first time in seven years.

4

EXORCISING THE GHOST

Eastern State Penitentiary. Photo by Andrew Garn; courtesy of Eastern State Penitentiary Historic Site.

One night when we were kids, my sister and her friends decided to play with a Ouija board. Like a typical younger sister I thought the older girls were very cool; they were in the eighth grade and allowed to wear trendy clothes and makeup, and gossip about sex and drugs. Being a lowly sixth grader I wasn't allowed to join them, but I did watch from the living room steps. They lit some candles, turned out all the lights, and sat in a circle around our glass-topped coffee table. They placed their pointer and middle fingers on the game's special planchette and started asking questions. I watched the wooden chip zip around the board under their fingers as they asked about boys, their friends, their future. They were doing it all wrong.

At the time I was obsessed with monsters and the occult; I was even yelled at by my sixth grade teacher for bringing in a book on witchcraft that had a drawing of a naked woman inside. "That's inappropriate, Margee," she said, despite assigning me a book that graphically depicted animal slaughter.

Watching from the steps, I grew increasingly frustrated, and finally, in a loud whisper, I said, "You guys, I'm pretty sure you're supposed to be asking to speak to, like, spirits and ghosts and stuff. It's not a Magic 8 Ball." I was met with three pairs of glaring eyes and a command to "shut up," but soon they did start asking questions of the spirit realm. The tone shifted from light and fun to more serious and dark. The indicator started moving more slowly; the answers became more obtuse and ambiguous. I watched as they quietly began to share their feelings of spirit presences in the room. "Do you feel that?" "Dude, whoa, this is freaky." They continued on, asking questions about family secrets from deceased relatives they felt hovering behind them, sending chills down their spines (so they said). Feeling satisfied and excited, I went to my room and made a plan for my own Ouija board experiment.

> > >

I left my occult-obsessed, Goth-girl adolescent phase pretty quickly, but I never gave up on imagining fantastic creatures, supernatural beings, and otherworldly adventures. There's only one problem: I've never seen a ghost. I've never felt a mysterious chill or heard a name on the wind. I've never had any kind of paranormal experience, and Lord knows, I've tried. I would look for Bigfoot on every hike, the Loch Ness monster in every lake, and a ghost in every church. I was secretly envious of everyone that shared frightful encounters with the paranormal and supernatural. There they were, wishing they could forget, and all I wanted was my own story, a real story.

While writing this book, I searched for ghosts in the most haunted places in the world. I ventured south of Bogotá to the former hotel and mansion at Tequendama Falls. The story goes that the indigenous Muisca people believed it was possible to jump from the falls, turn into an eagle, and fly away from the brutal enslavement of the Spanish colonizers—and so they tried. Hundreds lost their lives this way, but their spirits remained behind, bitter and seeking revenge. Ignoring the warning, Carlos Arturo Tapias built the Hotel del Salto in 1923 next to the falls as a retreat for rich Colombians who would come to drink, dance, and show off their wealth. One by one wealthy patrons began falling to their death into the falls. But the parties continued until a gruesome murder of a young and beautiful socialite occurred in the upstairs room, the murderer driven mad by the powerful energy of the falls. The blood-splattered walls were cleaned, but the victim's spirit remained, committed to bringing vengeance to all who trespass. It is said that if you look for her at just the right time, you can see her slight frame moving behind the windows, waiting and watching. The mansion was eerie, and the falls were beautiful, but I didn't see the ghost of the Hotel del Salto.

I went to Trans Allegheny Lunatic Asylum in West Virginia, where the ghost of Lily, a three-year-old child, is supposed to stalk the grounds, holding your hand and stealing your candy. Lily was born to a patient at TALA who was institutionalized after being raped and abused by Civil War soldiers. I didn't see Lily, though the asylum's true history of abuse was plenty scary. I went to Hill View Manor in New Castle, Pennsylvania, where the ghost of "Jeffery," also a young child, kills anyone who sees him within twenty-four hours. I didn't see Jeffery—just an old abandoned nursing home. I planned to venture out to Boston Village, aka

Helltown, Ohio, the site of satanic rituals, mutants, and ghosts. The village was taken over by Satanists who, under the darkness of night and cloaked in large black hoods and robes, used their dark sorcery, including human and animal sacrifices, to conjure spirits to do their bidding. The people were run out of town, fearing not just the Satanists but the mutants and insane who lived in the woods looking for their next victim. Right before heading out to cross the bridge where you can hear the ghosts of sacrificed babies cry out, I found out that it was all made up, another example of the growing "fakelore," or believable websites and online stories manufactured to be convincing. The town was taken in a massive eminent domain claim by the state—nothing more, nothing less.

I was getting frustrated. Where were the ghosts? I'd been not only to these legendary haunted places but to cemeteries, churches, and people's homes. Everywhere I went, there were people who insisted they'd seen something, but not me. It was becoming clear I couldn't do this on my own.

> > >

Around age six or seven, I remember asking my Sunday school teacher, "Where do monsters come from? You know the swamp thing and werewolf—where are they in the Bible?" She told me they weren't in the Bible; they were imaginary characters like the tooth fairy. I didn't believe her. I knew the tooth fairy was real! She brought me money. And she was wrong: the Bible is full of monsters, some of the greatest monsters I've ever heard of, from the notorious sea monster Leviathan and the Behemoth in the Old Testament to Revelation's First Beast, with his seven heads, feet of a bear, mouth of a lion, and ten horns. In fact, religious texts, including those we now consider mythology (but were once revered with great fervor), laid the foundations for most of our modern-day monsters, with each culture making slight adjustments depending on time and place. Indeed, you can learn a lot about a civilization by looking at its monsters.

Years later, I came to the work of Claude Lévi-Strauss, the prominent anthropologist who explained how our mythic narratives and stories of ghosts and monsters were created to bring meaning to the world, to explain things we don't understand in nature, society, and ourselves, and to bring control to the uncontrollable. Early cultures created larger-than-life beings and beasts, which went by different names and took on different physical attributes, to explain storms, volcanoes, hurricanes, and the wild animals that hunted our ancient ancestors. Imagine the sense of wonder they must have felt, coming upon the fossil of a dinosaur in the year 500 BCE or trying to make sense out of lightning or hail.*

Our early ancestors were incredibly vulnerable to nature in all its forms: predators, disease, extreme weather, and so on. In the book *Blood Rites*, Barbara Ehrenreich documents the vulnerability of our early ancestors: we were not at the top of the food chain but rather a very low-hanging fruit. Over three hundred thousand people were killed by big cats through the 1800s on the Indian subcontinent alone—and they had guns! Stephen Asma, a philosophy professor at Columbia College Chicago and renowned monster expert, comments, "Though it may seem a remote possibility to us now, during the formation of the human brain the fear of being grabbed by sharp claws, dragged into a dark hole, and eaten alive was not an abstraction." Being able to give these natural, unpredictable threats meaning and to turn predators into monsters that they could defeat brought a great deal of confidence and inspiration to societies at the mercy of nature.

My favorite monster of antiquity is perhaps the manticore, first described by Aristotle and then indexed by Pliny the Elder circa 23 CE in his book *Natural History*, which was the authority on all things monstrous up through the seventeenth century: "a triple row of teeth like a comb, the face and ears of a man, grey eyes, a blood-red color, a lion's body, and inflicts stings with its tail like a scorpion." Wolves became werewolves, dangerous dogs became chupacabras, human-eating snakes became dragons, and

---

*Other interesting misinterpretations of fossils: narwhal horns have been attributed to unicorns, mastodon skulls were seen as evidence of cyclops, and even Thomas Jefferson in the 1790s introduced the megalonyx, which he believed to be a great catlike creature based on the discovery of a large claw. It turned out to belong to a sloth.

squids and octopi became sea monsters—all to be defeated at the hand of humans. Indeed the monster as inspirational metaphor is still very much with us. During the 1930s the Hollywood Motion Picture Association decreed that every monster in a film must be destroyed by the end of the movie.

As the big questions about the elements and nature were solved, the threat of the unknown moved closer to home, as tribes of different races, religions, and cultures began meeting each other for the first time. Now the scary stories around the fire were about people from far-off lands standing ten feet tall with tails, horns, pointed teeth, and eyes of the devil. As Asma writes, "the Far East was a land of romantic and fearful projections for the ancient Westerners. Foreign people, such as Persians, Indians, and Chinese, were often linked with the strange and alien creatures of bogus natural history and mythology." While divisive, turning outsiders into terrifying monsters went a long way toward securing group solidarity, protecting resources, and rallying troops for battle.

Each progressive step toward civilized society brought answers to the big questions, and with each advance a whole cast of supernatural beings moved from reality to fiction. Monsters increasingly became representations of the taboo and the destruction that comes when we step outside the boundaries of civilized society. They became repositories for the imagination: we could imagine a fantastic beast that embodies all the things we are not, or that we want to be. But they were not real; there were no sea monsters or Titans. The big unanswered questions moved inward, to sin and salvation.

In the developing world the real monster was no longer "out there" on the battlefield or in the forests but inside and all around us, in the form of spirits, ghosts, or demons. These monsters were real: murderers, thugs, brutes, and thieves were proof that evil could infect any one of us. And these agents of the Devil, including witches, demons, and ghosts, would not be conquered with strength and weapons but prayer and faith. Belief in possession, hauntings, and witchcraft reminded people to stay on the righteous path of the Lord (or gods, spirits, or whichever supreme being a particular culture recognized) and fight their inner beasts tempting them to stray. This fear-based morality was and still is an incredibly effective form of social control.

Modern monsters continue to reflect the fears of our time, but largely as metaphor: Godzilla as the consequence of the dangers of nuclear waste, a zombie apocalypse as the consequence of societal breakdown, bio-mutant robots as the consequence of unbridled science and technology. Most people don't believe these monsters are actually real but vehicles to help societies deal with a changing world. But there is one monster that remains, that many people (across the globe) still believe exists, and that is a representation of death, one of our biggest fears: the ghost.*

> . > . >

In the United States (and even more so in Japan, as I would find), fear of the supernatural is extremely popular. Ghosts are always in the top five scariest monsters in ScareHouse customer surveys, and it seems there is always a new TV show about paranormal phenomena: *Ghost Hunters, Ghost Hunters International, Fear, A Haunting, The Dead Files, My Ghost Story, Fact or Faked*, and even *Celebrity Ghost Stories*. And that's to say nothing of horror movies—these are just the nonfiction stories of people obsessed with ghosts. Ghost hunting has even become a commercial activity: former institutions, churches, hospitals, and hotels are being bought up by eager capitalists looking to make the easy money found in offering paranormal investigations, and folks are lining up to pay them.†

I've toured a lot of historical sites and former institutions that offer their own paranormal investigations, and many of them

---

*A Huffington Post/YouGov Poll in 2012 reported that 45 percent of Americans believe in ghosts, and 64 percent believe in life after death.

†At Haunted Hill View Manor, a former nursing home, you can pay $65 to spend a day looking for ghosts, plus an extra $25 if you need equipment. The building is unheated, in a state of ruin, and staffed by a handful of guides; the overhead is almost nonexistent. The fewer amenities, the better!

sensationalize the "haunted" history of their buildings. For example, they create and share extravagant ghost stories, put props or "artifacts" in certain places, or change the temperature to essentially fake the paranormal data. This is entertaining for the everyday curious customer looking for a fun experience, but I wanted the real thing. I connected with a paranormal investigation group from Connecticut that consisted of a professional paranormal photographer, a psychic, a sound tech, and an experienced hunter. They had chosen a site that, according to the ghost-hunting community, is the most haunted in the United States. There would be no actors or tourist gimmicks, and the site's handlers observe very strictly enforced rules *not* to talk about the paranormal, share ghost stories, or suggest that the space is haunted. Oh, and one more thing—I'd already spent a night there. I was going back to Eastern State Penitentiary. This time I wasn't alone.

≫ ≫ ≫

I wish I could say I felt more comfortable returning to ESP in the dark for a second time, but I didn't. The forty-foot walls and massive main gates never cease to be incredibly imposing and unsettling, and now I had a new question consuming my mind: *What if this place is haunted?* I equally wanted it to be true and false at the same time. After a welcoming startle scare from Amy, I introduced myself to the eight investigators in the group, and then, as sociologists like to do, I slipped into the background, ready to quietly observe. Perhaps I could learn something about our fascination with and fear of ghosts, and—maybe—come away with my own ghost story.

≫ ≫ ≫

ESP handles paranormal investigators like anyone else who wants to rent their space. This means staff and guides are on-site for guidance and supervision only; they advise where investigators can go, what they can do, and how long they can be in the space, but nothing more. The rules seemed pretty straightforward: we could never be out of sight of the tour guides, we were not allowed into any of the cells that are blocked, and we couldn't go outside the building into the yard alone. My ghost group seemed at ease with these rules, quietly listening as they began to unload their equipment.

I watched camera after camera emerge from their bags. There must have been ten or twelve in all, appearing out of nowhere, like a Nikon clown car. They were all different sizes and shapes, some digital and some film, and even one I think was an original Polaroid. The most impressive was a large, black, atlas-sized, motion-sensor camera fastened to a tripod. This is the same camera that big-prey hunters use to capture distant, fast-moving animals like deer and bears. Then came the sound equipment: two digital audio recorders, a cassette recorder, several microphones, headphones, and a sound amplifier. This was beginning to look more like a real hunting trip; I half expected a rifle to come out next. Instead, there were some unexpected gadgets: a thermometer, an EMF meter (which detects changes in electromagnetic fields), plus a tennis ball, a larger plastic ball, and a smaller denser ball. I instantly thought of the two scary twin girls in *The Shining*: "Come play with us, Danny." (This actually was pretty appropriate, as it turned out.)

The team split into three groups and took off in different directions. I went with Tom, the seasoned, experienced hunter and group organizer; Julie Griffin, a photographer (check out her book, *Ghostly Photographs*); Leslie, a psychic; and Teresa, a sound specialist. We headed slowly down the pitch-black cellblock, the only light coming from two small pin flashlights and the light radiating from the central rotunda, where the guide sat perched in the middle on a tall chair. From there he could watch all three groups. I had to laugh—the prison was built for easy surveillance, and it was still being used that way.

The group spread out ahead of me. I hung back to give them some space and watched as they touched the walls and looked all around, taking it all in. The building is mesmerizing, and had it been my first time there, I would have been doing the same thing. But I was happy to focus my full attention on the investigators. If I expected to see a ghost, I would need to follow their leads.

Leslie had stopped a quarter of the way down the cellblock. In a whisper she said, "Do you see him?" She pointed down the hall. "There's a tall man with a big belly standing in the doorway at the end of the hall." Tom, who might be six foot four and 350 pounds, found a way to approach her stealthily and whispered, "You see him? What's he doing?" Leslie replied that he wasn't doing anything; he was just staring at her.

⋆ ⋆ ⋆

Leslie learned she was psychic when she was a child growing up in a haunted house. Since then she has always been able to see ghosts and spirits, and she can act as a medium. This may sound like an unusual occupation, but Leslie is far from alone. Mediums and psychics have been with us since the dawn of time, and belief in their abilities is still widespread across the globe. There have been countless studies attempting to prove the abilities of psychics, all with dismal results. Most of the best psychics, mediums, and fortune-tellers are instead gifted in the practice of perception and observation. They feign receiving messages from the spirit world when in reality their messages come from the living: a person's clothes, hairstyle, makeup, age, gender, race, and culture. This "cold reading" is not a new phenomenon, and you could spend a whole book, or more, making sense of it.* But I don't think Leslie is a cunning or manipulative cold reader; she honestly believes she is psychic.

Research, of course, has yet to prove that anyone actually talks to spirits or that ghosts even exist (that doesn't mean it won't be proven one day—who knows what kind of discoveries science will make in the future?). What we do know is that some people, like monks, nuns, and shamans, report a high degree of spirituality,

---

*For a good overview of cold reading, check out *The Full Facts Book of Cold Reading: A Comprehensive Guide to the Most Persuasive Psychological Manipulation Technique in the World* by Ian Rowland; *Guide to Cold Reading* by Ray Hyman; and *Cold Reading: Confessions of a "Psychic"* by Colin Hunter. And my favorite: *An Honest Liar*, a documentary about James "the Amazing" Randi, who dedicated his life to exposing fakes and charlatans.

out-of-body experiences, and communions with God, nature, or some higher being, and yes, some can even see ghostlike figures. They may go into trancelike writing for pages and pages or speak in unknown languages. And while some shamans use psyche-delic drugs like ayahuasca or peyote, most practice concentration and prayer to move into their state of communing with a higher being—and their brains reflect this. Researchers have performed EEG and fMRI scans on meditating shamans and nuns, and it is clear that they enter into a different type of brain state. Even their visual cortices are active—meaning they are likely having hallu-cinations or visions. This ability to feel a greater sense of connec-tion appears to be easier for some than others. Are such people gifted? Is what they are seeing real?

＊ ＊ ＊

As I watched Leslie, my eyes grew wide, and my jaw literally dropped. I was speechless. I had never been with someone *during* a paranormal encounter, and I was completely unprepared for the intensity that was quickly building. I had assumed I would observe the group as they walked around ESP while taking photos and "feeling" energies, maybe pointing out signs of paranormal presences. But as Leslie stood fixated on the doorway at the end of the corridor with Tom and Julie flanking either side, I found myself inching closer, squinting my eyes, and following her finger pointing down the cellblock. My mind was racing: *What does she see? What does it look like? I want to see it!* I strained my eyes and leaned forward, and even though nothing was blocking us, we all remained behind the motionless Leslie. I couldn't make out any-thing through the dark doorway, but we stood in silence, hold-ing our breath until Leslie broke her gaze, dropped her hand, and said the man had disappeared. Everyone let out a breath.

We began moving down the cellblock, with the others paus-ing frequently to take photos with different cameras. Team mem-bers were meticulous with their process, ensuring images were captured with a variety of shutter speeds, angles, and exposure times, plus making lots of other careful adjustments to the esoteric

EMF meter and thermometer. The space was silent except for the sound of the camera clicks and flashes that echoed through the empty cellblock. Everything was in slow motion. The ghost hunters moved carefully and deliberately, and I was suddenly strongly aware of my own clumsy and loud presence. I began to take each step as if on broken glass. I obsessively checked my cell phone to make sure it was off. I feared shattering their delicate silence.

About halfway down the cellblock, Leslie stopped again.

She stared straight ahead, peering down the walkway. I saw nothing in front of her. "Hi there, my name is Leslie," she said to the empty space. "What's yours?"

, , ,

Are ghosts real? Science may be unable to answer this question definitively right now, but it can offer insight into people who say they have had supernatural experiences. Often, the ghost is in the machine. Sometimes this is a simple matter of mechanical or electrical explanations for paranormal activity: noises and subtle sensory signals given off by HVACs, radiators, or faulty electric systems. But there are other machines out there that reveal a lot about why we might see ghosts.

The first machine is simple enough—a speaker. Richard Lord, an acoustic scientist, and Richard Wiseman, a psychologist at the University of Hertfordshire in southern England, conducted an experiment with unsuspecting crowds attending a concert in London in 2003. Throughout the concert the audience was exposed to infrasound, which is inaudible sound waves of 20 hertz or less—essentially, tiny vibrations in the air. The crowd reported more feelings of uneasiness, sorrow, revulsion, fear, and chills down the spine when the infrasound was turned on. In an exhaustive overview of the research, Michael A. Persinger found the reported symptoms hold up across studies, even under experimental lab conditions.

These findings give weight to researchers like Vic Tandy, who suggest people who report supernatural encounters have simply been exposed to infrasound without realizing it. Our body picks up these inaudible sound waves through our ears, our skin, and even our eyes and registers the slight vibrations as a sign that something is not quite right. In fact, extremely low-frequency sounds are often to blame for a phenomenon known as the Hum,* which a small percentage of the population can hear in certain regions. The causes are diverse, from a manufacturing plant to mating fish, but the Hum has real consequences; it causes sleepless nights and nausea, and in the UK it has been linked to three suicides. Since we cannot hear it or see the source of the vibration, it makes us feel uncomfortable and our defense system is triggered, preparing our body for threat. This is the same process that alerts animals of an ensuing catastrophic event. For example, in 2004 animals retreated inland in droves hours before the Indian Ocean earthquake and tsunami; both of these phenomena produce infrasound, as do other naturally occurring phenomena like avalanches, volcanoes, and geomagnetic activity. Infrasound can also naturally occur by passing through and vibrating human-made machines like wind turbines and duct systems. A large, empty building with lots of structural defects—say, an abandoned prison or a rotting old mansion—would be a prime location for naturally occurring infrasound. Their floorboards and old ducts and pipes are loose and ready to rattle inaudibly if, for instance, a strong gust of wind happens to blow through. In that moment, your body may "hear" the vibrations even if you don't. Having experimented with infrasound myself, I can attest to the associated feelings of uneasiness and discomfort. In fact I now consider it a must-have for ScareHouse.

The second machine suggested to leave us feeling we're not alone in this world is aptly called the God Helmet, invented by Stanley Koren and Michael A. Persinger in the late 1980s. Assuming that paranormal experiences are not supernatural at all but a result of disturbances in our brain, Persinger believed if he could disrupt the brain's functioning, he could simulate this "sensed presence." To do this, Persinger and Koren created the God

---

*Locations where the Hum has been recorded: Bristol, Birmingham, Hertfordshire, and Strathclyde, England; Taos, New Mexico, and Kokomo, Indiana; as well as Canada, Germany, Sweden, and Denmark.

Helmet by adding small electromagnets called solenoids to the inside of a snowmobile helmet, positioned directly over the temporal lobes. When activated, the God Helmet exposes the brain to weak magnetic fields—around 1 micro tesla—which for comparison is weaker than a refrigerator magnet. After numerous trials Persinger reported that he could trigger the feeling of a sensed presence; he had found God (and ghosts) in the brain.

The idea that scientists had discovered the source of God set off a whole flurry of controversy, much as the mirror neuron debate would do decades later, and a litany of challengers, including Richard Dawkins, who, in a PBS *Horizon* documentary, tried on the helmet with less than favorable results (he didn't sense any supernatural presences). Persinger's work was further challenged with sa cathing paper from Swedish psychologist Pehr Granqvist, who attempted to replicate Persinger's findings and instead found that suggestibility and personality characteristics predicted whether or not a person would have a supernatural experience— it didn't have anything to do with weak magnetic fields. In fact there is no scientific explanation as to *why* weak magnetic fields would produce such results. Strong magnetic fields, however, are a different story.

What has been proven and replicated is that transcranial magnetic stimulation (TMS)—targeted pulses of 1 tesla (which is more than a million times stronger than what Persinger's subjects were exposed to)—*can* give us an "out of body" or "sensed presence" feeling when positioned in specific locations in the brain.* For example, a 2006 article by Shahar Arzy found that repeated stimulation of the left temporo-parietal junction resulted in the subject perceiving a shadowy figure. Indeed, people who "sense a presence" in the room sometimes display a hyperactivation of the temporal lobe, which is concerned with body awareness and our perception of self and other. It is also the part of the brain that has been shown to light up on fMRI scans when nuns claim

---

*It can do a lot more than that, in fact: TMS is now an accepted therapeutic treatment for major depression, schizophrenia, and neuropathic pain, and potentially a treatment for Alzheimer's and Parkinson's.

to be in deep prayer and in union with God. Furthermore, individuals with temporal lobe epilepsy (i.e., excessive brain activity in the temporal lobe) sometimes experience something called "ecstatic seizures," which produce feelings comparable to supernatural encounters, including a "sensed presence," and feelings of heightened spirituality and euphoria. This condition, collectively referred to as Gastaut-Geschwind syndrome, also includes bouts of marathon and spontaneous writing.

While magnetic fields might mess with your electronics and make your lights flicker, it's impossible to experience one powerful enough to evoke a "sense of presence" in the natural world. Monks, nuns, experienced meditators, and those with temporal lope epilepsy have the ability, through practice or biology, to disrupt the communication in their brain and experience these supernatural feelings. So my advice for those who see a ghost or feel a presence around them: be sure to add visiting a neurologist to your quest for answers.

⋆ ⋆ ⋆

The anticipation was building. I looked over and saw that Julie was frantically snapping photos, Tom was adjusting and fidgeting with one of the gadgets in his hand, and everyone was shuffling and moving around with nervous energy and excitement. I watched Leslie nod her head, her hands slightly trembling, but I didn't hear anything. We gathered closer, and Leslie began to ask more questions. I watched in awe as she whispered in a shaking voice into the darkness: "Can we take your photo?" "Can we talk to you?" "What are you doing here?"

Leslie was talking to a young boy, probably around fourteen she thought, and he wanted us to follow him into the yard to play. I was frozen in a state of complete bewilderment. Was I really seeing this? As I followed Leslie's gaze and tried to imagine what she was seeing, I remembered learning during my first visit about ESP's youngest inmate, a teenager, who was protected and favored by the other inmates during the 1960s. Could this be his ghost? Without saying a word, we all followed behind Leslie as she started moving quickly down the cellblock toward the exit into the yard. My heart was racing.

Right before we reached the exit, the tour guide appeared behind us and startled the group with a loud yet gentle reminder that we could not leave the building without supervision. Like a parent flipping on the lights in the middle of a make-out session, he immediately sucked the energy out of the room. Leslie turned around and said the boy was gone. He never came back.

> > >

After about five minutes of the group exploring the cellblock independently, our quiet energy returned; it was time for the balls. I was overwhelmed with curiosity as I watched Julie pull out a half-green and half-black ball the size of a large grapefruit. *What is she going to do with the ball?* If it rolled down the hallway, would a ghost disrupt its path? Would its bounce bring a strange echo? Maybe the ghosts would roll it back, or they needed it for a game of spectral croquet. Fearful of breaking the mood again, I decided not to ask. I was caught up in the energy, hovering behind them at arm's length, observing intently, as if I were a ghost myself. I realized I was *believing*.

Julie leaned into one of the cells and ever so gently placed the ball just inside the frame. She adjusted it so that the vertical line between its green and black halves was perpendicular to the floor, then stepped back. The suspense was killing me. Part of me expected the ball to pop open at the seam and let out a searing ghost light or the souls of all who'd died in this place. Or *something*. But it just sat there. The team took several photos of the ball from all different angles and then quietly retreated back to the central rotunda, leaving the ball sitting in the frame. I still didn't understand, but I'd have to wait for my answer.

We headed down another cellblock, where Leslie said she felt a strong energy, and stopped in front of a cell about one-third of the way down on the right. As far as I could tell, there was nothing significant about that particular cell. It looked similar to the hundreds of others: crumbling walls, piles of dust and debris, random pieces of wood, steel, and stone scattered across the tiny cement floor. It was dark, with a single beam of moonlight coming through the small cutout on the far wall. Leslie and Teresa moved toward the cell opening, and I bit my lip as they stepped up onto the frame and bent down to duck under the bar blocking the cell. A lot of things happened that night I could never have predicted, but this time I knew exactly what was going to happen next. As I learned from Amy during my first visit, you cannot, under any circumstances, go into a blocked-off cell. As if by teleportation, the guide appeared and once again reminded the group where we could and could not go. It was startling, but I smiled. These folks were just like me, letting their curiosity lead the way. I flashed back to my sixth grade teacher: "Margee, that's inappropriate."

Settling for a spot right outside the cell, Teresa sat down and started organizing her equipment. First she brought out a digital recorder with an attached sound amplifier that looked similar to a megaphone. Then she pulled out an old-school cassette recorder, a model that must have been twenty years old or more. According to Teresa, they are better at picking up transient sound. I stood only about a foot away, watching intently. She labeled a cassette with the location, date, and time, popped it in, and pressed "Record." The whole series of sounds triggered a powerful sense of nostalgia for me; the ballpoint pen tapping the face of the cassette, the clumsy clanking as it slid into place, the satisfying click when the lid closed securely, and the coordinated and forceful push of the "Play" and "Record" buttons simultaneously. I was thirteen years old again and making mix tapes in my bedroom.

Teresa pointed the amplifier into the cell, moved her headphones back over her ears, and closed her eyes. I was completely transfixed, staring into the empty and dilapidated cell, straining my eyes to see into the dark corners.

At first the others tried speaking into the cell, asking if anyone was there and then if the ghost could make a sound so we could hear it, or if it had any messages to communicate. They spoke softly in whispers, and then everyone fell silent, and we waited in the dark, listening. My anticipation grew, my muscles tensed, and my whole body and mind were bracing for what might come next.

I didn't want to move or even blink for fear I'd miss something. I was ready. But all I could see were specks of dust floating in the moonlight, and all I could hear was the soft winding and the gentle hum of the cassette tape inside the recorder. Then a strange sensation of dizziness washed over me, a feeling that the world around me was in motion but I was completely still.

I felt an intense tingle starting at the top of my head and then moving all the way down my spine and through my limbs. My shoulders shuddered involuntarily, but my body felt warm, relaxed, and energized at the same time. I closed my eyes and admitted something to myself: I was feeling a ghost pass through me. The physical sensation was pronounced and had no discernible cause. I simply couldn't think of any other explanation. I'd read reams of research on paranormal phenomena and spiritual experiences, but I didn't recognize this moment from any textbook or experiment. I took a deep breath in and couldn't contain my smile: finally, my first paranormal experience.

⋗ ⋗ ⋗

To say I am a skeptic of the supernatural would be an understatement, but I've obviously never given up hope of being proved wrong. Our knowledge of the universe we inhabit has always been incomplete. Look how long it took us to figure out the world wasn't flat; even today we don't understand why planes and boats go missing in the Bermuda Triangle. So when I experienced that chilling, euphoric sensation standing outside the cell during the investigation, I felt a deep sense of discovery. Not only was I learning that ghosts are real, but *I felt the presence of one inside my body*. If the world *were* flat, I would be experiencing the equivalent of learning that fact because I fell off the edge. I would have this story to share for the rest of my life.

Once the excitement waned, my logical mind was attempting to find explanations that did not include the supernatural. I thought about infrasound, epilepsy, and the magic of TMS, but none of these explanations were plausible. It didn't quite feel like the "chills" that I get when I have a fever.* It also didn't feel like the shiver so many of us experience when listening to really moving music. That response, called "frisson," starts in the lower back and moves upward, and is accompanied by goose bumps (or pilo-erection), which appear when our sympathetic nervous system is activated, like during fight or flight.

The ghost, it seemed, had activated my sympathetic nervous system, but I didn't really get goose bumps, and it was deathly quiet in the prison—I certainly wasn't listening to any music. So it must have been something else: a ghost, momentarily taking residence in my body.

Still, I'm a scientist. My skeptical mind wouldn't let me accept it—to my dismay. I knew something had moved through me, but maybe I had just wanted to experience something so badly that my brain made it happen. Placebo and psychosomatic sensations can be extremely powerful and are widely believed to explain the paranormal experiences people claim to have. You want to see a ghost, so you'll see a ghost. You want to feel a chill, so you'll feel a chill. Our brain hates dissonance, so it will work incredibly hard—so hard it affects our bodies—to make our thoughts match our experiences. But, at some level, I always thought psychoso-matic sensation had the air of a scientist's excuse: I can't explain what happened to you, spirit medium, so I'll just say it's all in your head. Later, after I left the prison, I continued to search the literature for a logical cause. And that's when I stumbled onto an explanation I had never heard of before: ASMR.

Autonomous sensory meridian response is basically tingles down the spine. It is not a clinical diagnosis, or as of yet recognized as a distinct, objectively measurable response. The descriptions of the sensation are all relatively consistent: the feeling of chills and quivers down the spine that travel out through our arms and legs. The description that fit my experience at ESP

---

*Fever chills are caused by our muscles quickly contracting and relaxing to produce heat and fight off a nasty infection. When that heat goes away, it feels like a chill.

exactly was a carbonated beverage being poured under my skin. And unlike the fleeting feeling of frisson, ASMR produces a feeling of euphoria, relaxation, and calmness that can last as long as fifteen minutes. The triggers can be practically anything but generally fall into one of these categories: interesting sounds like nail tapping, clicking sounds, crinkling bags; soft voices like whispering or quiet instruction;* grooming and self-care like hair brushing, massages, and even clinical exams; concentrated tasks like repetitive folding. There is a proliferation of theories as to why these types of activities are triggers: Yale neurologist Steven Novella thinks it could potentially be setting off minor seizures in the brain. Professor David Huron posits that personal grooming activities are akin to the grooming habits we see among primates—it's a time to bond and be together. Others suggest that quiet voices and whispering *are* relaxing and inherently pleasurable, but they are skeptical that ASMR is a distinct response at work outside of normal vagus nerve activation. There has been much speculation about ASMR, but far too little scientific testing to merit any definite conclusions.†

It was enough for me, though. I had experienced an ASMR, probably from the combination of the whispering voices and the sounds of the cassette recorder. In the dark prison, with our ghost-hunting antennae up, we were excited and emotional, full

---

*The painter Bob Ross, who had a PBS television program for years, is an icon in the ASMR community. I myself was obsessed with him growing up and all through college; I even owned a Bob Ross calendar and couldn't drive through the Pennsylvania mountains without thinking about happy little trees. Something about Ross's voice, his quick brushstrokes, and the gentle sounds of his mixing paints on his palette trigger ASMR.

†Just as this book was going to print, Emma L. Barratt and Nick J. Davis published the first-ever peer-reviewed findings from a survey study of those reporting an ASMR experience: "Autonomous Sensory Meridian Response (ASMR): A Flow-Like Mental State," *PeerJ* 3 (2015): e851. While there were no psychophysiological measurements, their findings confirmed what I experienced and reported through my own research. They also found that inducing ASMR led to temporary improvements in symptoms of chronic pain and depression. Finally, there was a high prevalence of synesthesia, when stimulation of one sense leads to activation of another sense (5.9 percent, compared to 4.4 percent of the general population) in the sample, suggesting the two experiences may be linked.

of suspense and anticipation. This heightened state happens whenever we are aroused; our system goes on high alert, sensitizing us to anything in our environment. In other words, the safety was off my arousal system, and I was primed to experience a strong physical reaction.

Even though I had discovered a nonparanormal explanation for my response, I wasn't going to give up on my ghost story. This amazing response and truly awesome sensation only happened because I allowed myself to be open to the experience, to suspend my disbelief and "opt in." I ventured into a ruined old building with ghost hunters, tuning myself carefully to their frequencies. I strained my eyes in the dark and let the room wash over me. And boy, did it ever pay off.

> > >

We stood still and silent outside the cell door for at least ten minutes, collectively entranced, straining to see or feel anything. Even though I had just met these people, the focused co-attention produced a feeling of closeness and compassion. It reminded me of the times I'd participated in group meditations inside a traditional sweat lodge. (This is a phenomenon known as *vipassana* love: when strangers who meditate together express feelings of love, even though they've never spoken.)

Outside the cell, time stood still for me once again, and we likely would have stayed there even longer had one of the other teams not entered back into the rotunda, breaking the concentration and the silence. Teresa pushed "Pause" on the recorder, and I shuddered and shook my arms. Everyone came to life and expressed how excited they were to have captured such great recordings to analyze. I didn't say anything about feeling a ghost pass through me; I was still trying to maintain an unobtrusive position. But it was hard. Everything in me wanted to share what I had experienced, just as at Fuji-Q Highland.

> > >

Later I asked Julie why she'd chosen this profession. She's a skilled photographer who could be working for a newspaper or *National Geographic*. Why spend hundreds of dollars to hunt down ghosts? Her answer was simple enough: "It's fun; it's intriguing; it's an adventure every time." I realized I'd been expecting something epic and dark, like a desire to banish evil spirits from the earth. Instead, Julie said she didn't get scared that much. She liked the anticipation of the hunt, the immersion in the space, and the exhilaration that comes with engaging with the paranormal. The rest of the ghost hunters shared her sentiments: yes, they desperately wanted to prove and find evidence for what they so strongly believed, but they were also looking for friends who shared their passion and would join in the adventure. Friends with whom they could share stories of feeling tingles all over their body, without being judged. I totally got it.

I had started this adventure with the goal of understanding our fear of ghosts and hoping to have my own paranormal experience. I had thought it was all about our fear of death, our relationship with God and religion. What I learned is that, at least in the United States, our obsession with the paranormal is more about anticipation, excitement, suspense, and, most surprisingly of all, "fun" fear with friends. From the outside, nothing happened in the prison that night. We walked around, took photos, and listened to silence. No, I didn't come away with a better understanding of our fear of death (though I would before I finished writing this book), but I did come to understand the joy and thrill of really believing. It *was* exciting. Letting myself run with my imagination, suspending all disbelief, and getting caught up in the moment was exhilarating. I still consider it my first paranormal experience, even if it wasn't entirely supernatural.

> ❧ ❧ ❧

Before saying good-bye, there was one last thing to do: get the ball. Walking quickly and excitedly back to the first cellblock, I finally broke down and asked, "What's up with the ball!?" Julie laughed. There are no ghosts hiding inside, no special Ouija properties. It's just a ball, and it makes a very good test for unseen presences. You place the ball, take a photo, and then come back later to see if it has moved. If it has, then you've got ghosts. It was surprisingly scientific.

We walked back toward the cell where she'd carefully set it out, nervously anticipating what we'd find.

5

THE LITTLE HOUSE OF HORRORS

Entrance to the Daiba Strange School, right next to Happy Smile Playland and LOL Picture Shop. Photo by the author.

I have been to a lot of haunted houses, more than most—probably thirty or so in 2014 alone. I've been to the Guinness World Record holder for longest haunted attraction in the world (Factory of Terror, Canton, Ohio); to haunts with big animatronic creatures that breathe fire (Ghostly Manor, Sandusky, Ohio) or shoot machine guns; and to haunts with hundreds of actors in Hollywood-caliber makeup, who ambush you from across the street, some walking around on ten-foot stilts or dropping down on bungee cords out of nowhere (Terror Behind the Walls, Philadelphia). I've been to haunts that claim to be the most intense, thrilling, and extreme (Black Out, New York City) as well as the most kid-friendly and family-friendly and everything in between. But that's in the United States.

While US haunts have come a long way from witches, black cats, and mummies, their history and the haunted house season are inextricably linked to Halloween, which emerged as a time of celebration and fun in the late nineteenth century. Early Puritan settlers were staunchly against Halloween, a celebration they considered dark and diabolical. But immigrants from Ireland and Scotland introduced the States to the ancient Celtic festival of Samhain, which involved wearing scary costumes and lighting fires to scare away tormenting spirits. Over the years, American Halloween became a mix of traditions from Samhain and the Christian All Saints' Day (when saints are honored and the newly departed souls are prayed for), and then eventually expanded to include every monster imaginable, leaving us with the highly secular and commercialized holiday we have today (second in consumer spending only to Christmas).

Rituals like wearing costumes, lighting candles, wearing dark robes, and offering gifts (treats) were mixed and reimagined over and over, resulting in the traditions Americans know and love like trick-or-treating, bobbing for apples, and dressing up in costume—which can range from a traditional scary witch to a slutty nurse.* As children we love dressing up as our favorite heroes or villains, and as adults the ability to become someone else, to do things we would never do using the "loophole" of wearing a costume, for better or worse, is all too appealing. Haunted houses grew out of these traditions of confronting and sometimes mocking death and continued to evolve rapidly. But

---

*How a ritual to ward off evil spirits turned into a "moral holiday" where the standard norms and consequences are set aside (another example of a moral holiday is Mardi Gras) is a whole different book. For a great review check out Elizabeth A. Grater, "The Rise of 'Slut-o-ween': Cultural Productions of Femininity in Halloween Costumes," master's thesis, George Washington University, 2012.

the idea of building a space that is scary, or creating content that is meant to scare those who witness it, is certainly not a Western or American phenomenon. Indeed, structures built to scare the public date back as far as ancient Egypt, where temples and pyramids contained labyrinths, mazes, and statues that were not only visually impressive and intimidating but when triggered would move, all to scare away intruders.

Most Americans understand a haunted house in this same proud tradition—as a place you walk into and things pop out and go, "Boo." The US population is pretty well educated on the rules: you don't touch anything, and nothing will touch you (there are exceptions, but I'll get to that later). But outside the United States, there are no rules, something I learned firsthand in Bogotá, where haunted houses are just starting to emerge. I consumed as much scary entertainment as I could on my trips to Canada, Japan, and Colombia—from haunted houses to themed restaurants and ghost tours—to observe how people in different cultures engage with and create scary material. I was also secretly hoping to find a haunt that would leave me feeling just as excited and delighted as I was as a child, when I got my first taste of haunted houses in the form of a shabbily decorated school gymnasium.

Lucky for me I did find it, in the most unexpected place.

⋗ ⋗ ⋗

The commercialized American Halloween has been exported around the globe, but in many countries haunted houses aren't particularly connected to it. In Japan, the haunt season starts as soon as the temperature begins to warm up, because going to a haunted house (or *obake-yashiki*, as they are locally known) in the summer will give you a "chill" and cool you off. If this sounds silly, it's actually not—the "chill" you get from a scary experience isn't just a metaphor. Your blood rushes away from your skin and to your muscles to prepare for fighting or running, causing your skin temperature to drop.

Having been to Japan's amusement parks, I decided to experience its unique style of horror, "J-horror," as well. I started by exploring the "Mystery and Panic" attractions in Tokyo's oldest amusement park, known as Hanayashiki, which opened in 1853. The tiny park is squished into the busy city that grew up around it; it's quite surreal to see roller coasters and a Ferris wheel operating in the middle of a bustling city street; usually rides have a wide footprint on the ground in case someone falls off. Here a fall would land you in the middle of a vendor's cart. Everything in the park was dated and covered with the telltale signs of time—rusted and squeaky tracks and wheels, chipped Pokemon figurines, layers of dust on the plastic pastel flowers. It reminded me of the now-popular photographs of abandoned amusement parks; only this was still open.

The first two rides left me doubtful of finding a really scary Japanese haunt. Thriller Car: Western-Style Haunted House was a perfect example of old-school dark rides that emerged at the turn of the nineteenth century in the early years of the amusement park boom. Dark rides combined trolley rides with scary images and macabre scenes full of automated props, flashing lights, and sounds designed to startle the audience. These rides were the precursor to the linear walk-through haunted attractions of today. The Thriller Car, which looked as if it were an original from the mid-twentieth century, rolled along rusty tracks at around three miles per hour with jerky stops and starts while all the traditional American monsters made their appearances in the course of the five-minute ride: vampires, werewolves, and a dusty old skeleton draped in a torn cloak. It was kids' stuff, a simulacrum of horror, dulled by changing cultural expectations.

Next I went through the Ghost Mansion, which I thought would be Japan's interpretation of Disney's famous Haunted Mansion. Instead, it was an immersive audio haunt, which was also a first for me and something I hadn't seen in the States (though I'm sure it exists).* The story was in Japanese, and there was no translation. It's hard to imagine what I might have missed, but

---

*Amazing advances in virtual reality and 4-D technology—synching audio, visual, and environmental cues with 3-D animation—are among some of the best rides today (for example, the Transformers ride at Universal Studios), but this was something else entirely.

the experience was absorbing all the same. Audio cues can be just as powerful as physical startles, and these cues were perfectly timed with environmental responses: I could hear footsteps while the floor shook; a crack of lightning made the lights flicker in the room and then go out. My headphones were filled with disturbing sounds—heavy breathing, a woman screaming, a baby crying— all sending a chill down my spine.* The tour ended with a pair of fading footsteps and the bang of a door.

After experiencing the old-school attractions, I was ready to be really scared and see something more in line with twenty-first-century Japanese designs. I thought I had hit the jackpot when I found a haunted attraction called Haunted House: Pure Japanese-Style Haunted House, which is where my journey of cultural ineptitude began in earnest.

Over the course of my tours through nine haunted houses in Japan, I committed at least twenty mistakes out of cultural ignorance; it was a great lesson in how many of our social scripts we take for granted. For instance, at the end of the first hallway of my first Japanese-style haunt, I came to a wall with multiple doors, none of which were notably lit or demarcated as the way out. In US attractions, you are not supposed to touch anything, including things you might in your daily life, like doorknobs or light switches or windows, so I found myself in a quandary: How do I get out? I patiently waited for something to happen, until an attendant had to come and point me toward one of the doors. In the Haunted Hospital at Fuji-Q I surrendered my flashlight too early, forcing another attendant to track me down and hand me another,† and in two other haunts I mistakenly went through emergency exit doors. By the time I reached my last haunted house, I was essentially tiptoeing.

---

*According to the International Affective Digital Sounds index, which is a rating of salience of sounds (pleasurable, arousing, and controlling), all these noises are among the most disturbing to human ears.

†Guests were supposed to keep a flashlight with them at all times, but I dropped mine off at the first drop box, thinking it was no longer needed. The box was just for those exiting through the "chicken doors," a way out for people who decide they can't take the scary anymore.

In the Japanese-style haunted house, I began to notice the cultural differences in expression of scary material, and not just ones relating to my own American blunders. Rather than a studiously thematic and special effects–filled attraction, it featured several nondescript hallways with no actors, and no sound effects or props, which in turn led to disturbing glass display cases with traditional Japanese monsters, more like a horror museum than a haunted house. The first display consisted of a ghostly mannequin dressed in a traditional kimono with a pale drawn face with a wide mouth, extended arms, and, of course, the long black hair common to most female monsters, especially in Japan. As I walked by, her eyes lit up, and she launched forward, stopping just inches in front of the glass. I assumed this was a representation of the *Yuki-onna*, or snow woman, who is a tall beauty with long black hair and frosty blue lips who stalks and murders humans, either freezing them with her icy breath or killing them with a single look from her piercing eyes. Various versions of *Yuki-onna* appear in Japanese literature; like the vampire in the West, she is a popular monster in Japanese horror.

To me, there was nothing scary about the *Yuki-onna*, other than the slight startle when I triggered the animatronic. But perhaps, had I grown up in Japan listening to frightful stories of the evil snow woman, I would have felt differently. Our threat response is automatic, but what we fear is largely learned, and the science behind learned fears famously starts with drooling dogs, terrified babies, and electrified rodents (indeed some of the research conducted to study fear is itself terrifying, an irony I would soon come to fully embrace).

The story starts with Ivan Pavlov, who laid down the basics of classical conditioning by training his dogs to salivate at the sound of a bell through repeated pairings of the bell with the presentation of food.* John B. Watson took this formula to the next level with

---

*Classical conditioning consists of pairing an unconditioned response elicited by an unconditioned stimulus with a conditioned stimulus, which results in an animal experiencing the unconditioned response to the conditioned stimulus (which is then called the conditioned response).

his ethically dubious conditioning of poor Baby Albert. By pairing the presentation of a white rat with a loud, frightening sound he trained Baby Albert not only to fear the rat, but through repeated pairings to fear anything white and fluffy—demonstrating stimuli generalization, or the process of associating any similar stimulus with the original threat, and thus making it scary. The story doesn't end there: B. F. Skinner continued to pave the way with his Skinner boxes, where he exposed animals to varying schedules of reward and punishment. This resulted in the theory of operant conditioning, which has taught us the best methods of training our pets (and each other) to ensure they'll never forget. Conditioned learning happens very quickly when strong chemicals are involved, like our threat response. Through fear conditioning, you can train someone to be terrified of pretty much anything—even a fluffy white rabbit.

The next scene in the haunted house was also filled with traditional Japanese furnishings, all tattered, tarnished, and torn. In the center was another woman dressed in traditional formal wear, and when I triggered the motion sensor, she turned into a wolf-bear-human hybrid. I thought maybe this was a representation of the *Rokurokubi*, a monster that passes as human in the day only to reveal its true supernatural nature at night, when it extends its elastic neck to consume human prey. Hybrid creatures, which are found across cultures, are scary for many reasons. First, they often feature life-threatening physical characteristics, like sharp claws and teeth. Second, they are usually very large and can probably fly and easily overtake us. And third, they are novel-looking creatures that create a sense of aesthetic dissonance.

In addition to the hybrids, the haunt contained ghostly, eerily realistic mannequins—which is not surprising: Japan is known for its all too humanlike robots that have inspired both awe and fear. There is often nothing intentionally scary about human-looking robots; they are actually made to *comfort* humans. But responding with repulsion and aversion to figures and images that look almost but not quite human is essentially our brain raising a red flag because it's confused. Our body and our brain work based on prediction systems; just as my body braced and then jerked when the Dodonpa didn't take off when I thought it would, our brain determines threats based on expectations. Figures, images, and representations that look human but that we know on some level are *not* human violate our expectation and create a kind of "error" in our processing. Roboticist Mashairo Mori coined the term the Uncanny Valley in 1970 to explain this phenomenon.* And thanks to research from Ayse Saygin, professor at the University of California, San Diego, we now have fMRI and EEG data showing exactly what our brains are doing when we dip into the valley and come back out. Perhaps not surprisingly, Saygin's work shows that it is a result of errors in our prediction systems and essentially a miscommunication between brain circuits. One message arrives saying, "This is a human!" and another message says, "No! It's a threat! Abort!" Our brain gets confused.

Our Uncanny Valley reaction, or disruptions in our prediction systems, is not the same as being "hardwired" for specific fears. In general anything that startles us (by occurring rapidly and unexpectedly) via our senses can trigger our threat response: a loud sound, a blast of air, a flash of light, a strong smell (including pheromones that are released by different animals when they are afraid), and of course anything that causes pain. But research is still not able to prove that we have evolved to fear specific animals or stimuli like spiders and snakes. It's close, though; fMRI studies have shown the amygdala is activated when people are shown pictures of upside-down triangles and the whites of the eyes. Researchers like Sandra Soares from the University of Aveiro have found that some images (namely, snakes) trigger our threat response even when they are presented so quickly that our conscious or thinking brain doesn't have time to register them. Lynne Isbell from the University of California, Davis, calls this

---

*Mori created a chart of the Uncanny Valley: the y axis represents familiarity and the degree to which we like something, and the x axis is human likeness, or the extent to which something or someone looks human. Mori noted that as something gets more human our affinity for it increases—to a point. When something that is not human approaches too much similarity, our affinity drops into the valley, and we are frightened or even disgusted by the image.

the Snake Detection Theory, which suggests that we have evolved to selectively recognize snakes more quickly than others because of the threat they have historically posed; those of us who see the snake and run live to survive and pass on this valuable trait. Similarly a study by Vanessa LoBue of Rutgers University found that infants can point out creatures like snakes, frogs, and spiders more quickly than flowers in photographs.

Still, evidence of hardwired fears—meaning specific neural networks that respond only to specific stimuli—isn't quite available yet. As LoBue and other researchers like Isabelle Blanchette from the University of Manchester note, humans today can also more quickly identify modern threats like knives, guns, and syringes. It's likely we've evolved to recognize threatening characteristics but not specific threats, and those characteristics are going to change based on time and place. For example, which do you think is scarier—guns or snakes? Well, it depends on who and where you are. Elaine Fox from the University of Essex observed this after exposing humans to pictures of guns *and* snakes, and concluded that humans recognize threats based first on relevance rather than evolutionary threat—that is, are you more likely to be bitten by a snake or shot with a gun? Your answer will determine which you recognize first (and which show up more often in scary movies and haunted houses). In Japan, ghosts are a likely candidate to be chosen over both.

Most Japanese horror is heavily based on ghost lore, which was apparent in not only this traditional Japanese haunt but also all of the haunted houses I went through.* Religion in Japan is not organized the same way as in the United States. For example, a majority of the population identify as not religious, but in Japan that means they are not a member of a specific organization or sect, and instead identify as "Folk Shinto" (51.8 percent), which

---

*There have been many, many popular Japanese horror novels, TV shows, and movies based on terrifying ghosts. For example the *Shibito no koiwasurai* (*The Lovesick Dead*, 2001) and *Honto ni atta kowai hanashi* (*True Scary Tales*, 1991), both of which feature ghosts returning to haunt the living.

is the traditional Japanese religion. After Folk Shinto, Buddhism is the most widely observed practice, and in fact many Buddhist practices and beliefs have become intertwined with Shinto. Like most religions, both the Shinto and the Buddhist traditions (which again often overlap) share a belief in the immortality of the soul, but the ghosts, spirits, and *kami* (spirits worshipped in the Shinto tradition) in the Japanese traditions take on a much bigger role.

The importance of spirits reflects Japanese mythology, which is full of stories of ghosts, people who died a "bad death" and linger on Earth to torment the living. As Hayao Kawai, a clinical psychologist and Japan's former commissioner of cultural affairs, said, "Our mythology [does] not have stories where anyone lives happily ever after." There is still a strong belief in ghosts and spirits in Japan. A study of college students in 1993 found that 60 percent believe in *kami*. There continues to be a widespread use of psychic specialists, shamans, and other new religious authorities who can speak to the dead and conduct decontamination rituals for homes where there have been bad deaths. In fact, homes where someone has been murdered or committed suicide (called *jiko bukken*, or "incident buildings") are almost impossible to resell in Japan because of the widespread belief that the deceased will return in ghost form.* These beliefs rooted in premodern religion persist today, as Mary Picone states:

> From the earliest periods of Japanese history the spirits of those who had died bad or "unnatural" deaths, that is, violently, or of "polluting" diseases, or when travelling far from home, or whose corpses were not intact, or prematurely— particularly if they left no descendants, and who were not commemorated posthumously until they achieved the status of deified ancestors—were thought to suffer in the afterlife

---

*Real estate agents are required by law to notify new tenants of a death within the previous seven years. However, with low-income housing in high demand, many *jiko bukken* are now specifically being sought out for their cheaper rates, which are usually half the asking price.

and/or to be dangerous to the living. In short the fear of ghosts was one of the strongest elements of pre-modern religions and is still present in popular beliefs.

Each haunted house I went to was built around a story of a violent death or a troubled and abusive relationship that had contaminated the space, leaving it haunted with *Yūrei* (ghosts of those suffering a bad death) who would torture anyone who entered. I didn't see any witches, axe murderers, or chainsaw-wielding maniacs covered in blood and gore, all of which are normal and expected in the United States. Japanese haunts were also darker, mustier, and tarnished—perhaps more creepy than gory (though there was still plenty of gore). American horror and haunted houses feel more visceral, with monsters who are very much corporal or humans who are broken in some way, either psychologically or physically. It is a reflection of the evolution of the hero narratives in US culture—strong people of action taking on monsters in a fight to the death.* Traditional Japanese horror, for its part, is focused on the afterlife and the ghosts we leave behind. J-horror movies tend to be creepy and use silence and suspense to hint at the violence rather than explicitly show it. Its characters don't fight their demons like enemies; they try to escape the long fingers of their past. A great example is found in comparing the American version of the blockbuster horror movie *The Grudge* and the original Japanese version *Ju-On*. Both were directed by Japanese filmmaker Takashi Shimizu, but the original Japanese version is quieter, the ghosts are more humanlike, and the story is built around the cursed house rather than the characters.

---

*Stephen Asma, in his book *On Monsters*, notes how the characteristics of the monster and the hero change based on time and place. He cites the evolution of Beowulf: In Norse mythology he was a strong, aggressive, prideful warrior who killed the evil monsters whose only intent was to murder and destroy. In the twenty-first-century retelling of the story (produced by Paramount Pictures, directed by Robert Zemeckis, 2007) Grendel and his mother are not mindless monsters but victims of cruelty, abuse, and misunderstanding, while Beowulf is the egomaniacal bully.

᠈ ᠈ ᠈

Even after having gone through nine haunted attractions, I had yet to feel *really* scared, as I have a thousand times going through ScareHouse back home in Pittsburgh. I even ventured out to a haunted prison–themed restaurant called the Lock-Up, where miniskirted law enforcement agents handcuff you, lock you in a cell, and serve you food like Freddy Krueger Chicken Fingers* and Tombstone Mashed Potatoes. I also went to a Ghost Bar, which looked like a Spirit Halloween store had exploded inside a restaurant. Drinks were served in skulls, random body parts were strewn on the floor, and black plastic bats dropped from the ceiling if you clapped loudly (this is also how customers alerted their servers, who were all dressed as *Yuki-onna*). Both of these restaurants were great examples of how J-horror can quickly turn slapstick, more comedy than true fright.

But Japan has also produced some of the creepiest, most skin-crawling horror in the world, and I was determined to experience it firsthand. I spent some late, weird hours searching the Internet for more *obake-yashikis* and came across the YouTube trailer for a place called the Daiba School Horror (or Odaiba Strange School). As soon as the sun was up, I headed down to the Decks at Tokyo Beach.

᠈ ᠈ ᠈

It was a rainy and chilly day, perfect for spooky fun (and short lines, since the haunted house is located along the water). The Decks at Tokyo Beach is part of a massive beach entertainment complex, which also contains Joypolis—the Sega Theme Park—and as expected, it was completely empty, just like the Atlantic

---

*These were chicken wings arranged in the shape of a hand, complete with peppers for fingernails. It actually did gross me out. Also, halfway through the meal a prison riot breaks out, sirens blast, and a host of costumed scary characters run amok while being chased by the waitstaff. It was all plenty strange, but no scarier than murder mystery dinner theater staged at Hooters.

City Boardwalk in the middle of winter. I wandered around the multilevel entertainment complex and shopping mall in a total daze. As a stranger in a strange land, I hadn't had an extended conversation with anyone (except myself) in a week and had averaged about four hours of sleep a night. I honestly thought I was hallucinating when, in my wanderings past stores like Happy Smile Playland and LOL Picture Shop, I came across a dangling crucified corpse, wearing long black hair and a surgical mask and surrounded by red lights, cobwebs, caution tape, vines, and random severed body parts.

I stood staring at the facade behind it: the Daiba School. It was designed to look like the front of an old schoolhouse, complete with wooden shingles and rusty pipes covered in blood (on the other side of which was, unaccountably, a fluorescent pink electric pine tree). My bewilderment must have been obvious. The cashier started speaking to me in a very friendly and energetic voice. I walked over, smiled, held up my hands to the side, and made an "I only speak English" face that I'd perfected during my trip. She laughed, disappeared for a few minutes, and then came back with a calculator to show me how much admission was— 800 yen, or about $8—and made a welcoming, sweeping motion with her hand.

Despite the cashier's energetic and friendly demeanor, I was already more scared than I had been in my previous haunt visits— but for an unexpected reason. All the haunted houses I had visited to that point had been big productions, or at least inside amusement parks I presumed were inspected, safe, and adherent to strict protocols. This one *was* strange and out of place among the other fluorescent facades. Who knew what the rules were? I felt like a lost girl wandering into the wilderness or Suzy Bannion walking into the German dance academy in *Suspiria*. I hoped there wouldn't be an evil coven waiting inside.

After I paid, the cashier started talking to me and gesticulating with a serious look on her face. I was legitimately concerned. Was I missing important information? What if she was telling me I was going to have blood spilled all over me or a bucket of water dumped on my head? I had no idea what I had paid for, and I had already committed too many cultural faux pas to count. Seeing my furrowed brow and look of distress, the cashier came around and pointed to my camera and motioned to put it in my back-pack. From there she walked me around the schoolhouse to the entrance, pointed to a spot right in front of a black drape, and left. I stood on the spot she pointed to and waited.

> > >

Every social interaction we have is mediated by our ability to read, interpret, and respond to the nonverbal messages of the people around us; this ability is present in us from birth. From the moment we're born (technically as early as nine minutes after-wards; nothing earlier has been measured) humans show a prefer-ence for faces: we *love* looking at faces and very quickly learn how to differentiate between expressions. This skill is essential for sur-vival: being able to identify emotional expressions and respond appropriately will not only keep us alive in times of threat but also help us to build strong social connections. Imagine the alter-native: rather than fleeing from the angry mob, you run to them with open arms, or rather than comforting your distressed loved one, you turn away.

While all humans (barring those with sight impairment or certain kinds of disorders) have this ability, our culture, our phys-ical environment, and our genetics influence how we perceive, interpret, and respond to emotional expressions. For example, in the seconds between a startle from a scary monster and the jump of a customer there is a whole host of interactions. First, culture will have shaped the character of the monster—from teeth to tails. Next, the individual's genetic makeup is going to influ-ence how startled she is, influencing the activation of her threat response (high or low). Then, culture will again shape the nature of her response—whether she jumps ten feet in the air with a loud scream or only slightly shifts backwards with a tiny gasp. Our emotional expressions are a result of this complex interaction between genes, our environment, and our culture. This means how we interpret fearful expressions and how we express fear can change based on time and place.

I conducted some simple experiments with this on my own while in Japan, and later Bogotá. I asked complete strangers waiting in line at haunted houses to pretend to be an angry bear or monster. There was a vast range in expressions, from the number of teeth showing, to the deepness of the furrowed brow, to the extent to which their nostrils were flared, to how loud they growled, and to how aggressively they moved toward me with outstretched arms in a clawing motion. In general, the strangers in Japan were more reserved with subtler and softer features, the Colombians were slightly more extroverted, and the Americans basically attacked me.

> > >

I stood at the Daiba School alone, surrounded by skeletons, scary masks, and vines covering faux stone walls, with absolutely no idea what I was about to walk into. I'd been to the website, but it's only in Japanese, and the YouTube trailer I'd seen hadn't offered any clues about what was inside. What if it were some sort of experimental extreme haunt where they would kidnap me and lock me in a room? I was nervous but exhilarated; I felt just the way I had going through my first haunt as a child.

Out of nowhere a young man, probably in his late twenties to early thirties, with straight black hair falling just past his ears and in a plain black shirt and pants, startled me from behind. I jumped around, and he started speaking to me in Japanese but quickly stopped upon seeing my confused face and hand gestures, not to mention the blush I could feel on my cheeks. I was sure I had done something wrong. He smiled and bowed slightly and reassuringly, and motioned for me to stay where I was standing. About ten minutes had passed since I had paid, and there were no other customers, nor anyone else in sight.

Finally the young man, whose name I later learned was Yuurei,* returned with a page-size cardboard tablet with "Directions" printed in English. Relieved, I began to read: no cameras or cell

---

*Yuurei (not to be confused with *Yūrei*, the Japanese word for "ghost") Hirano turned out to be the designer and builder of the haunt and has set up haunts in Taiwan and all around Japan.

phones, no touching anything, no pushing. And then something I hadn't seen before: "caution not to get too scared and stand still" (I would soon see the motivation for this rule). Then Yuurei handed me another piece of cardboard with three lengthy paragraphs printed in English and pointed repeatedly to it while speaking loudly and aggressively. I slowly absorbed his gestures to mean "You need to read this; it's important."

＊　＊　＊

Every haunt I had been to in Japan, save the few throwbacks at Hanayashiki, required me to read or view an extensive setup to understand the backstory. At the Haunted Hospital, I had to sit and watch a video (which was very bloody and pretty graphic) describing the bad deaths that had occurred there and the evil they'd left behind. Perhaps this was another of those.

It was hard to be sure. Yuurei didn't speak any English, and I knew no Japanese. I had to resort to cues in his face and intonation, and as Maria Gendron, Debi Roberson, Jacoba Marieta van der Vyver, and Lisa Barrett Feldmon have shown, these too can vary from culture to culture. When Gendron and colleagues asked isolated Himba people from northwestern Namibia to identify emotions based on Western vocalizations, they were able to accurately identify basic affect (positive or negative) but could not ascribe specific emotional terms (angry, scared, surprised, happy, sad, disgusted). We learn through socialization how to tell when someone is being sarcastic (a less popular practice in Japan), when they're crying tears of joy, or when someone is "fun afraid," as opposed to on the edge of true trauma.

In terms of physical gestures, Jessica Tracy and colleagues find there is some evidence of "universal" poses—for example, stretching your arms to the sky in celebration (even blind athletes do this) or stretching them out to grab someone—but the intensity, the distance, and sometimes the purpose of a gesture are very much socially scripted. In Japan, making eye contact for too long is seen as a sign of aggression, and when you hand someone an object, you are expected to do it with both hands. Also, to the consternation of some tourists, the American sign for OK (forefinger and thumb touching, with three fingers extended) means "money."

＊　＊　＊

The story Yuurei told me to read was about students, including a young girl (the Snow Doll) who had been caged and tortured by an evil old woman and a young boy who had hanged himself in the school. The school, cursed from the bad deaths, is now haunted by an evil and malicious ghost, and it would be my job to go in and vanquish the evil spirit and save the caged and abused schoolgirl. My task would not be a simple one; I would likely confront the evil ghost, and I had to be brave. I would be given tools to help me: a light to guide my way and an Ofuda, which is a paper talisman with holy Shinto text that would banish the evil spirit.* I would have to find the fire inside the schoolhouse, recite the sacred text from the Ofuda, and then throw it into the fire, banishing the evil ghost and freeing the schoolgirl.

I got chills just reading the story. Yuurei handed me my flashlight and the small thin paper Ofuda. He took me to the entrance and pointed to the word on the piece of paper and said it out loud, then pointed to me, and I repeated it. He shook his head and shouted the word louder, I did the same, and then we both repeated it two more times, each time louder than the last. With my heart pumping faster, I gripped my flashlight (I wouldn't lose it this time) and held the Ofuda in front of me. I would be brave and confront the evil ghost inside, find the fire, repeat the sacred text, and then watch it burn, casting out evil and saving the girl. I felt a surge of adrenaline. Yuurei smiled and pulled back the curtain. It was time to be a hero.

＊　＊　＊

---

*Many Japanese place Ofuda on their homes to keep evil *Yūrei* from entering.

I walked through the curtains and was immediately startled by a series of well-placed effects: an air horn, a strobe light, and a blast of air. I made my way slowly down a tight hallway, my flashlight providing little resistance against the dark. I kept scanning from left to right, sure at any moment something was going to pop out. I was a ball of pent-up energy. I nervously peeked around a blind corner: all clear. I stepped around and pointed my flashlight down the long hallway. I gasped as my tiny light exposed a tall woman, wearing a long, white, tattered dress, eyes hidden behind long black ratty hair down to her waist. She was standing perfectly still in the tiny circle of my flashlight. I stood, mouth open in shock. Do I keep walking? I took a step forward, and all at once she started charging at me in a full sprint, arms outstretched. She was running straight at me, and I started screaming, shrieking really, and instinctively began backing up until I hit the wall behind me and there was no place left to go. I pressed tightly into the corner and pulled my arms and shoulders into my chest, hoping to somehow shrink away from the onslaught. "Oh my God!" I shrieked. "Oh my God! Oh my God! Oh my God!"

> > >

I noticed differences in Japanese haunted houses from the moment I got into my first line. Unlike the Americans I had been watching from behind the walls at ScareHouse for seven years, who instinctively walk single file as though they were back in grade school, Japanese visitors cluster in semicircles and move slowly—much more slowly—and in unison through the attraction. And when the shit hits the fan, Americans try to save themselves. We scream, we run, and we throw our arms in the air or hug them to our chests—just as I did when attacked by the ghost. Japanese groups are different: they crowd closer together with a small shriek and crouch down lower to the ground. One group of young men was literally bent over and practically kneeling as they approached the final scene at the Haunted Hospital.

This response represents a collectivist orientation, a cultural value famously found in Japan, where (for instance) sick people often wear masks to protect the public from *their* germs. In Bogotá, I found that huddling close together was also the norm, but it didn't matter if you were cowering with friends or strangers, and everyone's reactions were far more expressive. For example, by the end of my trip through the Castillo Del Terro at Salitre Magico (the one and only haunted house I could find in Bogotá) the woman behind me had wrapped her arms all the way around my waist and buried her head in my back, while the woman in front of me had pushed all the way into me so that my head was essentially on her shoulder. With each scare everyone screamed very loudly and pushed more tightly together. We jumped, pushed, and even fell over as a group, a moving, thronging mosh pit of fear.

But in this strange little Japanese haunted house I was alone. There was no one in front of me to hide behind, no one to cling to, no one to absorb a scare from the back or the front. It was just me and apparently a very angry ghost.

> > >

In all my years as a thrill seeker, I had *never* had a monster run straight at me in a haunted house. This isn't just a coincidence; haunted house actors usually do not charge full speed at customers from the front because it makes them back up (which creates crowd traffic) and sometimes act out in violence (people punch). For these reasons, it's more lucrative in America to "scare people forward." But no such rules were in play at Daiba. A ghost came charging at me, and I lost my freaking mind.

The evil ghost stopped abruptly not two inches from my nose. She was a good seven or eight inches taller than I, and from behind her hair I heard her breathing in a low, growling manner. I was whimpering, truly terrified, and shaking. Then, just as quickly as she charged at me, she was gone, her white robes flowing behind her, dissolving back into the ghostly dark. The encounter couldn't have lasted longer than twenty seconds, but it felt like forever.

In my stay in the Hole at ESP my perception of time also slowed, likely because I was intentionally focused on what I was feeling—not to mention, my muscles were killing me. In other words my insular cortex was extremely busy. This time there were two reasons this moment seemed to slow so much for me; for one thing it was entirely new, and for another, I was petrified. We pay more attention to scary and novel things; we have to create a whole new place to store them or figure out if they belong in an existing schema. For me I had to find a spot for "charging, raging ghost" to go into my folder of scary haunted house characters.

We have a vested interest in making sure we remember frightening situations so we can avoid them in the future; when we're scared, we record more layered and rich memories of the experience. David Eagleman conducted some really fun research to test this theory, including having volunteers free-fall backwards with no rope into a net. As expected, people perceived their own falls to last longer than others'. Yair Bar-Haim and colleagues also found that anxious individuals who are presented with a mild threat, like a photo of a spider, experienced time as moving more slowly. The more details and layers of experience we need to encode, the longer we feel it lasts. This is why childhood summers feel like they last forever, and then start to fly by as we age. When we're young, everything is new, and we've got many images, smells, sights, and sounds to record. But as we age, we tend to see and experience fewer new or novel events (but it doesn't have to be that way—go travel!). Finally, our brain interprets objects coming toward us as threatening, and therefore time is perceived to slow down as we work to process and encode every little detail for future use. These findings are based simply on people looking at floating disks on a computer screen; I couldn't help but wonder what the results would look like if the looming threat was this angry, charging ghost.

I stood up straight and again scanned the hallway in front of me. I had to force myself to keep going, but I made it all the way down to the end and then had to turn a blind corner. I held my breath anticipating another encounter with an evil ghost, but no one was there. As I began to relax again, the wicked ghost reappeared, this time from the side. She growled in my face, then quickly took off, perhaps through a hidden door. I screamed again, my fear feeling more genuine than ever before. I was being stalked by a ghost in my own personal haunted house.

Still, I had my mission. I had to look for a fire to save the little girl. I shined my flashlight all around the long, dark hallway; the walls were distressed, as though they had been beaten with a sledgehammer, and starting at waist level there were frosted windows, some with bloody handprints. Rooms were littered with various schoolhouse furniture; chairs, desks, and pencil boxes were strewn about the floor. Dark shapes passed by the windows, casting a shadow, only to pop out later from behind the next door. Finally I turned a corner and saw a glowing and flickering light. It had to be the fire. A loud, low thundering sound filled the hallway as I began making my way toward the light, and it surrounded me and got louder as I approached the flames. Then there was a sudden percussive bang—I jumped and turned around. The ghost was back, her face lit by the fire behind me, charging at me from behind, screaming and howling with her hands in the air. I sprinted away, like an animal. She chased me down the hall toward the fire. I shouted the sacred text and threw the Ofuda into the flames. In an instant the evil ghost disappeared, and the thundering stopped.

I was breathless as I walked the last few steps out of the haunt, passing a sign in Japanese that I assume said something about saving the abused girl and vanquishing the ghost. Yuurei and the cashier were both waiting for me at the exit with smiles on their faces, and they weren't the only ones. My screams must have been pretty loud, as groups of people had come over from the arcade to see what was going on. I clapped my hands as I walked out and said it was wonderful and bowed my head in thanks.

> > >

I learned you don't need a haunt with two hundred actors all playing different monsters to scare the crap out of you. All it takes is one ghost, out to find you wherever you go. This tiny, five-minute haunt with only one actor had made me scream and feel six years old again. I screamed more in that tiny haunt than I did walking through some of the top haunts in the United States with every high-priced animatronic and twenty-foot-tall monster available. Maybe part of it was due to my own state of disorientation and exhaustion, not to mention confused expectations. Yet I believe the key difference was how immersed I was in the story and the personal connection I felt with the girl and the ghost. Japanese culture is traditionally more future oriented and values the investment of time and energy into telling a story, knowing it will pay off down the road. Including the guests in a plot to save someone else also reflects a more collectivist perspective—it's not about getting through yourself and surviving but about being a hero. The time spent reading and preparing for the trip through the haunt effectively took me to a perfect state of arousal: I was excited and nervous but also feeling ready. By the time the first startle was triggered I was so engrossed in the story and the scene that nothing could have pulled me out of the moment. I was *part* of the experience, not just a passive viewer. I felt brave, confident, and truly fearless.

> > >

I spent the rest of that day exploring the waterfront, then started my long journey north to my hotel. Tired of sitting, I got off the train early and walked the last mile or so. It was around eleven thirty p.m., but I wasn't especially worried about safety. I'd been all over Tokyo, through the streets of Shinjuku to the temple at Asakusa, and I had not experienced any negative social interactions. No street harassment, no pickpocketing attempts, no rude or aggressive encounters at all. People even leave their bikes unlocked on the street, sometimes with personal items still in the baskets. This was mind-blowing; at home I don't even leave my shopping cart when picking out fruit. Usually if I'm walking alone in the States at night, I go through extensive what-if scenarios and have my mace in my right hand, finger on the trigger and ready to run. But walking home that night, I felt safe. I passed about four groups of what appeared to be Japanese businessmen, some of them obviously drunk and stumbling, but none of them said a word to me. They seemed to avoid eye contact. No catcalls, no "Hey baby, where you going?"

At the end of my eventful trip, thinking back, I couldn't help noticing how considerate and respectful the people around me had been. And yet the Japanese love so many forms of scary entertainment and create such spooky and disturbing horror. I wondered if the two were related and how the objective safety of a society is related to the engagement with scary material. I would get my answer when I went to Bogotá, Colombia. But I still had to confront one more fear before leaving Japan.

PART III
REAL FEAR

I went to the woods because I wished to live deliberately, to front only the essential facts of life, and see if I could not learn what it had to teach, and not, when I came to die, discover that I had not lived.

—Henry David Thoreau

6

MEMENTO MORI

Mist-filled path in Aokigahara Juki. Photo by Šimon Vahala.

My earliest memory is of bones. I grew up spending every weekend with my mother's family on my grandfather's expansive 123-
acre sheep farm in northern Baltimore County. I don't know how
old I was, just that I was shorter than the tall weeds growing in the
fields when my two older cousins asked if I wanted to see something cool. Of course I did! There were no sheep left on the farm,

and the barn had fallen into a state of ruin. I followed my cousins around the corner, behind the crumbling stone wall, where they crouched down into the dirt and started digging. What they uncovered and pushed in my face was not the adorable woodland creature I was hoping for. It was about seven inches long, grayish brown, narrow, with lots of little holes and rounded edges. They enthusiastically blurted out: "It's a sheep bone!" "You're holding the bone of a dead sheep. Blood ran through that! And look— they're all over the place!" I threw the bone and went running back up the hill and proceeded to cry my eyes out for the rest of the day (and later became a vegetarian for ten years). That's the day I learned that everything dies.

This lesson was brought home a few years later, when my much-loved grandmother, always ready with a fresh baked cake and a smile, passed away after years of struggling with Alzheimer's. I was angry and confused when I went to say good-bye at the side of her open casket. The body resting in the soft white satin didn't look anything like my grandmother. The mortician covered her naturally beautiful face with heavy concealer, blush, and eye shadow. She looked like someone else. I squeezed my eyes shut and tried to erase the image from my brain. But these are the images that stick with you. Just two years later her husband, my sheepherding grandfather, passed away from a bitter battle with emphysema. Two years after that, almost to the day, his son, my uncle, died unexpectedly. My mother's family was devastated. I stood in the kitchen and watched my mom and aunts cry and decided that I didn't want to deal with death anymore. I decided to lock it away in a remote part of my brain and ignore it when it tried to come out. When it came time to put down my beloved horse Cookie when I was seventeen, I told my mom to take care of it and not to tell me. I didn't say good-bye, I wasn't with him when the veterinarian came, and I didn't hold him in his last moments. I refused to think about it. People die; animals die; we move on. Or so I told myself.

♪ ♪ ♪

If uncertainty is the root of fear, then death is surely the most terrifying part of human existence. The topic of dying is as big as the
topic of living, and its reality is fundamentally unknowable. For
this reason, it has been the subject of centuries of research, philosophy, psychology, and folklore. Humans may well have been
pondering it for as long as we've existed. Fear of death and dying
is layered. First, there is the difference between death—the actual
state of nonexistence—and the process of dying. Second, there is
the difference between fear of your own death or dying and fear
of a loved one's death or dying. And then there is fear of what
happens to our souls after we die and what happens to the souls
of those we love. All of these are uncertainties, but they still only
scratch the surface: How will you die, for instance? In a fire? By
drowning? Being eaten by snakes? Peacefully, in a hospital? What
happens to your body? Where will it be laid to rest? Who will see
it? Touch it? How will it decompose? Will you go on to heaven or
hell? Will you see your loved ones? Will you haunt the earth or
linger in purgatory? If you lose someone close to you, how will it
change you? What is the difference between brain death, cellular
death, biological death, and vegetative state? When do you say
good-bye? It's a lot to think about—too much. Which is why most
of us go to great lengths not to.

Indeed, dying wouldn't be nearly so scary if we didn't have to
think about it. This is a unique torture afforded only to humans.*
As Ernest Becker famously stated in his 1973 work *Denial of Death*:
"This is the terror: to have emerged from nothing, to have a name,
consciousness of self, deep inner feelings, an excruciating inner
yearning for life and self-expression—and with all this yet to die."
So how do we deal with it? We create culture, religion, and narratives that give life and death meaning, that explain the creation
of the world, the existence of humans, and what it means to live
a good, meaningful life. We hold on to these stories tightly, of

---

*While it has been observed that animals mourn the deaths of their own, and
may even have death rituals (for example, retreating to isolation to die), only
humans—at least as far as we know—have the ability to critically contemplate
and theorize about their own death.

heaven and hell, an afterlife, a soul that lives on, of ghosts and spirit realms that bring us comfort over an entirely unknowable future. The idea that culture and relationships provide us a sense of self and meaning, and protect us from the anxiety of knowing we will die, is the foundation of a rich theoretical perspective, tested and supported in over four hundred studies, collectively known as terror management theory (TMT).

Every culture creates its own rituals that shape individuals' perspectives on death and dying, which can change over time: from the Viking burials sending the deceased (along with human sacrifices) out to sea, to the Tibetan sky burial, in which the dead are laid on the top of a mountain to be eaten by predators. There are fire burials in Bali in which the soul is released in an epic cremation ceremony, and then there are the skull burials of the Kiribati, where the deceased are exhumed and their skulls removed, polished, lavished with offerings, and placed on a shelf in the family home. Death rituals are a central part of the way communities function; they bring citizens together to process and manage the fear and uncertainty of dying. But culture is always evolving, and when death rituals change, our relationship to death and dying changes as well.

In America, dying has changed dramatically. For centuries, the sick and dying remained in their homes surrounded by friends and family. After a person died, communities came together to carry out rituals and practices that reflected their values and beliefs, allowing people to process together and reinforce their shared meaning of life. Today patients are kept in hospitals or nursing homes with access restricted to friends and family. As sociologists Philip Mellor and Chris Shilling have noted, doctors talk about dying in technical, scientific, and biomedical terms rather than plain ones; in some cases, family and friends do the same thing. We stave off the inevitability of death with one more test, one more drug, or one more procedure that could turn everything around. Even when these efforts fail, we still use euphemisms like "losing the last battle," as though immortality remained a possibility until the end. These thought patterns have brought the living some comfort, but they have also removed the realities of dying and the fragility of our bodies from our social consciousness. As Norbert Elias wrote in his book *Loneliness of the Dying*, "Never before have people died as noiselessly and hygienically as today in these societies, and never in social conditions so much fostering solitude." In fact, Elias found that even when outsiders, friends, or distant relatives are able to visit the dying, they are less willing to do so today. Death has gone from being a community event that bolstered unity and understanding to a quiet and hidden phenomenon, leaving us even more uncertain and afraid of mortality. A recent study published in the *American Journal of Preventive Medicine* by Jaya Rao found that only 26 percent of those polled in a national health survey had advanced directives, and the percentage of the population that believes everything should be done to save a patient's life, even in dire circumstances, has doubled since 1990. This is the unwillingness to think about death writ large.

This anxiety is compounded, ironically, by the fact that in the developed world people are living longer. Our workplaces, homes, water, and food are safer; violent crimes in the United States are at their lowest level in forty years; and the odds of being murdered or robbed are less than half of what they were in the early 1990s. US life expectancy has doubled in about a hundred years, and in just the past forty years, infant mortality has dropped from twenty-six per one thousand live births to fewer than seven. Vaccination has brought major diseases, such as polio and smallpox, under control, and advances in surgery and medication now allow those who would previously have perished to live long and healthy lives. New technology has given us answers to the mysteries of our bodies; we can replace bones and organs, even grow new ones in a lab.

Oddly, all this success has made people in the developed world, and not just Americans, more anxious about dying. For example, a study of Canadians found that the longer men have to live, the more they fear a premature death. Research shows, too, that people expect to die sooner than they're likely to, with women underestimating their age of death by eleven years. Subjects also mistakenly believe their cause of death will be far more traumatic and abnormal than the country's statistics suggest. Because we cordon off the experience of death from our daily lives, we tend to see it only when it occurs suddenly and traumatically—which in turn makes us believe those tragedies are more common than they really are.

In a broad sense, our expectations have changed, so that today, not only do we want to look young and beautiful, feel energetic, and keep our intelligence, but we want to live forever. The more threats we remove, the scarier the ones remaining become. The more we value and fixate on youth and beauty, the harder it becomes to confront our mortality.

> > >

My strategy of avoiding death seemed to work. More family members passed away; more pets were put to sleep. I even had a friend attempt suicide, and while I felt compassion, there was a big empty black hole in the space that most people fill with anxiety, fear, and sadness around death. Even after my sister's car rolled into a ditch when I was fourteen, and I saw the door pop open as we tumbled down a hill, I wrote in my diary: "We went around a curve and flipped, rolled and bounced into a ditch. I thought if we could get the car out we wouldn't have to tell anyone, but then I saw the roof was dented in and the door had jammed open . . . I thought it was fun, to tell ya the truth . . . isn't that strange?"

At some level, I've always known that my approach to death was not healthy. When it came to death, I was all intellect, no emotion. I fought to keep my emotional brain from taking over during my walk on the CN Tower, but now I had to do the opposite. I needed to understand death emotionally, and not just for the sake of my own humanity—although that was certainly an important goal. But how could I be an expert on fear, how could I work in a haunted house inhabited by serial killers and zombies and ghosts, if I refused to really engage with death? But my instinct to avoid it was strong. I couldn't face it in a funeral home or a cemetery or a war memorial—those were places for the living that offered comfort. I would have to go someplace that wouldn't let me run away, that would hold death front and center and force me to engage with whatever feelings emerged. I wanted to go to a place where death *lives*, where people not only confront death but seek it out.

I knew of only one perfect place to do this, and it was many thousands of miles from where I lived and worked: the Aokigahara Jukai Forest. Set in the foothills of Japan's Mount Fuji, it is a deep and lush green wood, a place renowned for its beauty and peace. At fourteen square miles, it is easy to get lost in—in fact, local business owners and residents tend to keep their eyes open for cars that remain there overnight. After the Golden Gate Bridge, Aokigahara is the second most popular place in the world to commit suicide, and it is known, locally and internationally, as the Suicide Forest.*

Aokigahara is a kind of space between living and dying—a quiet, still place where people disappear. I had been to other places you might describe this way, like a cemetery or a haunted house, and certainly more than a few dangerous places. But this was something different: a place where death was not a thing you were afraid of but a thing you might choose. To understand death, to really think of it with the focus and respect it so obviously requires, to break down the barriers I'd built against thinking about mortality, this was the place I had to experience.

My friends were petrified and convinced I would die there, for a variety of reasons. My spiritual friends were worried I would be overwhelmed with the negative energies filling the forest and take my own life. My paranormal enthusiast friends were convinced a ghost, a spirit, or some kind of forest creature would kill me. My academic colleagues worried I would get lost and either die from exposure or try to seek help from other tourists and end up murdered or held for ransom. And of course a few people thought I was going there to kill myself. I was the only one who

---

*About 100 bodies are found in the forest each year, but the number of successful suicides is difficult to know for certain. After 247 people attempted suicide in the forest in 2010, authorities stopped releasing the official numbers for fear it would only contribute to the popularity and intrigue of the destination.

wasn't worried at all, which was a problem because I knew that was a lie and precisely the reason I needed to go there.

> > >

Getting to the forest was an adventure itself. The idea of visiting it made little logistical decisions seem surreal and even darkly funny. When is the best day to visit the Suicide Forest? Do you go after breakfast? I'd spent my previous day at the Fuji-Q Highland, riding the roller coasters and screaming my head off. I contemplated the idea of a bus loop between the forest and the park: it could be the "thrill-therapy" loop. I immediately felt guilty for such an insensitive thought, but part of me was still riding the physical and mental high from my day of screams and laughs. Did that make me ridiculous? Was it immoral? I didn't know, which confirmed my decision to continue on.

I rode a series of trains and buses, and I couldn't help but wonder about the intentions of everyone around me. Was it possible that someone on this vehicle was going to take their own life? But passengers thinned with each transfer. In fact, I was the only one at the station boarding my last bus. I felt the eyes of a group of young girls on my back as I stepped on and realized that *I* was the conspicuous one. I displayed all the warning signs—a stranger, traveling alone, not dressed in hiking gear, sitting silently the whole trip.

I took my seat and tried to look like a happy tourist for the few passengers already onboard. I didn't want anyone to think I was going to kill myself or, just as disturbingly, to scavenge. This is another of the unsettling realities of Aokigahara: knowing it is a popular suicide destination, people now go into the forest looking to rob the dead of their valuables. Even worse is that some go looking for macabre souvenirs like bones, nooses, and the highly sought-after and profitable footage of finding a "real" suicide victim.

It may sound grotesque, and it is certainly appalling, but there is an appetite for real images and artifacts of death. There are a few plausible explanations as to why: one is the attraction/repulsion dynamic discussed in Chapter 3. But researchers Philip

Mellor and Chris Shilling suggest that because real death has been so far removed from our lived experience, we go looking for places and images that make the unknowable more known, making us feel more secure and in control. As Susan Sontag famously stated in her book *Regarding the Pain of Others*: "The feeling of being exempt from calamity stimulates interest in looking at painful pictures . . . and looking at them suggests and strengthens the feeling that one is exempt." This may seem counterintuitive: we are inundated daily with stories of tragic and gruesome deaths and the fictionalized representations in movies, in video games, and on TV, resulting in habituation or desensitization. But engaging with death from a distance, passively or symbolically, is not the same as confronting the reality.

Growing up on farms, I saw death everywhere, and I realized quickly that like most things, it's not the same as in the movies. From the barn cats that routinely left their eviscerated mice and birds in the horse stalls to the slaughtered deer strung up in the hay barn, its body ripped open with a bucket full of blood underneath (that was a fun surprise), it's not the same. But most people have no idea what a corpse smells like, what it looks like after a day or a week. The bodies most Americans do see are painted and preserved, and often unrecognizable, like my grandmother. So while youth today have likely seen more dead or mutilated bodies on the screen than their peers of a hundred years ago, they've never slaughtered an animal or felt its blood on their hands and seen the look in its eyes as it died. Not that these are things we need to do, or should do, or should try to expose others to. Rather, it explains the big question mark we have today when it comes to real death. According to research on dark tourism, people go to morbid sites to try to gain a deeper understanding of death. But as I would learn, we don't need to feel real blood on our hands or be in the room with a corpse to understand death; we just have to be brave enough to confront it.

I was cognizant that this was exactly what I was doing—going to a place where death lives to understand it better. However, there is a big difference between going to a place like Aokigahara to engage with emotions—grief, say, or fear, or love for someone lost—and going to exploit tragedy for gain, whether it be by scavenging from bodies or trying to record the lowest and most personal moments of someone's life. I had no wish to come across a dead person, but I decided that if I did, I would not photograph, collect, or share any information. I was going there to confront my own personal fears and deepen my understanding of death. No one else's life needed to be disrupted.

> > >

Eventually I was alone on the bus, looking at the sun shining brightly above the magnificent Mount Fuji, when a scary thought entered my mind. What if I came upon someone who was not dead but considering it or, worse, in the process of dying? This, to me, was more terrifying than finding a corpse or even dying myself. What if I couldn't save him? I don't speak Japanese, and I had no cell phone reception. Awful thoughts ran through my mind of trying to frantically untie knots that were too tight or trying to lift someone up who was too heavy. What if I couldn't stop the bleeding? What if I couldn't find help fast enough? I replayed the American Heart Association's hands-only CPR video in my mind: quick compressions made in rhythm to "Staying Alive" (how appropriate). My breathing (actually, my hyperventilating) naturally fell in step to the song, and for the first time I was starting to feel nervous about going into the forest. Any morbid or dark humor was replaced with real concern; I could handle finding a dead body, but I didn't think I could handle being witness to a suicide. I couldn't ignore death this time or run away, and the more I thought about it, the more anxious I became. My emotions seemed to be kicking in, and for the first time I *felt* maybe this wasn't a good idea.

> > >

I exited the bus at a tiny stop and stood alone on the side of a road, the massive Mount Fuji looming in the background and in front of me, an almost unreal place, vast and green and tranquil. Mount

Fuji is actually three volcanoes stacked on top of each other, so the ground in the forest is mostly dense, dark volcanic rock, which forces the trees to wrap and twist their roots around and into any available crevice, searching for a spot to anchor. Everything is covered with a layer of dew, and when the sun shines through the trees, light bounces off of the shiny rocks, dark green moss, bright green ferns, and undergrowth that cover the floor. The forest is alive with color and movement, truly a mystical scene. I hadn't even set foot inside yet, and I could see how someone would call this the perfect spot to die.

That's what Japanese author Wataru Tsurumi wrote in his 1993 best-selling *Complete Manual of Suicide*. His text, along with Seicho Matsumoto's 1960 novel *Kuroi Jukai* (*Sea of Trees*), which ends with two lovers killing themselves in the forest, is widely blamed for turning this forest into the top suicide destination in Japan. Both of these books are often found next to the bodies of those recovered from Aokigahara. But the lure of the forest doesn't start with the books. Japanese mythology paints it as a place filled with mystical beings and close ties to the spiritual world; in fact, many religious groups and cults have made the forest their home base.* And these aren't even the darkest realities of the forest. In the nineteenth century it was known as a drop-off location for a practice called *ubasute*, which is abandoning the elderly and infirm to perish alone in the woods. The forest is also rumored to be one of the Seven Gates of Hell. Finally, to avoid contaminating the home and leaving their loved ones with an angry ghost, those seeking to kill themselves venture into the forest, where their souls can haunt and torment all those who enter.

I took a moment to look around and try to gain my bearings. I started walking toward a trail opening, and from there my plan was to break off trail and (safely) explore. I had read about increased efforts to monitor the forest, that there are now daily

---

*The cult/terrorist group responsible for the Tokyo subway sarin attack in 1995, Aum Shinrikyo, built their headquarters at the base of Mount Fuji, where they murdered the brother of a cult member who had escaped, and stored chemical weapons and firearms.

patrols and security cameras at the entrances, but I hadn't seen anyone yet, and I didn't notice any cameras. But I did see a sign that made my heart skip a beat. The sign was written in Japanese, but I knew what it said: "Think carefully about your children, your family," and "Do not agonize over problems yourself. Please seek counseling." The signs were an initiative of a man who went to the forest to kill himself but walked back out and began an awareness and prevention campaign. I couldn't stop thinking about what I would do if I were to find someone. I was nervous; my mind ran through every scenario.

> > >

Committing suicide does not mean someone is not afraid of death. Understanding what leads to suicide, however, does teach us a lot about a society's relationship to life and death. In the predominantly Christian United States, suicide is considered a sin, punishable by spending an eternity burning in hell. But suicide is taboo even among the secular; it is considered to be one of the most cowardly and selfish acts a person can perform, bringing disgrace to one's family. And of course it's illegal. These taboos seem to have an effect—many Americans, even those in desperate situations, choose to keep living. But it does happen. In 2013 the United States was ranked thirtieth in the world, with 12.6 deaths from suicide for every 100,000 people. This is higher than the United Kingdom, Ireland, Germany, and Canada, but far fewer than Japan, where there are 21.4 deaths per 100,000, or about 70 per day, and 71 percent are men. The most often cited reasons for suicide in Japan are familiar: financial burden, depression, and love, similar to reasons across the globe. So what makes people in Japan more likely to kill themselves?

> > >

Japan is somewhat of a paradox. It has the lowest death rate among seventeen other similarly developed nations and the lowest level of violence (the United States has the highest of both). Yet even though suicide is considered a taboo to most Japanese, the country is consistently ranked among the ten countries with the highest suicide rates in the world. Part of this can be traced to the historical and traditional view of suicide as an honorable death under certain circumstances, whether it is done to avoid capture (as with the Samurai and the practice of seppuku), as an act of war (kamikaze pilots), or to avoid bringing shame on the family. While not as widespread, this sentiment continues to exist today. For example, in 2007 a government official under investigation for wrongdoing killed himself; in response, the governor of Tokyo publicly called him a true Samurai. And in 2014 a prominent doctor, Yoshiki Sasai, hanged himself in the midst of a scandal involving stem cell research, citing in his suicide note the heavy responsibility he felt toward his research group.

Japanese culture is more collectivist in nature than American culture; the Japanese value a strong sense of responsibility, but rather than the individual's needs and opinions, those of community and family come first and carry far more weight. For the few people who do commit suicide, they often see it as the right thing to do for their families.* Moreover, many emotions associated with depression and suicide, like feelings of vulnerability, weakness, and melancholia, have only recently become recognized as problematic and a sign that someone needs help.†

---

*Pressure to be successful and support their families can translate to extreme feelings of guilt and self-loathing in the face of failure. Japanese workers, referred to as salarymen (or career women), work longer and harder than is healthy, but there is little tolerance or acceptance of those who need help when they become depressed and overworked. This, along with financial worries, is cited as the leading cause of suicide among men. Studies support the correlation between suicides and increased financial burden; in fact the suicide help line number in the forest is connected to a debt counselor.

†Seeking treatment from mental health professionals is still stigmatized in Japan. There wasn't even a Japanese word for "mild clinical depression" until the introduction of antidepressants in 1999 by the Japanese pharmaceutical company Meiji Seika Kaisha. Eli Lilly had decided not to sell in Japan in the '80s because of a lack of demand, but with the introduction of the new diagnosis *kokoro no kaze* (which translates to "your soul has a cold"), mild depression became a "real" illness, treatable with medication. While overmedicalizing human emotions can lead to pathologizing normal reactions, in this instance it has connected people who need help with treatment. Now depression is largely accepted as a pathological problem, but there is still little support to address the social and emotional sides of the illness.

Things are changing in Japan. After 33,093 people killed themselves in 2007, the government finally took action, vowing to decrease the rate by 20 percent in ten years. Its efforts, including media campaigns, suicide hotlines, and the installation of blue lights in the subway,* have helped, and there has been a decline since 2009 (27,283 in 2013), but it is still the number one cause of death for men between the ages of twenty and forty-four.†

, , ,

As soon as I entered the forest, I had to stop. It is truly breathtaking. I looked out off of the trail and couldn't tell where the ground stopped and the trees started. Tree trunks, roots, and volcanic rocks covered with green moss and even some remaining snow twisted and tangled over each other, making the forest floor look alive, yet it was eerily quiet. This was the closest thing to a mystical forest I had ever seen, and it is no wonder that it is one of the most spiritual and sacred places in Japan.

I walked farther in and scanned for a spot to go off the trail and deeper into the forest. I found an opening and then searched for a tall stick to plant in the ground between two rocks as a guidepost. I was not the first to think of leaving a trail of bread crumbs, so to speak. Many who go into the forest to kill themselves tie a string, rope, or tape to a tree and carry it with them. Some do this to find their way back out if they change their mind, or as a guide to lead someone else to their body for recovery. Local authorities and volunteers have also used this tactic during their body sweeps, leaving a colorful spiderweb of strings and tape crossing from tree to tree. I didn't see any strings—just a few scraps of colored tape on the ground.

I walked in a straight line from my guidepost into the forest, instinctively stopping often to look around and lift up stones and

---

*Researchers aren't sure exactly why the blue lights work, but they're assumed to have a positive impact on mood.

†It's important to keep in mind that this statistic is also a reflection of the safety and long lives enjoyed by Japanese people more generally.

logs, but I didn't find the woodland creatures I'd grown up searching for. Finally I saw what I was looking for, a perfect arrangement of rocks and trunks, twisted into a nature-made chair. A large volcanic rock, slightly wet and covered in moss, was my cold but perfect seat, while a massive tree with a thick trunk offered its tangled roots as my two comfortable armrests. It seemed created just for me. I sat down and took out my journal to think about death, or in my case feel.

꘎ ꘎ ꘎

Thinking about death, even in a place like Aokigahara, is not as simple as it sounds. If you're not attentive and devoted, you'll quickly get distracted or back away from it—which is why I'd come all this way in the first place. It requires patience, even a little preparation, to do an exercise like this and expect to get anywhere. So I brought several different scales, activities, and journals to help me with my confrontation. Terror management theorists use a lot of different methods to force people to think about their own mortality. I'd decided to pursue one that is known to lead to positive outcomes and was developed from interviews with those who had near-death experiences (NDE). The "death reflection" task has four reflections to complete: (1) visualize your own death in detail, (2) imagine how you would handle your final moments, (3) engage in a life review, and (4) imagine how your death would affect your family.

I didn't have a hard time with step 1—I even had a little fun with it, in fact. I have always imagined I would die tragically, impulsively doing something far too dangerous: trying to jump from between the tops of cars on a moving train, roller-skating at breakneck speed down a steep hill, paragliding, whitewater rafting, base jumping. Something extreme would be my endgame. Instead of ending the exercise with a detailed image of how I would die, I had a new list of adventures I wanted to go on.

But I wasn't thinking about my own death yet, not really. It was as though I could actually see the walls I'd built up in my own mind, keeping death hidden away. I tried to break through them by conceding that I would likely die of one of the most common causes of death in America: cancer, heart disease, or stroke. This in turn made exercise 2, how I would handle my final moments, much harder. This is where discipline was required. I forced myself to walk through the disease progression from diagnosis to treatment, to that fateful day when nothing else can be done. How would I say good-bye to my friends and family? What would I want them to know? What if I forgot something?

After a few minutes of thinking this way, I felt tears welling up in my eyes. And then, immediately, I felt stupid. What was I doing? Sitting in a haunted suicide forest halfway across the world thinking about death—why? To make myself feel bad and cry? The world was full of people born into desperate situations, and I had gone thousands of miles to imagine my own death. What good could come of this? Had I been anywhere else, I would have gotten up, walked out, turned on some music, and gone about my day. But I couldn't leave; the next bus wasn't coming for an hour. I told myself this was just another new experience and to keep going. It was something new to try.

How would I handle my final moments? My first impulse was to die alone and not tell anyone. The idea of a long, drawn-out good-bye sounded too awful. But that answer was just another cop-out on my end, so I started thinking about what I would say to people. Then, suddenly, I got angry. This task was impossible. How in the world was I supposed to know how I would *really* handle my final moments? How could anyone know? I found myself yelling the question into the oppressive quiet of the forest, shattering its silence with my frustration.

Part 3 was easier: I had to review my own personal history, but I cheated a little, and I knew it. I looked back at my life chronologically, rather than emotionally. The question is really meant to bring attention to unfulfilled dreams, regrets, and feelings left unshared or unexplored, but all that was too much to reckon with, and I was amazed at how burned-out I felt after the previous question. Still, I told myself, at least I'd answered the question, and I hadn't run away yet.

The final reflection, on how my family would handle my death, was the hardest. I am not close with my extended family. I don't even know how many kids my eleven cousins have, who is married, or where they all live, and it would be a struggle to remember the last time I saw most of them. After my mom's parents and brother died, family gatherings became more rare, and kids grew up and moved away. And my dad's family—let's just say I learned more about fear during the yearly visits to see his family in Florida than in all my years working in the haunted house industry. But the distant, troubled nature of our extended family brought my parents and me closer together, and I know my death would destroy them.

Debra Bath found in her research that regardless of how people feel about their own death, they fear the loss of loved ones. I've seen this in my own data analysis of ScareHouse customers as well, with comments like "I fear losing my children more than anything in the world." I can't count the times my mother has told me she would trade her life for mine, and I know she would. And when I've been out on the metaphorical ledge, about to do something stupid, dangerous, and far too reckless, it was the thought of my parents' devastation that pulled me back. It wasn't *my* fears that controlled my behavior and kept me safe and alive; it was theirs. Without them, I do believe I would be dead. We often can be more kind to someone we love than to ourselves. Think about how amazing that is and what it says about the human species. We were built to be stronger together.

In that moment I was so thankful for my parents' unwavering support and love. I wanted to call them and tell them. I felt a surge of love and compassion for everyone in my life.

> > >

It may sound crazy to sit in the forest and find yourself yelling at no one, but mine was not an unusual reaction to the task. My flood of compassion and thoughtfulness, in particular, was typical. Recent studies looking at the impact of reflecting on death (using the same task I did) found subjects exhibited more generosity and greater concern for the group than for themselves.* But research is just catching up to philosophical wisdom that goes back as far as the Stoics in the third century BCE: confronting one's mortality is good for the soul. Thinking about our death can make us better people. In a review of literature, Kenneth Vail and colleagues found that "the awareness of mortality can motivate people to enhance their physical health and prioritize growth-oriented goals; live up to positive standards and beliefs; build supportive relationships and encourage the development of peaceful, charitable communities; and foster open-minded and growth-oriented behaviors." They found that people display greater empathy, forgiveness, compassion, love, creativity, and tolerance and they adopt a more egalitarian perspective and cognitive flexibility, meaning they are better able to appreciate different points of view.

Vail further reviewed studies that show confronting death can lead to better health-protective behaviors. Reminding people, in a subtle and supportive way, that they will die has been shown to encourage people to start exercising, stop smoking, eat healthier, and use sunscreen. Vail states: "In sum, conscious thoughts of death can motivate efforts to reduce one's perceived vulnerabilities, potentially motivating behaviors and attitudes that improve one's physical health." This is consistent with studies on aging that show as we get older and begin to realize we have a finite amount of time, we become more generous and more nurturing of our social relationships, focus on the positive, and reduce the

---

*Participants given this task in a laboratory environment were then given the opportunity to take from a limited supply of raffle tickets, good for a chance to win US$100; taking more tickets increased their chance of winning, while taking fewer tickets ostensibly left more tickets for future participants. Across three similar studies, among participants with initially stronger extrinsic goal orientations, the death-reflection condition reduced the number of tickets taken from the limited public supply. These results suggest that the reported elements leading to positive life changes following near-death experiences can be harnessed to guide the reprioritization of intrinsic over extrinsic goals in managing the awareness of death.

negative.* But you don't have to be eighty to appreciate that you have a finite amount of time; it can happen after a near-death experience or a simple reflection on mortality.

These positive outcomes offer a much-needed balance to the research findings from TMT that focus on the negative social consequences of bringing up death. Namely, when presented with images, ideas, or even locations that bring attention to our own mortality, we tend to become more defensive and more punitive toward outsiders, and cling more tightly to our values and to those who share our worldview. Basically, we circle the wagons. Yet these research findings are strongly based on context: Are you asking a New Yorker what it would be like to die in a terrorist attack or a young woman what she would want her mother to know before she dies? These questions take people to different emotional places, triggering different attitudes and beliefs.

Moreover, we can change how we respond to or engage with thoughts about death. For example, Eastern meditation practices, along with a variety of new religious and spiritual practices and mindfulness training, can turn confrontations with mortality into motivating, inspiring reminders to build strong supportive relationships, to live up to your own personal standards, and to always be looking for ways to grow and experience new things.

> > >

After I had worked through the task on death reflection, I moved on to some quotes I had pulled from various religious texts and works of philosophy and poetry. I skimmed over the poets, having read my fair share of Edgar Allan Poe, Emily Dickinson, and

---

*Molly Maxfield and colleagues found that older adults reminded of death were more forgiving of moral transgressors. Specifically, in two studies, younger (ages seventeen to thirty-seven) and older (ages fifty-seven to ninety-two) participants were reminded about death or a control topic, and then asked to recommend punishment for a moral offender in a series of vignettes. After a mortality salience trigger, older participants were lenient toward offenders, whereas younger participants were harsher.

even some work from the Graveyard Poets who were writing in eighteenth-century England, some years before it became cool to write scary stuff (which happened during the Gothic era). My eyes gravitated to the shortest quote I had copied on the bottom of the page: *"Memento Mori"* ("Remember one day you will die"). It's a famous Latin quote, found on everything from twenty-first-century Day of the Dead figurines sold in Spencer's to medieval Christian art. I had read it a hundred times before, but this time it gave me pause.

Even though the death-reflection activity had asked me to focus on my own death, I hadn't. Not really. My reflection had been on *dying*, not actually being dead. Dying is a social process. It involves people, relationships, and emotional processing. Death is . . . well, what is death? All I am certain of is that at some point I will cease to exist on this earth.

> ❧ ❧ ❧

I don't know when I abandoned my belief in an interventionist God and heaven. It may have been around the time my Sunday school teacher told me monsters weren't in the Bible, come to think of it. Ever since I let go of that faith, I've been jealous of my religious and spiritual friends, so confident and secure in their beliefs of what the world is all about. But I can't understand how anyone can assume his or her version of God or an afterlife is the right one. The only thing I feel certain of is that we will all die. Everything else is a story: maybe true, maybe false, but in any case told to make us feel a certain way. That's the point where I usually stop thinking about death. But this time I pushed forward. *The body I'm in will be gone,* I told myself. *These thoughts I am having will vanish. The people and animals I love, the things I own, will cease to exist. There will be no me.*

I looked at my hands, and the thought of death turned grisly. I imaged the skin drying out, becoming like paper and falling off. I imagined my body cold and naked on the forest floor, my blood becoming thick and dark, my gums pulling back, revealing fanglike teeth. I saw the animals that would come to feast on my remains like the bodies that are laid out on the mountaintops in the sky burials or among the Maasai tribes: wild dogs chewing off my flesh and pulling apart my limbs, scavenger birds plucking out my eyes and tugging on my exposed tendons. Then the bugs, maggots, skin beetles, and insects with more legs than I could count would infest every part of my body, burrowing underneath my loose skin and gnawing their way through my torso. The flies would come; they would lay their eggs inside my carcass, inside my skull. Their larvae would feed off my brain, chewing on all that is left of my thoughts, my memories, my love, my desires, my secrets. At some point, I would cease to be noticed even by scavenging animals. My body would be abandoned.

If this all sounds disturbing to read, it was even worse to imagine, alone in a strange place. I felt completely overwhelmed. I held on to the two tree roots at my side and stared into the forest, as the dark epiphanies kept coming. I realized the very memory of being in this spot, on my nature-made throne, will disappear when I do. I was on the verge of hyperventilating.

                                                                    ➣ ➣ ➣

The mental walls I'd built were officially broken. And while there's no such thing as bottled emotions, there's certainly a direct line between thoughts and physiological responses. And thoughts began pouring out, as if from an overstuffed closet, bringing along a whole bunch of feelings with them. All the things I wouldn't get to do ran through my head: I wouldn't see the Pyramids or the Great Wall of China, but more importantly I wouldn't have the chance to build better relationships with the people I love, to say things to them I had not yet managed to. I wouldn't get to keep growing, becoming a better self. I felt a tremendous sense of regret for all the things I hadn't done, and all the time I had wasted, all the times I avoided change, just because the known was comfortable and safe. Is that really living?

I curled my feet up onto my volcanic tree throne and hugged my knees. I let myself cry. And I cried and cried, harder than I had since I was a child. I started apologizing for all the important moments I had missed because I had shut down my feelings out of fear. I bawled, in between gasps for air, an apology to Cookie for not being there when he died, and as the words left my mouth, I felt an intense weight in my stomach, a pain as if I were being sucked into a black hole from the inside. It hurt so badly. I hadn't seen anyone else in this forest who might hear me, but in that moment I didn't care. I hugged myself and let out a wail into the woods.

> > >

Some confrontations with death are traumatizing, and not everyone processes them the same way. Resilient individuals bounce back and continue on with their lives. For others, especially those whose brushes with death are particularly traumatic, like witnessing a murder or having one's own life threatened, it's much harder to use the usual coping mechanisms, namely, clinging to beliefs and values to make sense of what is happening, leaning on friends, and finding confidence in ourselves. The outcome can affect us psychologically, and we may lose faith that the things we thought would protect us—our worldview, our beliefs, and our friends—actually protect us at all; the vulnerability and fragility of our lives are exposed. As Thomas Greening wrote, "What happens when we are traumatized? In addition to the physical, neurological, and emotional trauma, we experience a fundamental assault on our right to live, on our personal sense of worth, and further, on our sense that the world (including people) basically supports human life. Our relationship with existence itself is shattered." As a result, victims of confrontations with death may avoid any reminders of the event, experience flashbacks, withdraw from relationships, have trouble experiencing emotions, feel a loss of interest in enjoyable activities, or attempt to self-medicate with drugs or alcohol. The collective name for these symptoms is familiar: post-traumatic stress disorder, or PTSD.

TMT states that most people become more judgmental and punitive when confronted with their own mortality, but it turns out those who have PTSD do just the opposite. Tom Pyszczynski conducted studies with domestic abuse survivors from Poland, civil war survivors from Côte d'Ivoire, and US college students who have been exposed to trauma, and found that when confronted with their own mortality those with PTSD and peritrauma dissociation (which essentially means PTSD-like symptoms during or even before the traumatic event) judged moral offenses less harshly, were more lenient toward transgressors, and had more positive attitudes about issues like foreign aid. The authors suggest that this is because there is something wrong with their defense mechanisms, that they have "disrupted anxiety-buffering functioning." Pyszczynski states: "They do not deflect mortality threats through symbolic worldview defense, and they exhibit disturbance in affect after mortality thoughts." Basically, they confront death head on and then feel really sad about it.

But maybe this is not a disruption at all; maybe it's an improvement. Maybe those who once struggled to manage their emotions now have a greater appreciation for the full range of human experiences and worldviews. Maybe they are more generous to others because they suffered the most from lack of generosity. Maybe because they know what it feels like to be treated as less than human, they act with more compassion. Maybe it's because they recognized that life is fleeting and it's better to be open and kind, rather than defensive and prejudiced. Research on post-trauma growth supports this theory: traumatic events can offer individuals an opportunity to completely rebuild themselves and decide what is really important. This doesn't happen for everyone, however; some may come away with a blunted affect or feel emotionally numb—not necessarily cynical, or even vindictive, but rather they just don't care or don't feel anything at all.

> > >

After I ran out of tears to cry, and a nasty headache started setting in, I began to calm myself down. I pushed back into the base of the tree as far as I could, and wrapped my arms around the roots. I tried to commit every single image and every single feeling to memory. I never wanted to forget this day.

Curled up in my throne on the other side of the world from home, I felt vibrantly alive and full of love not only for my parents but for everything (likely helped along by some dopamine and the enkephalins in my tears). I felt safe, warm, and more appreciative of life than I ever had before. I closed my eyes, and I saw my own dead body where I had left it in the woods, but now the sun had bleached my bones a beautiful bright white, and the forest floor, having absorbed my remains back into the earth, was filled with the most beautiful green grass and wildflowers.

I don't know what will happen when I die, but instead of not thinking about it and running in the opposite direction, I now make it a point to remind myself, to *feel* it. I killed myself that day—just in my mind, but in a way that reminded me how possible it was to do it in reality. Confronting the fact that one day we will die helps us appreciate the gift of life and the support and love of others. But recognizing that you have the ability to kill yourself, that you have the power to end your own life, puts living in a whole new perspective. There is so much power in recognizing that simple fact, that each day is our choice: Are you going to live or die? And if you're going to live, what are you living for?

I felt a profound sense of control and freedom over my life and my body. Of the many feelings I had in Aokigahara, this is perhaps the most difficult to explain. It was more than an appreciation of being alive or feeling overwhelmed with my love for the world; it was a kind of self-ownership I had never experienced before. I wasn't along for the ride anymore. This is *my* life.

I was still nervous I'd come across someone contemplating suicide on my way out; even after all the contemplation and reflection I was still unsure what I would say. But I now trusted myself to say something from the heart, something compassionate, genuine, authentic, and true. Everyone builds his or her own relationship with death, and what is meaningful for me may be completely different from what is meaningful for you. And that is the beauty in life. (I'd still call for help because depression is a serious illness and requires professional attention, not ramblings from an overly emotional sociologist.) In that moment I knew I truly would do exactly what I wanted with the rest of my life. In plain English, this may sound selfish, but it means much more than indulgence—it means a life well lived.

Eventually I got up, unstuck my wet pants from my legs, picked up a rock from the ground at the base of my volcanic tree throne, put it in my pocket, and whispered two more words into the forest: *Memento mori.*

7

WRONG TURN

La Candelaria, Bogotá. Photo by Pedro Szekely.

The US Department of State's travel warning for tourists visiting Colombia in 2014 was as follows:

> Bogotá is considered high for terrorism, residential crime, non-residential crime, and political violence by the Department of State. The Department of State's Travel Warning for the potential for violence by terrorist and other criminal groups continues to exist in all regions of the country. . . .

Criminals are quick to resort to physical assault and commonly use knives and firearms in the commission of crimes. . . .

Theft and assault are frequent on-board public transportation. . . . Major accidents involving inter-city buses are a regular occurrence, resulting in deaths or serious injuries. . . .

Americans continue to be attractive kidnapping targets among foreigners because of a perception of wealth and perceived political significance for leftist groups. No one is immune from kidnapping on the basis of occupation, nationality, or other factors. The U.S. government places the highest priority on the safe recovery of kidnapped U.S. citizens, but it is U.S. policy not to make concessions to kidnappers.

This advisory was posted two weeks before I traveled to Bogotá. It didn't come as a surprise, exactly: Bogotá these days is an up-and-coming tourist destination, but it isn't far removed from being the murder and kidnapping capital of the world. This may not quite be travel brochure material, but it makes Bogotá an ideal place for a scientific study of fear. Do you go to haunted houses for a thrill when you have a very real reason to fear death or violent abduction? And how might your attitudes change if your neighborhood suddenly grew safe, within the span of a decade or two? I planned interviews with anthropologists, historians, sociologists, political scientists, and psychologists. I also checked out all the "fun" scary activities I could, but outside of physical thrills (paragliding, whitewater rafting, skydiving), the city had little to offer, for reasons I would become familiar with.

Bogotá is geographically vast, covering 617 square miles, and is home to over 8 million people (some estimate it may be as high as 12 million). This is a massive increase from the 5.4 million in 1999 and 2.8 million in 1973—much of which can be attributed to entire communities fleeing horrendous violence at the hands of leftist guerrilla and right-wing paramilitary groups that were ravaging the rural countryside. And of course there was the matter of Pablo Escobar's notorious Medellín cartel, as murderous and wealthy as any in the twentieth century. Into the first decade of the twenty-first century, Bogotá was characterized by constant violent political conflict and rampant trafficking of drugs and guns. Colombians lived with a constant threat of narco-terrorism, kidnapping, extortion, bribery, corruption, fraud, and violence. The homicide rate jumped from 39 per 100,000 in 1990 to 80 per 100,000 only three years later. And over 14,000 Colombians and foreigners are estimated to have been kidnapped from 2000 to 2007, making Colombia the "kidnap capital" of the world.

The travel warnings were enough to make anyone think twice, but I told myself the Department of State was just trying to cover its bases. A conversation began to unfold between my emotional brain, which was frankly pretty terrified of Bogotá, and my thinking brain (prefrontal cortex), which had decided I was going anyway. After all, I could be murdered or mugged or pickpocketed anywhere, right? Plus, I reminded my emotional brain, there was vast improvement in the country; peace talks were happening between the government and guerrilla groups (though one group did kidnap a Colombian general in November 2014), and homicide was down to 29 out of 100,000. New initiatives, my thinking brain continued, were curbing corruption and improving safety, and they had an impact—there were only 292 reported kidnappings in 2013. In 2007 the country had even started an Institute of Tourism, which successfully marketed the country internationally; foreign visitors rose from 0.6 million in 2007 to 2.2 million in 2013. That's a pretty good stat. Moreover, I would be staying with friends who were experts in the politics and culture of Colombia: my good friend and fellow sociologist Majo Álvarez Rivadulla, now a professor at Del Rosario University; her husband, Juan Carlos Rodríguez-Raga, a professor in economics at the University of Los Andes; and Laura Wills, also a professor in the Economics Department at Los Andes. Between the three of them and the wisdom from about four other friends with PhDs in political science, anthropology, history, and psychology, I convinced my emotional brain to calm down.

> > >

My first night in Bogotá with Majo and Juan Carlos was an eye-opener. I had assumed traveling through Bogotá would be like traveling through any other big city (I'd been to New York, Rome,

London, Paris, Tijuana, and other cities); I just needed to be smart, keep my eyes open, avoid shady strangers, and keep valuables close to me at all times. But there were a few surprises. For example, not all of the people in police uniforms are cops, and not all taxis are real taxis. While corruption has declined, there is still plenty of impure motivation afoot: real cops may still ask for bribes, cars will run you over, and everyone will try to give you counterfeit money. Streets could suddenly turn dangerous in the space of a block, and the soldiers armed with machine guns— well, it was hard to convince myself that they were there to protect me. I parried many of these concerns with one lifeline, an object that could summon help at any moment: my iPhone.

This turned out to be a mistake too. As soon as Majo saw me walk in clutching my shiny new iPhone 5c she said, "Oh I would love to have an iPhone, but it will just get stolen. You definitely cannot carry that in your hand or have it out in public." Poverty is rampant in Bogotá, and muggings are common, especially of comparatively rich tourists. I would have to leave my phone hidden away and inaccessible at a moment's notice—talk about foreign. But even that didn't change my fundamental outlook. A city was a city, and I'd been to many. My thinking brain was still certain that my emotional brain was just a worrier.

> > >

A little over half (50–60 percent) of all Americans will experience a traumatic event in the course of their lives.* For most people, after a threat has passed, all the hormones and chemicals

---

*This percentage varies widely. Some researchers put the exposure to trauma at two-thirds of the population, others at 50 percent. Differences in definition of traumatic event, sample size, and location may explain the varied rates. In general, acute traumatic events involve experiencing, facing, or witnessing a death or a serious injury to yourself or others. Chronic traumatic situations refer to ongoing exposure to threats. The traumatic events most often associated with PTSD for men are rape, combat exposure, childhood neglect, and childhood physical abuse. The most traumatic events for women are rape, sexual molestation, physical attack, being threatened with a weapon, and childhood physical abuse.

released during fight or flight go back to baseline within about six hours. It's normal to experience depression, confusion, and anxiety for days or even weeks afterwards. But humans are an incredibly resilient species, and eventually a majority of Americans return to their normal homeostasis. But about 8 percent of trauma victims do not return to baseline and instead develop PTSD.* Studying why some people develop PTSD while others do not (even when their traumatic experiences are the same) provides critical insight into what is happening in our brains and bodies when we're afraid. The goal is to develop better interventions for those who do struggle or, better yet, figure out ways to prevent it altogether.

Kerry Ressler and colleagues at Emory University found that those who tend to "bounce back" from trauma show stronger connections between their "thinking" brain, the prefrontal cortex, and their "emotional" brain, the hippocampus (in the limbic system). This is important because when we're scared, the messages from our thinking brain take a backseat to survival. It may be oversimplified, but think of it as a race car speeding around a track without a driver: the pedal is to the metal, but there is no clear destination. If we're able to keep the driver in the seat, we can steer the car and tell it when to slow down around the curve and when to speed up across the flats. In a threatening situation this translates to our thinking brain (specifically the medial prefrontal cortex, which suppresses the amygdala) telling ourselves, "Calm down. Everything is OK. We're going to get through this."

Genes play a role as well, particularly one called FKBP5, which is involved in hormonal response. Clinical neuroscientist Negar Fani studied low-income, inner-city residents (who have

---

*The rate of PTSD varies widely too. In the general population about 7.8 percent will develop PTSD in their lifetime. The rate is higher for women (9.7 percent) than men (3.6 percent) and significantly higher for veterans. Statistics vary, but the US government estimates about 30 percent of soldiers who have spent time in a war zone experience PTSD. Lifetime experience of PTSD in the general veteran populations ranges from 6 to 20 percent depending on type of deployment and the war in which they fought. For more information visit the website of the National Center for PTSD at the Department of Veteran Affairs.

a relatively high rate of traumatic experiences) and found that PTSD developed more often than average in those with a certain expression of the FKBP5 gene. The expression of the 5-HTTLPR gene, which controls levels of serotonin during times of threat, is also correlated with different stress sensitivity. Research has also found that people who can easily produce neuropeptide Y, which switches off the threat response in your brain when a crisis is over, respond better to stress. Those who have "efficient" dopaminergic and opiate systems deal better with stress as well. Other genetic differences that have been linked to PTSD include brain-derived neurotrophic factor (BDNF), monoamine oxidase B (MAO-B), apolipoprotein E (ApoE), regulator of G protein signaling 2 (RGS2), and gamma-aminobutyric acid. In fact, according to twin studies, heritability may account for as much as 40 percent of the variance in who develops PTSD and who does not.

These biological differences help explain why witnessing a violent crime can completely destroy one person emotionally and psychologically, while another person can process and work through it in a short time frame without much disruption of her everyday life or any long-term consequences. (There are also those folks who have no response at all, but we'll get to that in another chapter.) Nevertheless, even with efficient systems with well-balanced hormones and all the "right" gene expressions, our ability to deal with trauma and everyday stress is dramatically limited without the support of other people. People need each other: friends, family, and neighbors. These informal social ties in times of stress make us feel supported, cared for, and loved. During a time when a person's worldview is under attack, friends and community remind him that everything is OK. This is true at the individual level and the societal level: citizens need to know that they are being taken care of and supported during times of crisis, meaning communities need respected and trusted police forces, governments, fire departments, and religious leaders. When that safety net is gone, crisis, trauma, stress, and violence all become a lot more difficult to deal with. This may be one reason that countries with long histories of upheaval have a hard time bouncing back.

> > >

On my third day I planned to spend the afternoon on a bike tour of La Candelaria, the oldest neighborhood in Bogotá, which was founded in 1538 by Spanish conquistadores. La Candelaria is beautiful, with lots of Catholic churches and rows of old pastel houses packed together on tiny narrow cobblestone streets. This section of the city is right in the heart of downtown Bogotá, home to numerous famous museums, government buildings, and universities. It is also believed to be the most haunted space in the entire sprawling city.

I took a cab with my friend Laura to the University of Los Andes and told her I was fine to walk the rest of the way to the tour company on my own. She asked, politely but firmly, if I'd memorized the map and her phone number in case I needed anything—and of course I hadn't. I hadn't memorized a phone number since I was sixteen, and I probably hadn't memorized a map ever: both tasks were entrusted, these days, to my smartphone. "Got it," I said brightly, holding up my phone. Laura looked at me with a very serious face. What if my phone were stolen? Could I get to my destination without the help of GPS?

I felt stupid. Majo and Juan Carlos had warned me, but apparently I had not translated their wise advice into action on my part. I was completely unprepared. I hastily wrote down Laura's number on my arm, along with her address. I promised I would be OK; I could get to the destination on my own. "It's ten in the morning—I'll be fine." But Laura was not persuaded. She insisted she walk with me at least halfway. Laura is an expert on politics in Colombia and a regular guest on local and national news outlets; just a week prior she'd met with candidates running in the 2014 presidential election. And she was telling me, in no uncertain terms, to get it together, listen, and face facts. I didn't want to admit it—to myself or to her, or to anyone—but for the first time in a long time, I was scared—for real.

Laura walked with me to the bottom of a hill leading into the old city; from there she told me the roads to take to get to the tour company. As soon as she left my side, my brain started with the what-if scenarios: I had brought my passport with me, but what if someone stole it? I hadn't brought my ATM or credit card, because I'd read that kidnappers would force you to empty your bank account. But what if a robber didn't believe that I wasn't carrying it? What if he forced me to bring him to where I'd left it—at the home of Majo and Juan Carlos and their newborn baby boy? What if the clothes I was wearing were too flashy? What if someone thought my knock-off sunglasses were the real thing?

By the time I reached the tour company, I had completely forgotten about ghosts, spirits, and the supernatural. I didn't pay any attention to the beautiful historic architecture and four-hundred-year-old churches around me. I just walked with my shoulders up, chin out, eyes straight, and my "don't mess with me" face. And then, much like my flashback in the elevator on the CN Tower, an image came into my mind, one I hadn't thought about for a long time.

> . > . >

I grew up in a rural middle-class suburb where no one bothered locking their doors, but for eight years as an adult I lived in poor neighborhoods with high crime rates.* It's what I could afford as a graduate student. Over those eight years and two different homes my tires were slashed five times, and eventually my car was totaled right in front of my house. I had rocks thrown at me all the time and garbage dumped across my sidewalk, and I was routinely verbally harassed by men and women, kids and teens of every race and ethnicity. There were at least three break-in attempts (a boyfriend had all his tools stolen and then had to "buy" them back) and routine calls to the police. The man who worked on my house and lived on the third floor was shot in the head (though

---

*The relationship between poverty and violence is beyond the scope of this book, but to get started check out anything written by Yale sociologist Elijah Anderson.

not while at home). The flowers I planted were trampled (at both homes), and my retaining wall was torn apart, its bricks thrown on the street and against my house. A bullet shattered my house-mate's car windshield. Even as I shamed anyone who refused to come to my home, I was building fences in my backyard, installing alarms and cameras, and staying inside. Eventually my house became a fortress. But surprisingly what pushed me over the edge was not violence directed at me but between others.

One night in late summer 2013, I called the cops, as I'd done before, to do a drive-by and break up a fight outside my house that I had lived in since 2007. Just like at ScareHouse, but under completely opposite circumstances, I hid behind my blinds, as I always did, and watched the cops ride by with their lights on. The street quieted, and I went to sleep, frustrated and anxious as usual.

The next day I came home from work around four p.m. to at least twenty kids in the middle of the road screaming at each other. Apparently this was round 2 of what had started the night before. At the beginning of the year there had been two days of street fights three blocks from my house in which about seventy kids and adults brutally beat each other, ending with multiple arrests and injuries. The fallout lasted for weeks, and I feared the same was about to happen right in front of my house.

I pulled over, and as I was calling 911, I saw something I will never forget as long as I live: a young girl, no more than fifteen, with pink flowers on her jeans and yellow barrettes in her hair, slammed the head of another young girl into the sidewalk. My car window was open, and the sound of the girl's cheek hitting the cement was stomach-turning, a kind of muted crunch. The girl with the yellow barrettes then tried to lift the other girl up by the straps of her orange tank top, but they snapped under the weight of her body, pulling them both to the ground where they continued to beat each other. After that it was a blur: children were on top of each other, kicking, punching, and screaming.

Just like death, real fights don't look anything like fights in the movies or on TV. They are not graceful; punches don't land squarely, if they land at all. Bodies move and fall in ways that are completely unnatural; arms and legs twist back, and necks bend at 90-degree angles. But the most striking difference is in the face. Pain, fear, and anger contort people's faces in ways that are truly, instinctually terrifying. As I mentioned in a previous chapter, we start learning from birth how to recognize and read facial expressions, and sitting in my car on that day all I saw and felt was fear. I burst into tears and screamed, "Please, please tell them to come faster" into the phone as I watched in horror, too afraid to get out of my car, feeling utterly weak and powerless.

My heart was racing, I was sweating, and my hands were shaking as I wiped my tears away. But when I looked back up, what I saw filled me with a new emotion entirely. Standing on the porches and sidewalks around me, adults, parents, and other children were not shaking in fear as I was—they were laughing and *filming*. My tears dried immediately, my fear switched to anger, and I felt a powerful rage rise up in my chest.

Just then three patrol cars arrived, and everyone started running.

I knew that what I did next was stupid; I had been on the receiving end of retaliation for talking to cops in my old neighborhood. But instead of flight, my body was all fight. It was as though I was outside my body, watching myself get out of the car, run over to the officers, and scream, "I saw what happened! So did everyone on this block who just ran inside!" I turned and shouted to the houses, "This is wrong! Why are we tolerating this? You should be ashamed! Get out here and try to stop this! These are children!" The cops then asked me if I were OK, and I screamed at them, "No, no, I am *not* OK!"

I went into my house and tried to calm myself down, but just broke down in tears again. Not only was I heartbroken and confused over how such a violent situation could be one of the most terrifying of my life, yet a comedic relief for those around me, but I had put a target on myself and my house (confirmed by various comments shouted at me as I went inside). As at so many times before, I couldn't decide whether it was safer to stay inside or leave. If I left, my house was open for vandalism or robbery, and

I was open to being jumped while walking to my car. If I stayed, I wouldn't get jumped, but people could still break in. I was too embarrassed to call anyone or expose them and their property to danger. I was paralyzed with fear; I stayed up all night, watching secretly out my window. A patrol car was parked at the corner, but it wouldn't be there forever. Eventually, I would have to leave. I would have to go to work; I would have to go to the grocery store; I would have to live my life. I had had this same argument in my mind many times before, as have thousands of others. It's not fun.

The next morning I pushed myself to walk to my car. What other choice did I have? But I was tired, tired of going to bed every night anxious, waking up in panic attacks, and being a prisoner in my own home. I moved within two months, and on my last night there, wrapped in blankets on my living room floor (too afraid to leave the house empty before closing paperwork was signed), I woke up twice to the sounds of chains clinking and then slamming as people tried to break into my tightly locked U-Haul parked out front. I felt my heart rate go up and my chest get tight. I told myself this would be the last time I went to sleep scared.

> > >

When I arrived at the tour company, I introduced myself, took a map from the guide, and went to look at the bikes. I put my hand on a bike seat, estimating the height, looked down at the paper map in my hand, and saw it was shaking.

I felt ridiculous and self-conscious. I shouldn't have been scared. There were no present threats—only a slide show of previous violence playing in my mind. I needed to get my emotional brain and my thinking brain talking again. No, I hadn't ridden a bike since 2006 (at least not one that wasn't bolted to a gym floor), and true, I was afraid to ride through the busy streets of Bogotá, where traffic lanes, lights, stop signs, and one-way roads are just suggestions. And yes, it was a neighborhood with high rates of street crime, so certainly, there was a need for vigilance and concern, but I was safe—I would be with a group and a guide.

There was no need for my body to go into full threat-response mode. I told myself to snap out of it: *You're Margee! You test your limits and push yourself in new directions! Now get on that bike!*

But I could not get on the bike.

I have never chickened out of anything once I've decided to do it. After months of abandoned prisons and suicide forests and thousand-foot drops, I never imagined riding a bike on a haunted tour of an old city would be the adventure I would back out of. Before I could even really think about what I was doing, I told the guide I was not feeling well and apologized for wasting his time and walked out. My executive functioning had completely surrendered to my limbic system. I was essentially thinking with the brain of a bird.

In a daze, I started walking down the street, only in the opposite direction of where I had come from. I had no idea where I was going. The layers of self-recrimination started piling on. What was I doing? I was not making rational or smart decisions; I'd just traded a safe, public, guided tour for wandering around aimlessly alone. I had a general idea of where Laura and I had walked from, but the narrow cobblestone streets all looked the same, and I couldn't remember which were safe to walk down, so I just kept walking, one foot in front of the other, eyes straight ahead but not really seeing a thing.

The storefronts started turning into residences, and the buildings started to look shabbier and covered with more graffiti. I was lost and becoming more and more nervous. My mind was spiraling through a series of plays starring me in every bad scenario imaginable. One-act numbers not fit for Broadway: "Kidnap Girl!" "Margee the Victim!" "The Idiot Who Kept Walking!" I was doing the equivalent of running up the stairs instead of out the door in every teen horror movie ever. As I passed a series of hostels, which are all over La Candelaria and cater to student backpackers, I thought of the especially violent mugging and sexual assault of an American and her friends a few years prior. "The Hostel Episode," starring yours truly.

I just wanted to get someplace safe where I could sit down and look at my GPS and make a plan to get to one of the several museums I knew were close by. I searched every street for a café but somehow ended up going deeper into the old city and was soon surrounded by row houses. I looked up into the sky for any landmark that would help orient me, but I couldn't see above the buildings. I was trapped in a labyrinth, and the walls felt as if they were closing in.

I saw an opening along the line of row houses and made my way toward it, hoping it would reveal a park or churchyard where I could sit and feel safe enough to gather myself. I turned into the opening and was excited to see it was in fact a courtyard, but my excitement quickly turned to pure terror.

⋅   ⋅   ⋅

I lived in violent neighborhoods for only eight years, but when I moved to a safe neighborhood, I realized what a dramatic impact it had on my well-being. Even when it's incident-free, living in a constant state of fear (whether it be a violent neighborhood, a war zone, or an abusive household) is draining. The body is always in its hyper-vigilant, "ready to run" mode, which is physically, emotionally, and cognitively exhausting. You are constantly processing excess cortisol and adrenaline, which disrupts your other systems. Among the effects are a weakened immune system, digestive problems (such as ulcers and irritable bowel syndrome), decreased fertility, heart disease, weight gain, metabolic syndrome (sometimes called "prediabetes"), sleep problems, fatigue, memory problems (the hippocampus shrinks), a slowing of cognitive processing, difficulty concentrating and controlling impulses, and depression. I experienced nine of these symptoms and went to the doctor more frequently than at any other time in my life, though not once did I or the doctor connect any of my symptoms to my home life. After I moved, I had more energy, and I felt better, happier, and excited. I also felt an intense remorse for those who don't have the privilege to leave. The fact that anyone can be productive or functional while living in constant "high alert" mode is a testament to how strong we really are.

Chronic stress and fear are the reality for many who live in poor and violent neighborhoods. In fact, a recent study from Kerry Ressler found higher rates of PTSD in residents of certain violent parts of Atlanta than among war veterans. In interviews with randomly selected patients at Atlanta's Grady Memorial Hospital, Ressler found that 67 percent of those interviewed had been a victim of violent assault, 33 percent had been sexually assaulted, and half knew someone who had been murdered. By Ressler's assessment 32 percent of those interviewed met the classification for PTSD—compared to 8 percent of trauma victims in the general population and 11–20 percent of veterans who fought in twenty-first-century wars. This is doubly unfortunate, because it means that they are not just more likely to experience trauma but also more likely to have a hard time processing it.

The higher rate of PTSD in violent neighborhoods is not a result of people with unfortunate biological predispositions ending up in the same dangerous place. Our environments shape our brains. Judy Cameron, a professor in the Psychiatry Department at the University of Pittsburgh, states that a person's sensitivity to stress is a result of the complicated interplay of genes and early life experiences. To explain this complicated relationship Cameron uses a simple but perfect metaphor: a cookbook. Our genes are like sets of cookbooks inherited from our parents—we're stuck with what's in the book (DNA). But that doesn't mean there isn't room for some individual creativity and outside influence. Your cookbook may contain recipes for both a hearty stew and a tangy salad, but you're more likely to make the stew on a cold winter night. The same goes for gene expression: different environments (including physical and social environments) will influence how our genes are expressed. This is called epigenetics. However, environmental influence has a long arm, and gene expression can be passed down from one generation to the next. This epigenetic inheritance is a critical finding. Scientists once thought an embryo's epigenome was wiped clean of epigenetic tags and rebuilt (in the cookbook metaphor this would be like throwing out your mother's list of favorite recipes and building your own).

But it's not: some epigenetic tags are carried over generation to generation. In the context of how negative environments like toxic water or soil, smoking, or drug and alcohol abuse affect our gene expression, this can be rather daunting. We like to think that we are born with a clean slate, but we do carry both the burdens and the benefits of our family.

From the moment we are born our environment is working on us at every level, and we respond with the tools we have, passed down from our parents. There is no sense in separating nature and nurture. Who we are is the result of a constant adaptive feedback loop between our body and our environment. But we are not entirely hostage to the brain our childhood and our parents built; we do have free will, we can make choices, and we can change who we are. Just remember, some people have to work a lot harder and against both biological and environmental obstacles to do so.

> > >

Stone walls enclosed a small courtyard with a few benches, surrounded on each side by row houses and maybe a few businesses, whose entrances were all covered with low awnings. It couldn't have been more than one small block. One thing was clear: this was not a place for tourists. Every head turned as I walked into the yard, and all activity came to a halt, creating an eerie silence inside the walls. I felt a wave of panic wash over me, just as when I had walked out of the Hole at ESP—only there was no Amy around to tell me it would be OK. My whole body was shaking, my heart was pounding in my chest, and my ears started ringing. I was going to turn around and walk right back out, but saw out of the corner of my eye that two men had moved in front of the opening. Was this a coincidence, or were they blocking me in? I tried, as inconspicuously as I could, to scan the walls and buildings for another exit. Without making eye contact I saw men and women, some sitting, some standing, and quite a few lying on the ground in various locations under the awnings. Finally my eyes landed on another exit diagonal from where I stood.

I was scared to move. Everyone was staring right at me. I had already received a handful of unnerving looks in the thirty or so minutes I had been walking. I was not as obvious as a lot of other tourists, with their oversized backpacks and tennis shoes, but maybe that would have been better; locals know what to expect from tourists. What did I look like to them? A woman dressed in jeans and boots, walking erratically and sweating profusely.

I could feel the energy and intensity behind everyone's eyes, and it was paralyzing. I feared if I moved too quickly or in the wrong direction, I would trigger the onslaught of a violent attack. But just as I knew I couldn't stay hidden in my house forever, I knew I had to leave that square. I wanted to communicate somehow that I was not a threat. I forced a goofy smile and shrugged my shoulders just slightly as in "silly me" and casually pointed toward the far exit. "Oops," I hoped I was saying. "Didn't mean to interrupt your day. I'll show myself out." As I walked toward the gate, measuring my steps to appear calm, I could tell two men had fallen in line behind me.

I felt my body instinctively brace itself.

> > >

There really isn't a "one size fits all" when it comes to treating trauma victims. Everyone has his or her own process. But research has found several effective and promising interventions that can help a person navigate the dark side of fear. There are the pharmacological interventions: namely, selective serotonin reuptake inhibitors (SSRIs).* There is also vagus nerve stimulation and transcranial magnetic stimulation, cognitive behavioral therapy,

---

*SSRIs do not add more serotonin to the brain; they simply make the serotonin that is already there more available by blocking the transporter and stopping the reabsorption. This allows serotonin to do its job of helping other parts of the brain function more efficiently. SSRIs are the most prescribed drug in the world, used to treat phobias, depression, anxiety, PTSD, and PMS, and sometimes even used as a preventive measure for patients undergoing long-term treatment.

psychotherapy, alternative therapies, and spiritual counseling. Or, my favorite option and among the most interesting of recent interventions, how about erasing the traumatic memory altogether?

Most people have a memory they would like to forget, or at least strip of all meaning and emotion, so it blends in with the other unremarkable information we store. It may sound like *Eternal Sunshine of the Spotless Mind*, but some new interventions are close to accomplishing this feat.

The problem with traumatic memories is not so much the facts of the event but rather the emotional response triggered upon remembering, which makes us feel as if we're experiencing the trauma all over again, apparently like what was happening to me while walking through La Candelaria. From a survival perspective, it's important that our brains are able to do this: we don't want to forget how scary the gigantic alligator is. But in cases of trauma, it can be maladaptive and lead to fear generalization in which similar stimulus or context triggers a memory recall and threat response, like poor Baby Albert, to intense flashbacks and PTSD.* The question is, then, how do we keep the memory but leave the trauma behind?

Our memories are not like digital photo albums that we can open and view perfectly preserved. Each time we retrieve a memory it is re-created anew. It's more like going into a kitchen pantry and making your favorite meal: the essential ingredients are basically the same, but it tastes a little different each time you make it. When we remember things, we're picking out words and images, ideas and feelings, that seem to go together to re-create an experience in our brain. Each retrieval is re-created based on the last one, making memory an active and ongoing process.

Scientists call this the memory reconsolidation theory, and they believe it is a much more accurate view of how our brain really

---

*Even those without PTSD can experience intense emotional recalls of experiences when presented with a stimulus that reminds them of the trauma; for example, witnesses to mass shootings may experience panic attacks when hearing a loud bang.

works: we experience something and encode the facts and associated sensations, which remain stored until they are retrieved, reconsolidated as a memory, and then encoded again. Next time you tell the story, you're recalling the memory from the last version you told, not the original "hard copy." For example, now when I remember my experience of being stuck in the elevator at the VA, I also immediately think of my walk on the CN Tower *and* my time in the Hole at ESP, and honestly, the memory is not so bad anymore, since it's now connected to exciting new experiences and personal growth.

Remembering is an active process, which means we can introduce manipulations and interventions. It is a little unsettling to think that your early memories have probably changed many times over the years, but it also offers real hope for those struggling with trauma.

The goal with reconsolidation interventions is not to change the facts or content of an event, but to disrupt the process of emotional encoding, either with some careful therapeutic coaching or with medication. For example, Emily Holmes discovered that if you play a repetitive, highly absorbing game like Tetris within six hours of viewing especially disturbing or traumatic material, it reduces the salience (or emotional weight) of the memory and reduces the occurrence of intrusive recall, or thinking of it without trying. Basically this happens because the part of your brain responsible for emotional encoding is too busy watching falling blocks and trying to figure out where to put the crazy Z shape. The actual events of the trauma are still stored, but the images and strong feelings have been washed out by the colorful falling blocks. Holmes's research offers exciting evidence for the efficacy of interventions immediately following crisis and for those who suffer crippling flashbacks. We could soon see prescriptions for emergency Tetris sessions for recent victims of trauma.

There are also pharmacological options: beta-blockers such as propranolol that can disrupt reconsolidation and detach the association of strong emotions with memories. This treatment has proven effective in a number of animal studies but has shown mixed results with studies of veterans with PTSD. Not everyone thinks this type of emotional manipulation is 100 percent ethical or a good idea. The President's Council on Bioethics issued a statement of caution, warning that this type of manipulation is disrupting to one's sense of self. Admittedly it is scary to think about how malleable our memories are or to consider the idea that we may remember things that didn't happen. It can be hard to accept that we forget a lot of things; most details in fact are so unimportant that they never return to our awareness. But if you think recalling every experience with spiders when you see one is frustrating, imagine having intrusive recall of everything all the time. We have to prioritize and organize what we remember, and our brain is really good at remembering the important stuff. But when that important stuff is also destructive, interfering with our ability to live a good life, then maybe it's OK to forget. I agree with researcher Elise Donovan, who wrote, "Veterans who cannot function in society due to PTSD have essentially already lost their sense of self. The ethical issue is not how treatment may affect them, but whether withholding research and treatment that may alleviate the condition is justifiable."

> > >

As soon as I realized the two men were following me, I wanted to break into a run. But I did my best to walk at a fast yet calm and untroubled pace. I heard several people cough and a few people spit, but no one said a word. They just watched me.

As soon as I made it through the square and onto the street, I picked up my pace. I knew I should turn around to see where the two men were, but I was too afraid to look. I kept walking for at least three blocks and finally turned my head and saw the two men had stopped a block past the square. Feeling a sense of relief, I broke into a small run and didn't stop until I reached a café, probably seven blocks away.

I stormed through the café door with more energy than I would have liked. The last thing I wanted was more attention, but I couldn't help it. The barista immediately noticed I was out of breath and shaking and asked if I was OK. I said yes and tried to smile and focus on the coffee menu on the wall in front of me and dig out some cash from my pockets, but my hands were shaking too badly. I could feel the tears forming behind my eyes and pressure building in my sinuses. I'm sure my face was turning red. The barista motioned for me to have a seat at a table and take a second to calm down. I did not want to cry; I knew if I started, it would be hard to stop. Instead I practiced my breathing exercises—inhale for a count of four, and exhale for a count of four. And then I pulled out my journal, in an attempt to bring my thinking brain back online, and started writing.

I struggled to collect my thoughts. There I was, hiding in a tiny café, in a city where life has improved significantly, but where—compared to the United States—poverty, crime, violence, political conflict, and instability are everyday realities for a vast majority. I'd had a brush with what it might be like to live in those conditions, and it had done a lot more than give me a good scare. It left me with a crisis of conscience.

In my journal I saw a folded-up magazine article a friend had given me about an experience called "Extreme Kidnapping." Back home you could pay $500 to have professional gangsters abduct you at gunpoint and hold you for four hours. And if you want more, it's yours for a price. I felt as if I was going to throw up. Didn't this amount to the kind of violence tourism that made Americans seem not only ridiculous but desperately out of touch with the realities of political instability and poverty?

This thought hit home with me. I was frustrated, confused, panicked, filled with self-doubt. I was completely uncertain about what I was doing and who I was. Was my whole pursuit to understand how we enjoy fear at its core exploitative, insensitive, and fundamentally amoral? Or worse: Did my work at ScareHouse actually perpetuate violence by glamorizing it? My whole worldview had been challenged. In Bogotá I was plagued by nightmares every night and spontaneously broke out in tears at least twice a day. I didn't know if I wanted to write this book, and I was ready to get out of the fear business entirely.

> > >

After an hour of breathing slowly and journaling, I still felt unsure about what I was doing in life, but I did at least feel confident enough to get up and leave the café. As time passed and I walked through the city, I grew increasingly frustrated by the energy I had spent on being scared. For what? Nothing had even happened to me. In fact the worst thing I'd experienced was my own self-induced threat response, but I certainly wasn't feeling relaxed in the post–dopamine and endorphin soup, like after the CN Tower. I was starting to understand why everyone here asked, "Why would anyone go to a haunted house to be scared in Colombia? You can just walk out on the street!" I always thought they were exaggerating, but maybe they were right after all.

Once I finally found my way out of the old city, I went to meet with Esteban Cruz Niño, an anthropologist who studies violence, fear, and mass murder in Colombia. He literally wrote the book on Colombian serial killers: *Los Monstruos en Colombia Sí Existen*. My meeting with him could not have been more perfectly timed. I essentially had just experienced the reality of his hypothesis on fear and Colombians: that because Colombians are exposed to and experience real violence routinely, they have no desire to seek out or engage with symbolic violence (like horror movies or haunted houses). "Real life," he said, "that is the horror story."* He cited the lack of a profitable commercial horror or thrilling industry; for example, a new TV drama, *Dr. Mata* (a kind of mash-up of *Breaking Bad* and *Dexter*), failed to do well in the ratings with anyone other than the young and rich, a

---

*The hypothesis that countries with low levels of actual violence have higher levels of engagement with symbolic violence (scary material) seems to make intuitive sense, but there are many counterexamples, like Mexico, which hosts a successful horror movie industry despite high crime rates. And at the micro level there is high engagement with scary video games and horror movies by deployed soldiers and high engagement by groups that have high levels of violence in their communities, like gangs.

small segment of Colombia. Compared to Americans, Niño said, Colombians do not think about fear in terms of "potentiality" but rather "eventuality." Rodrigo Duarte, who is the director of a horror genre film festival called Zina Zombie Fest, made a similar comment: Americans are hyper-paranoid about everything that could potentially happen, but probably won't, while Colombians live their lives among real threats every day without complaining. (I noticed that lots of people in Colombia are reluctant to say anything negative about their country.)*

Niño's words rang true after what I had experienced not an hour prior to my meeting with him. My American paranoia, exaggerated by my former experiences in violent neighborhoods, had turned me into a frightened mess. There are a number of explanations as to why I was so obviously a target in the tiny

---

*Bogotá does have a history of horror films, albeit small, and I had seen several paranormal-themed tours and entertainment. But as everyone I interviewed in Bogotá pointed out, they serve a different purpose. Rather than being strictly for entertainment, they are avenues of explaining and coping with the real violence people experience there, or as a source of hope and spiritual guidance. Duarte said Colombian horror films use black comedy and a satirical approach to tackle everything from guerrilla warfare to the NARCO wars. He explained that sometimes filmmakers do this to make a political point, but it is also a way to take ownership and control over the conflicts and real "monsters" that threaten Colombia. Historian Sebastian Quiroga, the producer of *My Ghost Story* for the Biography Channel in Latin America, affirmed what Duarte and Niño pointed out, and added that ghost stories are created and shared as a way to pass along warnings of violent groups (guerrilla, paramilitary, or drug) without using real names for fear of retaliation. I would add that while the circumstances may be different, all storytelling generally serves similar purposes across time and space; just as our ancient ancestors were turning predators into monsters, so every society finds a symbolic way to tackle its great white whale.

Zina Zombie Fest is dedicated to bringing independent horror films to the people—not just in Colombia but all over Central and South America. It began as a cinema club and expanded into a festival dedicated to bringing films that could not be shown in the popular malls. Duarte now travels internationally, working with other film festivals, filmmakers, and producers to provide a venue to show great independent work. The Zina Zombie Fest is in its sixth year and continues to grow. The festival has achieved a great deal of support and legitimacy, even securing funding and sponsorship from the Ministry of Culture.

square; it could have been gang territory, a popular drug-dealing location, or a place to do drugs. They could have wanted to rob me or kidnap me, or both. Or it could have been a decent community of longtime residents in La Candelaria who are sick and tired of the young tourists trashing their neighborhood and staying up until all hours of the night drinking and partying (a common sentiment among the older residents). Just as I perceived them as a potential threat, so was I to them. The men following me could have been watching to make sure I wouldn't return, or waiting for the right moment to rob me, or they could have just been walking in the same direction. I could have narrowly escaped the most dangerous environment I'd ever been in, or I could have just freaked myself out because the situation reminded me of the last time I felt legitimately frightened for my safety. For all I know, I could have been in more danger walking home at eleven p.m. in Tokyo a few months earlier. But that's the thing with fear: reality often doesn't matter; it's all in the perception.

Yes, vigilance is good, and it was appropriate for me to be alert as a tourist in a rough neighborhood, but I didn't need to freak out to the extent that I did. The next day, when I asked Laura, who was born and raised in Bogotá, how she deals with constant threat, she shrugged and said she accepts it as a reality but doesn't let it control her life. I wanted to do that.

> > >

Americans are a paranoid bunch. We're afraid of all the wrong things because, as sociologists W. I. Thomas and D. S. Thomas pointed out in 1928: if you believe, or in this case feel, something is true, it has real consequences. It doesn't matter if there is no monster under your kid's bed. He's going to end up shaking, crying, and sleeping with you. Thinking, intelligent adults do the same thing, as David Ropeik points out in his article "The Consequences of Fear":

From transgenic food to industrial chemicals, from radiation
to mobile phone towers, the new technologies of our modern world have offered us wonderful new benefits, which also
pose a host of new risks. Some of these risks are physically
real. Many are only phantoms of our perceptions. Both contribute to an undeniably real sense of worry and apprehen-
sion that extends far beyond the next 24 hours.

Nevertheless, the truth is that even though the United
States ranks pretty low in safety compared to other industri-
alized nations, most Americans are safer today than they ever
have been before (and living longer, as we learned in Chapter
6). According to the Pew Research Center, which analyzed data
from the Centers for Disease Control (CDC) and the National
Crime Victimization Survey, rates of nonfatal violent crime
decreased 72 percent between 1993 and 2011. Gun violence is
also down: fatalities from a firearm were 48 percent lower in
2010, and violent crimes with a firearm decreased 75 percent
since 1993, when gun violence peaked.* In real numbers there
were 1.5 million nonfatal gun crime victims in 1993; in 2011
there were 467,000. Property crimes like burglary, motor vehicle
theft, and other theft have declined 61 percent in the same time
frame. But people are panicked not only about violent crime.
As Ropeik states, we're worried about a whole host of issues we
have no control over, namely, how our environment filled with
all kinds of new agents is affecting our health and safety. It is as
though every threat we remove makes the remaining that much
bigger, stronger, and scarier. The fears that are likely to influence
our lives—cancer, dementia, heart disease, diabetes—are hard
to wrap our minds around, since there is often little we can do
to predict or avoid them. All this leaves us feeling insecure and

*Violent crime did sneak up in 2011, and the United States does have prob-
lems with guns: we have more homicides by firearm than most developed countries, and even though we only account for 5 percent of the world's population,
we own 35–50 percent of the world's civilian-owned guns.

vulnerable, with no opportunities for confrontation or resolution. These fears hang on us in the form of stress and anxiety. We zero in on what we can control, becoming obsessed with what we eat and drink, where and how our kids can play, where we go and whom we talk to.

Much of this misperception about crime rates and risk has to do with media exposure. We see news from across the world within seconds of it occurring, making anomalous and tragic events seem more common and closer to home than they actually are. According to our emotional brain, we may be living in Colombia or Afghanistan or Iraq. There's also more time dedicated to crime reporting in our national news nowadays. In 2013 the Pew Research Center released *The State of the News Media*, which reported that local markets' crime reporting is down—17 percent of all news coverage in 2012, from 29 percent in 2005. But on the national level ABC, CBS, and NBC increased the amount of time spent covering crime on their morning and evening news shows, most significantly for their morning shows, during which crime coverage rose from 9 percent in 2007 to 14 percent in 2012. This, along with the constant barrage of fear-triggering marketing of consumer goods, leads Americans to think violent crime is more prevalent than it is.* But just because we're more aware of child predators and shark attacks doesn't mean they are more prevalent.

Media exposure and misperception of threat are only part of the problem. As my colleagues in Bogotá reminded me, they too have an abundance of media exposure to violence, so how can Laura say she doesn't let it control her? As Niño pointed out, maybe it's the difference between preparing for the potential versus the eventual. Preparing for a potential threat focuses attention on avoidance, so it's more passive: "Don't go there, or do this, or say that because bad things *might* happen." Whereas preparing for

---

*The academic terms for these consequences are *familiarity, group polarization,* and *confirmation bias.* See Daniel Gardner's *The Science of Fear: Why We Fear Things We Shouldn't.*

an eventual threat focuses attention on engagement and is more active: "*When* this bad thing happens, you can do this, and afterwards, you can do this." The first perspective restricts us; the second empowers growth.

The consequences of this misperception/fear/avoidance dynamic extend beyond a nagging concern over whether the new plastic is really safe to drink from, or if you should go check out a new restaurant in "the bad part of town." At one end of the spectrum it can lead to the negative psychological, physical, and social consequences discussed above in response to trauma (especially isolation and chronic stress), while on the other end it can lead to what may feel like minor changes in your behavior in an attempt to make you feel safer. But these minor changes carry a heavy cost in the form of lost opportunities for developing emotional flexibility and resiliency. And we're passing this on to the next generation: today's overprotective or "helicopter" parents are raising kids who have never had the chance to test their own limits, to confront a situation that is stressful or scary and learn to trust their own abilities, to fall down and learn they can get back up and be OK—a critical skill called "distress tolerance." Just because we're more aware of the damage that can result from trauma doesn't mean everyone should put their child or themselves in a bubble. In fact that is one of the worst things you can do.

Child development researcher Roger Hart found evidence of this shift toward overprotection when he recently followed up with adults he studied as children. At the time (over thirty years ago) Hart was interested in how children spend their free time, and he found that they were allowed to wander far distances, walk through neighborhoods unsupervised, swim, climb trees, and generally play on their own, and they were fine. Today, the same kids who were allowed to roam free in their youth do not allow their own children to stray more than five feet for over five minutes, because they're too afraid something could happen. Children (and adults—it never stops) are powerfully shaped by the expectations placed on them, and if the message they are getting is "You can't handle this," they will internalize that message and believe that they can't handle it. There are ways to keep your child safe and also let them test their limits.*

Stress management is a skill we learn over time. Just as our immune system becomes stronger by producing more white blood cells when exposed to pathogens, so can our self-esteem bolster our sense of resilience and courage when we're exposed to manageable threats in a supportive environment (not trauma). Without these opportunities we are essentially an immune system with no white blood cells—fine as long as we hide in a bubble. But we can't stay in a bubble, and who would want to?

We have the ability to be strong and resilient, but we have to have chances to prove that to ourselves so that we *know* and we *feel* that we can handle it so that, like Laura, we don't let fear control our lives. I was starting to think maybe there was a place for what Niño called symbolic violence, but what I would come to call voluntary high-arousal negative experiences, or VHANE.

That night, on my way home with Majo and her newborn son, I passed through a protest that had turned violent in front of the community college. Tear gas filled the air, officers in riot gear and gas masks with machine guns were everywhere, and broken pieces of a stone wall littered the road. I felt the gas burning my throat and couldn't look away from the frightening scene. But it barely earned a passing glance from the driver, who rolled up the windows, or from Majo, who moved a blanket to cover her son's nose and mouth. Just another day in Bogotá.

> > >

---

*This is not to say that parents should allow children to run amok wherever they want (though extremists in the free-range parenting movement come pretty close), nor should parents purposely expose their children to challenges or threats they are incapable of understanding or managing—that's where parenting comes in. Parents have to know and understand where their child is developmentally and what their child's comfort level is, and then make a rational decision. Finally, there's a difference between unstructured or unsupervised playtime and neglect, and a big difference between facing and overcoming a challenge while playing with friends and growing up in an unstable, stressful, and violent environment. Check out Roger Hart's Children's Environmental Research Group (cergnyc.org).

On my last night, I ventured out alone once again. This time it was for a tour of the Central Cemetery of Bogotá, which since 1836 has been the resting place of the most famous, respected, and notorious Colombians. It was an unconventional affair, equal parts history and haunted house–style thrills and scares, and it was very well done.

Several scenes were of the traditional, slasher-flick breed, and they were plenty gruesome—a suicide by hanging and an axe murder among them. But the moment that stood out to me was not gory at all. It was a scene staged at the grave of a murdered kidnap victim. The actor playing the ghost of this person, a young man of slight frame and weight, sat at the base of his tombstone, facing out toward the crowd and hugging his knees. He spoke of how, just the day before, he'd been with his wife and children, complaining of the mundane aspects of daily life. He would give anything, he said, to return to his home and his loved ones. Sensing the moment, I turned to watch the crowd react. I saw two women embrace each other. A man appeared to be wiping tears from his eyes. A young couple squeezed closer together.

Something occurred to me as I turned over this scene in my mind. These stories offered more than just a fireside scare. They are the fabric of folklore; they bind together communities. From ancestral folktales of monsters and beasts that keep kids from wandering off into the woods to ghost stories Colombians share to warn each other of violent groups (guerrilla, paramilitary, or drug) without using real names for fear of retaliation: these stories are a way to create and share experience and culture.

Before visiting the cemetery that night, I had never experienced such a wonderful balance of thrill, laughter, suspense, and history. This tour had scared people, used depictions of violence, and made people uncomfortable. Yet it also left people feeling proud, confident, thankful, and with a sense of solidarity. Here, I thought, was the evidence of how thrilling, dramatic, scary, and, yes, even tragic material could make you feel better and more whole. It was not insensitive, as I'd feared in my dark moment in the old city. Done right, it was fun, illustrative, moving, and maybe even a little bit healing.

In these spaces you can feel something you have never felt before, or recall a difficult memory accompanied by friends in a safe environment, and this time maybe you can store it with a little less fear and a little more fun. Creating an experience with the right amount of fear to push boundaries and leave people feeling confident, with the right amount of fun to leave them feeling wonderful, and all within a context that is not exploitative or insensitive, is a tough challenge—one that many, many places have failed at. But I saw and learned firsthand it was worth doing.

And if anyone should try to do it, I thought it should be me.

PART IV
BRINGING IT HOME

Always do what you are afraid to do.

—Ralph Waldo Emerson

8

BUILDING THE BASEMENT

Photo courtesy of ScareHouse. Copyright Rachellynn Schoen.

You never forget your first contact with a corpse.

In the summers, my parents used to take our family to the Steppingstone Farm Museum in Maryland, where they hosted a Scottish Highland fair. One warm day in 1991, amid the cicadas and the low wind, I slipped away to explore on my own and wandered into an old blacksmithing shed. I nosed around, investigating the oddly shaped tools, pulling on the chains hanging from the rafters, and lifting up the heavy, rusted horseshoes. Everything was covered with a solid inch of dust. Behind the workbench I noticed a short hallway with a tiny rope strung across the entrance with a sign reading "Do Not Enter." Naturally, I slipped under the rope, batted through some cobwebs, and snuck into the back room, which was empty save for something on a chair in the corner, covered by a white sheet.

It was a body.

My heart and my feet stopped. "Hello?" No response. I tiptoed closer and held my breath as I listened for signs of life. Nothing. I lifted the bottom of the sheet just enough to reveal two tattered brown shoes. My gaze moved up the legs to very old wrinkled hands. I dropped the sheet and jumped back. I was alone in a dark room with a dead man. All around me were rusted farm tools, which is to say, murder weapons.

In a flash I could see the whole story: in a heated argument, some seven-foot, 350-pound Scottish blacksmith had attacked his grandfather with a thresher or a sledgehammer or a sickle. Where was this monster now? Had he hung the "Do Not Enter" sign to hide the corpse? In any case, I knew I should run. But I couldn't move. I had to see the rest of the body. I closed my eyes and pulled the sheet down over the figure's head and prepared for the worst. When I opened them, I was nose to nose with the wrinkled, smiling face of an old man with two perfectly blue eyes staring right at me. Despite the lack of gore I still jumped backwards, screamed, and ran out.

I didn't stop running until I reached my family and told them what I had found. One of my dad's friends quickly set me straight: my corpse was a wax figure of an old blacksmith. It's funny: my first reaction was disappointment. There went my "tall tale" of finding a dead body I was already imagining sharing with friends. But it left me with an idea. Later that day, and then every following year, I asked my friends if they wanted to check out the old shed and then proceeded to give them a good scare. In the end, the old man wasn't my first corpse, but that barn soon became my first haunted house.

There was nothing inherently scary about the wax black-smith—quite the opposite. He was smiling and kind looking. And there wasn't really anything scary about the shed either (other than being old and full of intimidating things that could kill you). But as I walked friends over, I told the story of the Scottish black-smith stashing his dead grandfather in the back room of an abandoned old shed after a tragic fight, and it was done. The scene was set: as soon as they saw the wax figure, even without the sheet, my friends would scream. I was an evil child, but my friends loved it.

I had learned a lot from my blacksmith-haunted house. Put this same figure on a park bench or in a shopping mall, and he might look out of place, but he wouldn't be scary and certainly not the stuff a fun thrill is made of. It was the place that I found him—the rusted old tools, the dark room behind the "Do Not Enter" sign, the story I told of murder and mayhem, and the invitation to experience an adventure that made the difference. We all knew, even me at some level, that the shape under the sheet wasn't really a dead body, but it was exciting to suspend our disbelief, to allow ourselves to get caught up in the story and feel close to something dangerous and taboo. This is why we like to go to "scary" places: when done well, they can create an emotional experience with real social and psychological benefits.

> > >

What is a haunted house? It depends on who you ask. For most Americans a haunted house is a space you go with your friends to walk through single file, where monsters, machines, and animations pop out and go, "Boo." But within this basic formula there is a tremendous range that divides the haunted attraction industry into three broad categories. First there are the backyard haunted houses that are thrown together the last week of October for the neighborhood kids, although mostly they're for the people doing the building and the joy they get from the creative process (and watching the kids react). Next, there are mid-level haunted houses, most of which evolved from former Jaycee (United States

Junior Chamber) haunts in the 1970s and '80s.* These are the traditional, family-friendly, $5-ticket haunts run by small charities, schools, volunteer firefighters' associations, and other nonprofit groups to raise money. Then there are the mega-haunted attractions. These are the attractions that bring in over thirty thousand people a season (some, like Terror Behind the Walls at Eastern State Penitentiary, are getting over a hundred thousand) with high-tech, high-quality, Hollywood-style sets and designs, and lots of paid professionals rather than volunteers.[†]

Finally, again depending on who you ask, there may be a fourth type of haunted attraction, which emerged in the twenty-first century: the "extreme" haunt.[‡] These are haunted attractions where the actors interact with customers and expose them to extreme circumstances like being restrained, touched, blindfolded, and exposed to torturous scenarios. This has divided the haunted attraction industry, and ScareHouse has been squarely in the middle of it. Apparently, so have I.

⁊ ⸱⸱ ⁊ ⸱ ⁊

---

*Jaycee, the leadership training and civic organization that started in 1920, began finding abandoned buildings and creating its own small haunted houses in the late 1960s and into the '70s. Jim Gould and Tom Hilligoss, members of the Bloomington, Illinois, chapter, wrote a book on how to build and create a haunted house. The book was well received by the organization's chapters, and at the next convention in 1975 Hilligoss built his booth into a small-scale replica of a haunted house. The response again was so positive that he formed the Haunted House Company, which supplied Jaycee chapters with masks and materials for their seasonal haunts. Hilligoss traveled around the country, sharing his expertise on haunted houses and how to make them successful.

†Many of the largest haunted attractions are run as nonprofits, or fundraisers for nonprofits. To find out how your local charity haunt spends its money, see charitynavigator.org.

‡I have a feeling that as entertainment continues to mix and merge mediums and environments, the whole idea of differentiating between haunted houses, immersive theater, interactive performance art, virtual reality, and video games will be meaningless. There will always be traditional haunted houses; each generation needs to experience the thrill and fun of walking through a haunted house as scary characters and monsters pop out at you.

My first introduction to the concept of extreme haunts, a term laden with misunderstanding, confusion, contention, and straight-up disagreement, was when someone asked me what it was like to help create one. This was news to me; I never considered the work I had been doing with ScareHouse's interactive attraction, the Basement, as building an extreme haunt. I was just listening to data.

I had been conducting qualitative analysis on open-ended questions from ScareHouse customers since 2008 using the grounded theory method, which involves coding answers with themes, concepts, and categories that emerge from the data (as opposed to starting with a set of codes and applying them *to* the data). I probably have the most entertaining codebook in academia: I have an entire category called "Monsters" with individual codes for zombies, ghosts, witches, demons, serial killers, and so forth, and a category of "Ways to Die." By counting the number of times a code is applied I am able to chart trends over time—for example I predicted the rise (and now fall) of the zombie craze back in 2008.

One category emerged quietly in 2008 and then slowly started to grow and then explode in 2011: an uncategorized code I just called "interactive." I applied this code whenever someone would mention how much he or she would like to be or was almost grabbed, touched, removed, or lost from their group when going through ScareHouse. (Like most haunted houses, ScareHouse doesn't allow physical contact between customers and monsters.) More and more, customers seemed to want us to remove the barrier between the actor and the customer to make it feel more active, more realistic, and therefore scarier.

The data presented quite the challenge and raised a lot of questions. How would we create a scary interactive experience that felt real but was also safe? After many, many conversations with Scott Simmons, owner and creative director at ScareHouse, we decided to try an experiment inspired by the interactive or "immersive" theatrical productions that put the customer *in* the performance, where actors can touch you, like the groundbreaking theatrical experience *Sleep No More*, put on by Punch Drunk Productions in New York, and the Pittsburgh-produced, one-on-one interactive experience *STRATA* by Bricolage Theater.

In true pilot-testing experimental fashion, we reached out to the *STRATA* cast and hired actress Ayne Terceira, who was the perfect mix of professional talent and unnerving character. We set Ayne up with two large antique chairs, a small table, and a flicker lightbulb in the middle of the ScareHouse basement, which by day was an eight-lane duckpin bowling alley but by night was a pitch-black echo chamber. We left the character development up to Ayne, who decided on a Victorian-era wife and mother. Our only direction was: "Ask them questions, touch them (no bathing suit areas), and scare their pants off." And that she did. We didn't charge for the experience we called "ScareHouse Secrets," which lasted just five minutes and basically consisted of sitting customers in the dark until Ayne would appear and go into an improvised interrogation.*

The customer reactions were amazing; after the first initial scream and string of swear words, they would begin to laugh nervously and move around in their chair, and then leave with a big smile, just like my friends after I took them to my blacksmith haunted house as a kid. I talked to every customer afterwards, and while a few people didn't "get" it, most said that being alone in the dark combined with the uncertainty of what Ayne would do or say next pushed them to a state of anticipation and exhilaration they'd never felt before. They were terrified and loved it.

The next year ScareHouse created a new immersive, interactive, scary, and thrilling experience built on the lessons we had learned from ScareHouse Secrets, called, appropriately, the Basement.

> > >

---

*Actors would approach customers in line and invite them if they wanted to learn the "ScareHouse Secret," and only those who said yes were brought in to meet Ayne. They were told to take the actor's hand and that they would be away from their friends for at least five minutes but they could leave at any time.

From the very beginning, the mission of the Basement was clear: to create an experience that was scary, interactive, and engaging. We wanted to make the scenes feel intense and "out of control" to the customer, but in reality they were staged, scripted, and very safe. As Immanuel Kant wrote in the *Critique of Judgment*, fear is only fun when experienced from a safe place. To that end, the Basement was built on the principles of informed consent. Customers had to voluntarily choose the experience (which was a separate ticket from ScareHouse); be over eighteen; understand what the experience entailed, including potential risks; know that they could leave at any time; and realize that they were under supervision of surveillance cameras, security officers, and management and working with trained professionals.* Once these principles were in place, we created the first season of the Basement, which consisted of twelve scenes in which customers interacted one-on-one (or two-on-one) with characters survey data told me were scariest: clowns, demons, nurses/doctors, butchers, criminals, naked people (though our actors were only made to seem naked in the dark), and witches.

This is when I learned that what I was calling "interactive" the haunt world was calling "extreme." And, to put it mildly, it pissed a lot of people off—from other haunters to churches to feminist bloggers. As Pat Konopelski, who opened the Naked and Scared attraction at Shocktoberfest in Reading, Pennsylvania, which customers go through in their underwear, said, "You think you've made it when you're in *Time*, on CNN, but no—it's when you show up in the homilies." I understood religious organizations having a problem with the Basement; we had demons and witches, which I'd known since Sunday school went against church doctrine. But it bothered me that other haunters and feminist bloggers were

---

*We developed a list of Frequently Asked Questions and a waiver everyone had to sign that explicitly stated the rules and the "safe word" they could say at any time to end the experience and be escorted out. All actors had to pass background checks (as do all ScareHouse employees) and go through training on what they could and couldn't do. We hired actors with experience in reading and responding to audiences and customers—namely, those with improv, immersive theater, or performance art experience.

upset. I have no problem with the word "extreme." A lot of what I've helped to create in the Basement *is* extreme. I have a problem with the assumption that "extreme" automatically means unsafe, exploitative, traumatizing, and offensive.

The Basement adopted the same policies regarding safety as the haunts upstairs: background checks on all employees, building according to fire and safety codes, Department of Labor posters everywhere, and a handbook of protocol and policy over twenty pages long. And of course surveillance cameras and security on-site.* The Basement also adopted the same policy ScareHouse has observed since it opened: there would be no scenes depicting sexual violence, no scenes with helpless female victims, and no use of derogatory words for women.† The horror industry is very much a male-dominated world, and more than a few extreme and traditional haunted houses have scenes in which women are victimized and abused.‡ We live in a world where women are undermined and exploited, where threats of violence are real and present. And as I confirmed in Bogotá, fear can be traumatizing when it's too close to real life. There is enough sexual violence in view on any given Saturday night out; my colleagues and I saw no need to ratify this terrible reality by showing more of it in our haunted house. Just like the main haunts in ScareHouse, the Basement would offer

---

*The entire issue of safety in the haunted attraction industry *should* be a concern. Some of the most dangerous haunts I've seen are traditional small-town haunts and hayrides where anything goes (imagine flamethrowers around black plastic and dried hay with a sixteen-year-old driving a five-ton tractor full of kids and teens—talk about scary). There's no federal oversight of haunted attractions, and local oversight varies drastically by county and state. Many haunted houses use volunteers who are children; most do not perform background checks.

†This was difficult to police at times, as actors would say these words—to men and women—impulsively when immersed in a scene, and they would apologize afterward, but the fact that these words flow off the tongue so much more readily than other types of words speaks to how normalized violence against women is in our culture.

‡I don't want to bring any attention to the "extreme" haunts that I think are disgusting, so I'm not going to mention them by name except to say that there is a contingent of the haunted/extreme attraction world that is built more for its creators than for its customers. These individuals do not want to build people up but rather watch them break down.

an alternative to these kinds of spaces by creating a thrilling, scary experience that flips existing power dynamics.*

The first full season of the Basement was a massive success and sold out most nights. We even opened it for three off-season events: Christmas, Valentine's Day, and a special event in the summer. All sold out. I collected over two hundred customer response surveys, and the results were overwhelmingly positive: 91.4 percent said they would return the following year. I was proud of what we created in the Basement, but I was left with so many questions. For example, I asked customers to rate the Basement on how intense, thrilling, scary, uncomfortable, and revolting they thought it was. My predictions on the results of these ratings were way off: people thought it was more thrilling and intense, but not scarier. According to the analysis of the answers to "What can we do better?" people wanted it scarier. This was a puzzling thing to hear, because we'd designed the Basement with a series of experiences that were absolutely terrifying. For instance, some customers had their throats "slit" with a plastic knife. How was that not terrifying? How much scarier could we get? How much scarier did we want to get? Thankfully, before we rebuilt the Basement for a second year, I had been learning a *lot* about fear. And to top it all off, I had a meeting with someone who would help give me a whole new kind of insight into the subject.

➤ ➤ ➤

Greg Siegle, associate professor of psychiatry and director of the Program in Cognitive Affective Neuroscience (PICAN), is an expert in the field of emotion research. He's received millions

*The Basement does contain sexualized content, but none of it is meant to simulate or even come close to sexual assault. Each scene that involved some sort of sexual content did not include any suggestion of assault, while the scenes that were more violent did not involve sexuality. Finally, when it came to violence or harassment, the actors were exposed, not the customers. Men and women routinely grabbed or attempted to grab and say crude, out-of-context, and inappropriate things to our actors, even after an explicit explanation before entering the Basement that they were *not* to harass or touch the actors. These customers were made to leave.

of dollars in grants from the National Institutes of Health. His résumé is enough to intimidate even a seasoned researcher, but luckily, I had spent the past year growing ever more courageous.

Despite his prominence in the field, Greg turned out to be friendly and welcoming instead of elitist and smug like so many research directors I had met before. He even invited me to get hooked up to what he called "the shock box" to test my psycho-physiological fear response. In other words, he offered to try to scare the hell out of me and then measure the response in my brain and body. Naturally, I was all too happy to do it.

A week later Greg greeted me with a friendly smile and an outstretched hand. Outfitted in comfortable dark jeans and a polo shirt, with straight, dark brown hair down to his shoulders and an almost (but not quite) hipster beard, Greg was just about the most approachable and warm researcher I've ever encountered. Not necessarily what you'd expect from the doctor whose job is to test your fears, or so I thought.

Greg knows fear from every perspective. He understands the power of inciting fear and therefore does not take the subject lightly. The model for his lab is the same model we use in the Basement—one built around the principles of informed consent. Before Greg began any of the fear testing with me, he walked me through the basics, but not the specifics, of what we would be doing. We discussed that to truly explore my fear reactions, we would be doing things unlike any usual lab protocol—things that might provoke surprise, fear, or intense reactions. I said, "Sign me up!" You might think this somehow ruins the testing results— and indeed, advanced knowledge of a threat does affect the way we experience it. But without a discussion of expectations and a knowledge of what you are consenting to, the chance of inflicting trauma is high. Greg and I talked for a good two hours before we began, so by the time he started actually testing my fears, I knew I was in a safe place with someone I could trust. As I would observe later, during our own study, he approaches every participant with the same consideration and concern. Fear is something we can play with, and achieve positive outcomes, but only when handled responsibly. This is a lesson I desperately want to teach to the rest of the makers and creators of thrills and chills.

I was familiar with the devices Greg was using to measure my psychophysiological responses; I'd spent my academic career reading studies that deployed them. But as I have learned time and time again, things are different in real life and hit you in ways you could never imagine. First there was a galvanic skin response device that measures the sympathetic nervous system via electrical conductance of the skin. Basically, it knows how much you're sweating. Next, the electroencephalography (EEG) device, which was an intimidating black crown adorned with ominous, spidery legs that attach to different parts of your head. Its "feet" are actually nodes placed at specific points around the head to measure the electrical activity created when neurons are firing in synch.* Different firing speeds or oscillations represent different kinds of brain activity. Slow oscillations, or theta waves, represent around four to seven firings a second and indicate a more trancelike state, often observed during times of drowsiness or meditation. Alpha waves comprise neural firings at about eight to thirteen times a second, reflecting a kind of idling brain state, awake but relaxed. Next is beta, which describes firing between thirteen and thirty times per second. Beta waves show up when people are active, paying attention, and thinking. Finally, there is gamma, capturing arousal states of over thirty oscillations per second. Gamma waves suggest a person is fully engaged and aroused. This is also the wave state that has been observed when Tibetan Buddhist monks are meditating on the idea of "pure compassion" (benevolence, nonreferential compassion)—when the brain is "all in."

Once the EEG and GSR (galvanic skin response) devices were on, Greg pointed to three computer screens in front of us and said, "This is your brain, and these are your brain waves." At first I didn't understand what I was looking at. Two screens showed what looked

---

*The EEG Greg used, made by a company called Emotiv, retails for only about $750, compared to the larger and much more expensive $80,000 EEG that Greg's lab uses for studies that require detection of weaker signals than we were going to be working with. This new portable EEG was actually designed for gamers who play online role-playing games as wizard characters who wanted to be able to cast spells with their brains. So thank you, gaming industry, for making affordable EEGs available to the research community, who can now go out of the lab to undisclosed locations to collect data in more suitable environments. Commence your spell casting.

like recordings from a polygraph machine or EKG monitor, with lots of squiggly waves jumping all around. But the screen closest to me had four outlines of a brain, each to represent theta, alpha, beta, or gamma. The changing colors indicated higher or lower waves and location (front, back, left, or right). It all just looked like a psychedelic screen saver, but when Greg had me run through a series of calibration tests, the connection between what I was doing and what I was seeing on the screens started to click. Greg asked me to close my eyes for ten seconds and then open them.

"See this here, the pattern, that's a little bit of alpha, so your brain goes into an idling state when you close your eyes."

Seeing the response on the screen, I realized I was standing behind a peephole looking into my own brain. Suddenly I was nervous. What if my brain and my body responded to fear in unexpected or unusual ways? What if I wasn't really scared of the things I thought I was? What if I didn't have a startle reflex? And this time it wasn't just me behind the peephole; Greg was there too—in fact he would know how I was responding before I did, and he would be the one startling *me*. Of all the scary, thrilling, strange experiences I'd had over the course of my investigation, this one, I realized, was the most alien, the most exotic, and the most revealing. There may have been no gore or monsters or towering heights, but there was no question this was strange and scary.

＊　＊　＊

"SMACK!" Greg clapped his hands loudly in front of me suddenly. I screamed and flinched backwards into my chair, completely and utterly surprised. I knew at some point he was going to test my startle, but had no idea when it was coming and couldn't help but laugh at and appreciate my own automatic response.

I looked at the monitors and then at Greg. This was a moment of truth for me. For years, more years than I could remember, I'd been telling people I love scary things and haunted houses because I have a sensitive startle reflex. It might sound like a trivial thing, but this was my chosen career, and a big part of my identity: the woman who loves to be scared.

"Well?" I asked, as I searched the monitors for some sign, still not really understanding fully what I was seeing.

"Yes," Greg said, "you do have a sensitive startle reflex, and we just proved that. We're measuring cortex, and this shows you had a big attention reaction and then in many ways stopped thinking."*

I was at once relieved and thrilled. I am sensitive to startles, and furthermore, they apparently shut down my thinking brain. I was observing live what I had experienced and read about for so long. My adolescent self who told my friend that I like haunted houses because they make me feel primal and get me "out of my head" was pretty much exactly right. I'd felt it on the roller coaster at Fuji-Q Highland, in the haunted Daiba Strange School, and in theme parks and dark caves my whole life.

Without skipping a beat Greg said very politely, "If it's OK, I'd like to touch you right here." He lightly touched my upper right shoulder. I said, "Sure." I was expecting some sort of upper arm squeeze.

Unexpectedly, he slapped me in the shoulder.

Again I was completely surprised. Here was this polite, friendly, well-respected, and esteemed researcher, and he had just slapped me on my shoulder. Greg asked if I was OK and then went on to explain how my brain reacted. First, my EEG showed beta waves—my body went instantly into alert mode. Then, quickly, I took a step back cognitively, as evidenced by theta waves. The EEG, Greg explained, didn't show any high arousal, but the GSR did measure a high sympathetic response. Here's what this meant in layperson's terms: I was hit, and my body said, "Ouch!" In response, my brain told me to take off. My default response, it turned out, was flight rather than fight (at least cognitively).

Next, Greg pulled out what looked like an iPod. It was the electronic muscle stimulator (EMS), otherwise known as "the shock box." The base of the device generates electricity that is sent through wires to two two-by-two-inch conductive pads that

---

*EEGs, especially portable devices like the ones we were using, only measure activity in the cortex. To measure activity deeper inside the brain requires invasive surgery, so it's usually restricted to primate and animal studies.

adhere to the skin. This model was actually designed for physical therapists, who use it to relax muscles, but as Greg said jokingly, he's more sadistic with it.

Greg attached the pads on my forearm close to my elbow and said we would be counting down from five, after which the EMS would be turned on. Anxiously, I counted down and then felt a small vibration underneath the pads. It didn't hurt at all; it was relaxing. As he turned the intensity up he explained that my sympathetic nervous system was showing a big response. I also had a significant increase in alpha and theta waves, but not beta. Greg said this in a way that made me think that was not completely normal, but I had no idea if it was not normal in a good or bad way. I didn't have much time to think, though, or really enough "thinking brain" online to think; I was in a trancelike, relaxed meditation state.

And then he turned it up some more.

The relaxing, soft vibrations rapidly turned into electrifying waves of pain. Ten thousand tiny needles were pricking my skin, then burrowing deeper into my muscles all the way to my toes and my bones. The pain was sudden and fierce, as if I'd stepped on a blowfish with every part of my body.

I shouted, "OH! OUCH!" Greg quickly turned it off.

The pain of electric shock is often compared to fire, needles, or knives, but in truth all these sensations leave a distinct mark. Your brain has different pain receptors (called nociceptors) that influence how you perceive different painful sensations. That's why getting punched in the face feels different from burning your hand on the stove. Personally, I have been exposed to electricity quite a few times, mostly from electric fences around the barns and stables when I was growing up. My worst experience happened when I backed into the end of an electric fence, hitting the spot right behind my elbow—my funny bone. It was an unforgettable wash of pain, tsunami-sized waves radiating from my arm through the rest of my body, vibrations of dull but agonizing ache. I instantly dropped to the ground, overcome by what was easily the worst pain I'd ever felt. The EMS was nowhere near that bad, but I could definitely tell it was in the same pain family.

Greg showed me how my sympathetic nervous system had spiked and what my brain waves looked like when I'd screamed. I stared at my brain in a state of pain; it was gratifying to see a visual, almost tangible representation of something that is completely invisible, a recognition that pain is real and not subjective. But then Greg told me to look at my hand: I hadn't realized it, but I had instinctually retracted my fingers and curled them into my palm, turning it into a claw. This is due to muscle contraction during electric exposure; it's the "can't let go" response that happens if you grab on to a high-voltage wire.

Greg continued to experiment with different shock settings and various other fear-inducing objects, and apparently something in the way I was responding to the various stimuli led Greg to the next test, which would open my eyes to a whole part of myself I was completely unaware of.

Greg told me he wanted to shock me again, and this time, as he put it, "I want you to flip it off. I'll tell you when it's going to come. Anticipate it, but turn it off. So get in that space."

Even though we hadn't talked about the idea of "turning off" pain or sensation, I knew exactly what he meant. There was a trick I had taught myself as a child, when my feet would fall asleep at school assemblies or other too-long meetings. Rather than experience those aching pins and needles as painful, I'd learned to tell myself they were a positive sensation ("That's what sleeping feet feel like, let them sleep," my young self said). I've used this trick my entire life: when my horse bit my thumb, when I watched scary movies or attended haunted houses and wanted to feel in control, and when I'd decided not to deal with death. And so, sitting in Greg's lab, I told myself that instead of feeling pain when the EMS was turned on, I would pretend it still felt good, just more soft, relaxing vibrations.

Greg started up the EMS again, this time turning it up much farther than before, and I told myself it felt fine, good even. Greg narrated what he was seeing as he continued to turn the dial up: "I can already see the high-frequency stuff [gamma] is completely gone, the attention systems are off. Beta is gone; gamma is gone. Alpha and theta a little, sympathetic nervous system still up. Let's see what happens when we turn it up." He turned the dial up higher and looked back to the screens:

"Nothing, nothing."

He turned it up a little bit higher and asked if I was still OK. I told him it was fine, it wasn't bothering me. And, truly, it wasn't. I could feel it, of course, but once I decided it wouldn't bother me, it didn't. Greg turned off the EMS, and I just sat there quietly. I wasn't really sure what had just happened, but Greg seemed to think it was interesting, which made me nervous. I'd long assumed this trick of mine was something everyone could do, but now I wasn't so sure. Was something wrong with me?

Greg turned back to the monitors and explained that what he had seen was a completely different response from the one I had before. The GSR showed that my sympathetic response was high, and explained that my limbic system had responded to the shock, but the EEG was different: "Theta is up a bit, compared to where it was before. This is a completely different response. So you just shut it all off. And you actually did shut it all off." Greg pointed out that my pupils didn't dilate, and I was able to answer his questions, so while my body was experiencing pain, I was not translating those sensations to a conscious unpleasant state. He said my theta and alpha waves during the shock mirrored the response he sees when people are under anesthetics. Basically, when I told myself the EMS didn't bother me, I was going into a kind of trancelike state as a form of self-sedation.

Surely this was a bad thing. It wasn't like the many, many times my executive functioning, or thinking brain, had shut down during the course of my high arousal adventures; in those instances I very much felt fear and pain—I just couldn't think rationally. This was different. I looked at the output from the GSR and could see that my body was registering pain. But I had somehow managed to disconnect myself, or at least my mind and therefore my experience, from my body, so much so that as I read those graphs, I actually felt bad for my own body—suffering by itself, abandoned by my brain. All the times in my life that I'd used this "trick," my body was still in pain; I just wasn't around to experience it. Greg, who was still looking at my active brain waves, could see that I was struggling to make sense of this, and thankfully he explained the picture, which was slightly different from where my dark, strange brain had taken me.

There are various methods employed when people try to diminish their threat response. First, you can suppress it: you focus your attention on masking the external signs of fear. This is more common in certain cultures; for example, Japanese study subjects tend to suppress or mask their reactions in the presence of others when compared to being alone, while Americans don't. But suppression doesn't result in a diminished physiological reaction; in fact, the increased attention put into masking can actually increase arousal. Second, some people "shut it down": their threat response just stops altogether. This is an automatic response that the New School's Wendy D'Andrea has found in her research with trauma victims. Those who had significant symptoms of trauma exposure experience a "blunted autonomic response," meaning that their sympathetic nervous system puts on the brakes, essentially turning off their threat response. This is not just a prefrontal cortex shutdown; this is a physiological reversal of the threat response complete with a decrease in heart rate and skin conductance. It has a purpose as a response to dangerous situations, but it has dreadful consequences. Individuals who experience this response may say they feel numb or empty and can struggle to overcome it long-term.

A third way people diminish their threat response is known as the vigilant/avoidant response. Christine Larson observed this response when testing participant reactions to photos of spiders while the participants were in an fMRI. She found that arachnophobic individuals showed a spike in activity in the amygdala within thirty milliseconds of seeing a spider and then showed an immediate drop in activity as they quickly shifted their attention elsewhere. The avoidant response can be problematic, because in order to extinguish a phobia the person has to be able to stay engaged long enough to form new memories of the experience, this time with a happier ending. Eventually the goal is for a phobic individual to become habituated to the stimulus, which is the basis for a common form of phobia treatment called exposure therapy.

But a strong sustained fear response, while not subject to the problems of avoidance, is not desirable either—it ends in negative rumination and chronic stress. Rather, the goal is to move toward the center, to what was observed in nonphobic individuals: a sustained amygdala response, followed by a natural return to homeostasis. It's not unhealthy to react with a little fear when you see a spider, but ideally the response should be smaller and slower, a sparkler rather than a bottle rocket. Those who show lots of strong communication between their cortex and their limbic system tend to navigate the waves of arousal and stress the best: they are able to be physically and mentally alert, and their messages from the prefrontal cortex are getting through and being read loud and clear.

One way researchers, including Greg, have found to help people stay engaged so they can work through their fear is by introducing social support, say from a parent or other caregiver. For example, James Coan found that when you're afraid, holding the hand of a loved one even for as little as forty-five seconds, significantly decreases your response to a perceived threat. As Greg explained, "Paradoxically you make something safe, and you allow fear to happen." This is likely due to the hormones and neurotransmitters—namely, oxytocin, opioids, and dopamine—that are released during the threat response and that can create feelings of closeness, bonding, affiliation, and love. This is just what Shelley Taylor found in her study of the biological basis of affiliation under stress. This makes sense evolutionarily: we are more likely to survive a predator attack, fend off enemies, and reproduce with sexual partners if we actually feel close to the people we're with when we're in a high arousal state.

The fourth way people can diminish or try to diminish their threat response is perhaps the most difficult: cognitive reappraisal, the same practice of actively redefining an experience and assigning new meaning that Candace Raio found to be ineffective in "real-world" stressful situations. But it is possible, and this is what I had done when Greg had told me to "get in the space" and shut down my fear response. It's an effective strategy, but it's difficult to pull off, as researchers James Gross and Gal Scheppes have shown, because depending on the threat, you might not have the time or the resources, either mentally or physically. I was not the only person on Earth with this ability, but it's not particularly common either.

This realization scared me, and I asked Greg what it meant. On the surface it didn't seem like a great thing; wasn't I cheating somehow? Isn't this exactly what I trekked all the way into the Suicide Forest to *stop* doing? Hasn't this whole year been about me experiencing fear? About being aware and reflective of what different experiences make our bodies do? How can any emotion be real if it can be manipulated? What does it mean if fear and pain become optional? Isn't that the definition of a monster?

Didn't it make *me* a monster?

Luckily, I was talking to the monster expert himself. Noting the concern on both my face and in my EEG readouts, Greg shared the long history of research looking at Tibetan Buddhist monks and their ability to diminish their pain but also engage with feelings of pure compassion and love. Studies with fMRIs and EEGs show that those who are skilled in the practice of mindfulness meditation (like interoception, it brings awareness and concentration to one's body and its biological experiences) report less experience of pain, and their brains show less pain as well. The areas in the brain that process pain actually shrink as they refocus their attention and reappraise what they're experiencing. So while mindfulness meditation essentially involves "shutting down" pain, it doesn't happen through a process of suppression, repression, or trying to ignore it—rather, it brings *more* attention to the experience and deciding what to do with the physiological response.*

For example, imagine you're driving on a highway in the middle of a rainy night. Your tire blows out, your phone is dead, and the closest house is down an unkempt, cluttered gravel driveway, at the end of which is a run-down farmhouse, with a single light in the window. From the moment you feel the car shuddering, your

---

*Studies show that attempting to ignore pain, or alternatively focusing intently on pain and how *much* it hurts; praying; and hoping all actually increase the psychophysics and self-report of a pain experience.

threat response has likely kicked in. And as you trudge toward the house, your imagination is probably running wild with visions of *Halloween* and *Psycho*. But there is another choice here: you can stop, breathe, and thank your lucky stars that there is a farmhouse nearby that might have a phone you can use. This doesn't mean you have to blunder forward like so many horror movie victims, of course. You can still be alert, but in this scenario you're not working yourself into an irrational panic and running up the stairs instead of out the door when you first spy the bloody chain-saw. Usually it takes practice to develop effective skills of reappraisal—at least when it comes to changing your psychophysical response and not just your subjective experience. But researcher Fadel Zeidan at Wake Forest University found that even one training session in the Tibetan Buddhist meditation called *samatha* can reduce the experience of pain and pain-related brain activity.

As Greg talked through this research, I tried desperately to keep my composure and reminded myself that he was dispensing valuable information about the neural basis of fear. But inside I was struggling and spinning. The picture Greg was painting of human emotions made sense, until I tried to place myself within it.

I'm not a Tibetan monk and have never been trained in their meditative practices. Even though we had just met and I was there researching for my book—not as a patient—I already trusted Greg, and I had to ask the next question in the most explicit way possible.

"So am I broken?"

Greg laughed and said, "No. You are one of the people who is practiced in the ninja arts of emotion. And you are a ninja."

Greg assured me my emotions were still very much present and very real, even if I was a ninja. He reminded me of the total bliss I had told him I felt when I went skydiving and rode the roller coasters; he said in those instances I chose to engage. According to Greg, one of the biggest mistakes we make when thinking about fear is trying to separate it from other high arousal states like pain, or being really excited, or laughing, or being sexually aroused. A lot of the same brain mechanisms are present in all these states, and it's up to us to give them meaning, as when

I switched from fear to anger during the street fight outside my house. Our sympathetic nervous system becomes aroused, and then we interpret the arousal with cognitive manipulation and coordination between the limbic system and prefrontal cortex. This is why I switched from fear to anger so quickly during the street fight, and why people scream and then laugh at scary things when they know they're safe, and why makeup sex has a reputation for being especially hot—the situation has changed, but the body is still in high arousal territory.

Those who have learned reappraisal naturally, without extensive training in mindfulness meditation, tend to be those who have experienced and had to endure the full range of physiological responses—whether it be pain, fear, anxiety, joy, or compassion. For example, studies of endurance athletes have found that the most effective pain-coping mechanism is not attempting to ignore pain but rather reappraising it. They do not label the feelings or sensations as pain at all but as positive and rewarding sensations that are part of the reason they love what they do, like people who drench their food in punishing hot sauce and football players who say they love getting hit. Other athletes tell themselves that the brain and the body are separate during performance, just as I did when I felt pity for my body. Monks and the very religious likewise endure suffering as part of their devotion, but rather than their suffering leading to desperation, anger, frustration, or sadness, they meditate on pure compassion and in doing so experience overwhelming and powerful sensations that can only be described as love.

There is another group skilled in the art of reappraisal, for whom emotions and sensations are two toolboxes full of the most interesting, fulfilling, fun, and thrilling toys on the planet: the bondage, domination, submission, and masochism (BDSM) community. Published studies of this group aren't numerous, but the ones that do exist focus almost exclusively on personality characteristics and disputes over whether or not BDSM represents pathological behavior—that is, whether it can be seen as a disorder (it's not). A 2013 study in the *Journal of Sexual Medicine* found something very interesting: as a group, the BDSM community had more

214 - Bringing It Home

favorable psychological characteristics (less neurotic, more extroverted, more open to new experiences, more conscientious, less
sensitive to rejection, and higher subjective well-being) than the
control group. To put this another way: most of those who are voluntarily being tied up, beaten, pierced, and tortured are doing so
not because they're working through some psychological trauma or
abandonment issues but simply because they enjoy it. This is only
one study, and much could still be learned by further investigation, but it appears for the moment that people interested in BDSM
may be emotional ninjas too. The common thread, the defining
characteristic of emotional ninjas, is mindfulness, or the ability to
recognize and understand their bodies' reactions and choose the
meaning they want to give it, to take the experience into their own
hands and make it work for them, physically and psychologically.

I wouldn't have thought I had much in common with Buddhist monks, ultramarathon runners, or BDSM aficionados, and
certainly not all at the same time. But regardless, I wasn't a monster or broken. In fact, I felt as if I just found out I have a superhero
ability, like some *X-Men* character. Dr. Kerr, Emotional Ninja.

But still, I felt like an odd fit for the cape and mask. Do most
emotional ninjas also have panic attacks? And a sensitive startle reflex? And like thrilling and scary activities? My superpower
seemed to conflict with other things about me. I'd never seen a
study showing a positive correlation (a link) between anxiety and
thrill seeking. In fact, the latest research suggests that aversion to
haunted houses and other scary activities could be a marker of
anxiety in children. And most treatment for anxiety is focused on
reducing arousal, not seeking it.

Greg said in many ways I was all over the map. When I'm not
bracing, I have a sensitive startle, but my first response to a lot of
the novel stimuli Greg presented was to take a step back, assess,
and then decide if I wanted to engage with it. Why this might be
the case is hard to say, exactly. There's still a hole in fear studies:
most of them happen in the lab, where creating a sense of uncertainty is difficult and researchers are limited in how scary they
can really get. Even in the context of informed consent, it's still
lab research.

So what if fear looks different in the real world? Most of the studies I have used to try to understand the *upside* of fear have come from lab research looking at the *downside*. But how did I know that research was appropriate? For example, in the lab it would be impossible to see how someone responds to being blindfolded, restrained, and locked in a coffin, or made to feel as if they've been cut with a knife on purpose. The lack of data is a real problem.

Greg suggested we fix it.

> > >

Wouldn't it be great, Greg offered, if we could get a protocol together to collect real data? I had taken careful notes on what people felt as they walked through ScareHouse, but they were just my notes. And Greg had used fancy instruments to understand what I felt, but it was only my reaction to being slapped in the arm and shocked a bit, nothing too scary. What if there were a way to combine the two? I would have the chance to test what I wanted—no more extrapolating from studies testing fear in the lab. We could be testing fear in the real world. We could start to answer so many questions: Who was choosing these activities and why? What do they feel like before they go in, and do they feel different when they come out? How does going through a scary experience change the way people think and feel?

The idea was simple: test people who were going through ScareHouse—specifically, my part of ScareHouse, the Basement. We would recruit participants only from customers who had already chosen to participate, which protected the university from any thorny liability issues. Then participants would be hooked up to the EEG, asked a series of survey questions, and exposed to fifteen minutes of various standard emotional and cognitive stimuli. For example, they would see pictures of scary and happy images, hear startling sounds, and be asked to think about something negative (ruminate), hold hands with their partner, and do frustrating cognitive tasks like counting backwards. Participants would then go through the Basement and afterwards return to answer more questions and go through the fifteen-minute cognitive and emotional stimuli exposure again (so we could measure change before and after). In return for their participation we would agree to send them a picture of their brain waves from their EEG report. It would appeal to their inner zombie.

And so Greg and I opened the first-ever fear lab inside a haunted house—and not just any haunted house. The 2014 Basement was entirely redesigned to take customers through a thrilling, frightening, and boundary-pushing experience built from what I had learned from my year of adventuring and my work with Greg. It would be the first scientifically designed haunted house that would leave customers feeling wonderful.

And so we set about rebuilding the Basement.

* * *

By the time planning started for the second season of the Basement, I had changed. Significantly. I had been around the world, not just riding roller coasters or leaning over the edge of buildings, but confronting difficult emotions, opening myself up to new experiences, and learning how strong I really was. I felt confident, happy, and more secure in myself, my beliefs, and my purpose in life than ever before.

More than anything, I wanted to share what I had learned about the benefits of physical thrills and psychological chills. But I knew that many of my experiences were far out of reach of most people. How could I capture the thrill of the roller coaster; the chill of the Daiba Strange School and paranormal investigations; the raw, visceral excitement of standing on the edge of the tower; and the personal growth found in confronting death? I wanted to create an attraction unlike anything I had ever seen or experienced. With the help of an amazing cast and crew, co-led by Crystal Rupp and me, I did just that.

First, it starts with choice. While the Basement 1.0 was built around principles of informed consent, I worried we hadn't done enough to make sure customers understood the experience they were agreeing to. I realized this after my year of experiencing one too many haunts (some of them "extreme") that had liability waivers but did not do a good job of informing me of what the experience would entail (they weren't scary or fun or informative or a growth experience). Moreover, I'd read countless reports of experiences at haunted houses, some extreme, some not, immersive theater productions, and entertainment events in general, free or otherwise, in which customers were simply not taken care of when it comes to physical and emotional safety. For example, some extreme haunted houses do not have a safe word, meaning there is no way, other than honest-to-God running for your life, that you can exit the experience in a safe and supported manner. Other extreme haunts that do have safe words have developed scenes in which actors, dressed as plant customers, say the safe word and are then further tortured. To me, this is 100 percent no different from legitimate torture and kidnapping. Customers must always, always know they are in complete control of their experience; it is *their* choice to engage, and we are there for *them*.

Catherine Hartley and colleagues recently published a paper on the importance of control in not only the response to fear but overcoming fear. The study consisted of randomly assigning subjects to stress (in this case a mild shock) in an escapable condition, an inescapable condition, or the control group. Afterwards they underwent fear conditioning and were then tested on extinction (no longer fearing the stimulus) and spontaneous recovery (fearing it again). They found that exposing subjects in the escapable condition to the stressor *improved* their fear extinction and prevented the spontaneous recovery of the fear. The opposite was true for those who were in the inescapable condition: they experienced worse fear extinction and showed an *increase* in fear expression the next day. This is a critical finding for the importance of choice. Knowing you can leave and choosing to stay is empowering; being forced to endure is the opposite. Just as playing Tetris can work as a kind of inoculation against developing PTSD, so too can exposure to controllable, chosen stressors help us deal with future real stressors. As Hartley states, "Our data suggest that clinical interventions involving the cultivation of a perception of control might ameliorate the excessive fear that is characteristic of anxiety disorders." Choice is critical, and any establishment that does not make choice explicit, understood, acceptable, and trusted is doing harm.

Informed consent doesn't mean that you have to walk a customer through an entire experience. Rather, it's explicitly stating the risks and dangers, both physical and mental. With this in mind I updated the information on the ScareHouse Basement website with more detailed explanations of what customers would encounter, was explicit in explaining the waiver when customers checked in (including customers for whom English is not their native language), and hired the most professional, talented, and trained scientist to be the first actor guests would encounter. Dave Malhorn, fellow professor and actor (who was also in *STRATA*), played the part of the doorman. Just as I had to turn over my trust to every professional I worked with during the year, I wanted customers to feel that they could trust the actors inside. Each night before every guest entered, Dave made sure they understood exactly what they were choosing to experience (and pointed out customers who were maybe not quite ready for the experience or were potentially dangerous to the actors). From there on in, every customer knew they were safe, and as Greg had said, you make something safe, and it allows fear to happen.

Next, the people. I'll never forget exiting the Takabisha and turning to give a friend a hug or high five, only to find no one, or the long walks through the world's first penitentiary in the middle of the night with Amy. Without her support after being in the Hole, that night could have turned traumatic (along with a few other adventures she attended with me—she quite literally saved me from drowning at the haunted Penfield Lighthouse in Connecticut). I benefited enormously from my time alone, but we are better together. So we set up the Basement to be experienced with a partner. Timing was also critical; the entire experience would last about forty minutes, the same amount of time I was on the CN Tower. Our startle response is saturated after about twenty minutes (after that, surprises don't make us jump anymore), but we still are in the throes of the threat response, in an arousal state and feeling afraid. Just as I moved in and out of feeling pure terror while on the EdgeWalk, I wanted people to have those moments when they are still engaged with fear but able to take a step back and think about what is happening and what they are feeling so they can learn about their own threat response in a safe environment.

Next, I thought about what I felt on the roller coasters—that intense, fast, out-of-control shock to the body that comes from whipping around corners and down steep drops. How could we re-create that feeling in a haunted house? There was no way we could literally get people traveling at sixty-two miles per hour as on the Eejanaika. But maybe there was a way to trigger that "stomach drop" feeling just by manipulating movement. I wanted this sensation to happen early on in the experience, to really get the arousal system going and create a sense of disorientation and confusion.

Tracy Campbell, who is a nurse researcher by day (not surprisingly, ScareHouse employs a large number of people who work in research), would be in the first scene playing an overworked librarian. Tracy is at most 110 pounds and five foot two, but because she is small, people don't brace themselves or expect her to grab, push, pull, and throw them around—which she did. Her role is to startle customers entering the Basement and immediately push them back into a row of doors set against the wall at a 60-degree angle. The doors move and bend (but not break or fall) when people fall into them, which creates a feeling of insecurity, forcing customers to brace their bodies forward, just as you do when preparing for takeoff on a roller coaster (as I experienced on the Dodonpa). Next, Tracy pulls them quickly to the ground and practically drags them over to the next part of the experience. But it isn't until a few moments later that the real "oh shit" moment comes: Tracy pushes the customers back into two chairs and proceeds to place bags over their heads, thrusting them into darkness. After that Tracy is a masterful manipulator of their movement—she carefully but aggressively pushes them forward and pulls them backwards, creating the same type of sensations we feel when whipping around curves and speeding along coaster tracks. Without being able to see, customers are unable to anticipate and adjust their balance, and their proprioception is thrown out of whack, making them feel further out of control.

Then I wanted to replicate my experience of being alone in the dark at Eastern State, to feel the terror that comes when our sight is lost, when we have to turn to our other senses to figure out what is happening around us. To accomplish this, we borrowed the Boy Scouts' resilience-building exercise of following a rope through the woods while blindfolded. Only instead of blindfolds we use bags, and instead of confronting trees, roots, and rough terrain, customers encounter two actors, each equipped with a whole bag of instruments that feel cold or hot or spiky or sharp, who make ear-piercing sounds. For about five minutes (which in the dark feels like forever) customers have to navigate a rope (of many textures) in total darkness. This, according to some guests,* is the most terrifying part of the experience. The uncertainty, the total darkness, the complete lack of awareness of what is lurking not two inches from your face leave every customer to confront the reality I discovered in my abandoned prison cell: that the scariest thing of all is your own imagination. Around this time, the actors also separate the couples, who always attempt to stay connected, and the response is intense. So many people simply refuse to continue on without their partner or play a desperate game of Marco Polo to find them.

Trying to capture the intensity I felt during my paranormal investigation was tricky; that experience was built around an eerie and scary space, filled with silence, anticipation, and sensation. Just as we had done two years prior, we reached out to Ayne Terceira, who continued to work closely with us from the very beginning. She not only understood what I meant by "eerie, anticipatory, silent sensation" but turned it into one of my favorite scenes of the year. With long black hair down to her waist—just like the iconic Japanese snow woman—inch-long fingernails, and the perfect combination of uncanny, unsettling, and unpredictable, Ayne

---

*Elijah Wood and Rose Leslie came through the Basement and stated that being in the dark on the rope was their favorite part, and in fact they gave the entire experience rave reviews. Definite highlight of my year.

became the spooky pew sitter. The scene is utterly unnerving; looking just like the evil ghost I encountered in the Daiba Strange School, Ayne welcomes customers into her candlelit church to sit in one of her pews, and then proceeds to silence them by shoving tissues in their mouths and sewing their lips shut with a disposable toothpick and floss.* All the while infrasound, just like what I'd learned about with the ghost hunters, pumps from a speaker in the background as she runs her long, sharp fingernails across their necks and arms—a popular trigger for an ASMR reaction. It leaves customers with chills running down their spine.

My adventuring wasn't all about physical sensation, though. I was also forced to engage with and think about things I usually block out. That's what happens when you open yourself up completely to feel; whether it's fear, love, joy, happiness, or sadness, when you let one in, they're all in. As I've learned, the lines between them are fuzzy at best. I wanted customers to have a chance to explore their own personal and relationship boundaries in the context of a safe environment. These boundary-pushing scenes would also be great opportunities to play with popular scary monsters, like deranged clowns. In one scene, our actors are instructed to play with the power dynamics with customers—for example, putting them in positions to play the role of the hero or helper (helping the clowns with makeup or finding stuffed animals) or the follower (having makeup put on them or choosing games). This forces our customers to reveal the boundaries of their behavior, which enables our actors to push them out of their comfort zone. In other scenes customers are challenged to think about the relationship with the person they'd come in with. For example, in a scene with a doctor, partners have to decide what, if any, medical procedures they would carry out, and with what instruments, on each other. In other boundary-pushing scenes customers have to figure out how they would respond to a demon who is attempting to steal their body, and what to say and do with a Shakespeare-reciting harlequin whose only goal is to ask

---

*Everything in the Basement, including the bags that are put over people, is single use.

the customer (of any gender) to be his spouse. In each of these scenes the actors respond to the customers, backing up or pushing further to find out where that individual's boundary is, and then giving it a nudge.*

As I learned from my years of reading survey responses, and throughout my journeys and many brutally honest conversations with strangers, sometimes it's the things inside us that we fear the most—the things we have seen, have done, or had done to us that we feel ashamed to admit to ourselves, much less to others. Yet there can be great relief in sharing our most shameful moments, as Vincent Felitti, who helped develop the adverse childhood experience score, has found in his own practice. Just the act of telling someone else a shameful thought, memory, or experience can lighten the weight of it. To that end we created a confessional complete with nosy priest who asks very leading questions of the customers, but only after making it clear that there is no outdoing his own pathological curiosity and need for detail, thus creating a space where the person can admit their own hidden or feared thoughts and feelings. Sure they can lie, but why would they? They have no reason to think their secrets will leave the room. Our actors don't know the truth from the fiction, and there is no real judgment. In a therapist's office there is confidentiality, but in a haunted house there is anonymity.

While confronting death was one of my most challenging adventures, trying to replicate the experience was actually one of the easier scenes to re-create. We built a coffin, complete with foam padding and satin sheets (it actually was really comfortable). Customers are brought into the scene by a priest and instructed to kneel at an altar in front of the coffin. After about ten seconds, Death enters the room. The actor who plays Death, Nick Noir, has black dreads down to his waist, several facial piercings, no eyebrows, and porcelain white skin—and that's when he's not in his Death costume, which is the iconic large black cloak, complete

---

*Of course, some people were willing to go far outside the rules the actors had to follow, resulting in more than one customer being asked to leave for not observing Basement rules.

with scythe. His very appearance has customers screaming, but when he starts talking, really preaching, about their impending death and has them choose who will be buried, customers completely lose it. One customer—whichever one did not volunteer—is put into the coffin for one minute, and the other is dragged away by the harlequin. The time duration is critical: up to about twenty seconds the experience is novel and interesting, but after the twenty-second mark customers begin to question how long they will be kept inside, and that is when panic sets in. But interestingly the reactions once people were put in the coffin followed two consistent patterns: either people completely freaked out and started banging and screaming to get out (many of them saying the safe word and being let out of the Basement entirely), or they said it was comfortable and relaxing. This highlights how important perception is in fear: some people felt closed in, claustrophobic, and trapped, while others felt safe, comfortable, and warm.

Finally, I wanted to bring my experience in Greg's lab into the haunted house. An actor brings customers in total darkness to sit side by side, where they are then cuffed to the chair, told to hold hands, and then tied to each other. The actor then proceeds to "cut" the customers with a (safely) electrified plastic knife wrapped in tin foil. Because the customers are touching, they feel each time their partner is cut as well. Ideally, because they are holding hands, both customers release oxytocin. The goal is to bring customers closer to each other, to bond together and create a memory they'll have for the rest of their lives.

After several other scenes that combine boundary pushing with physical thrills, customers exit the Basement and return to the spot where they checked in, collect their belongings, and are welcome to sit down and hang out, giving them an opportunity to reorient themselves and bring their "thinking" brain back before they go back out into the real world.

I only missed one night of the 2014 season. Every other night I spent in the lab, in the scenes, or, more often, outside, waiting anxiously for customers to exit, to hear their story, to learn and grow together.

＊ ＊ ＊

By the end of the season we had collected almost 100 brain scans and over 250 customer surveys. Most of these people were in their twenties or thirties, with slightly more women than men (51 percent, 45 percent), which mirrors the demographics from ScareHouse's customer survey data (and gives further weight to the fact that scary material is not just for men). We're still working on analyzing the massive amount of data, and the findings so far have been beyond enlightening. But there's one finding that I care about the most and that makes me feel prouder than I ever have before: people loved it, and they left the Basement feeling *wonderful.*

Participants had to rate their mood on a scale of one to ten before they went into the Basement and then again right after they came out. Not only did their mood change significantly, but the change was positive: being scared significantly made people feel better. Preliminary analysis of the survey data also shows that a majority of respondents felt they'd challenged their fears and learned something about themselves. In correlating the survey responses to the EEG data, we found that those who were the most open and ready to engage with the thrilling experience got the most out of it; that is, they left happier. And not only were participants saying that they felt better, but EEG data showed they were more relaxed; they didn't overthink or stress out about the cognitive tasks, and they didn't ruminate or worry as much. Basically their "mental chatter" shut down, and things didn't bother them to the extent they did before going through, just as I had experienced on the CN Tower EdgeWalk. Those who came to the Basement ready to engage, and even slightly anxious, reaped the biggest benefits—in other words, the biggest fans were people just like me.

We had collected statistically significant data with evidence suggesting why those who are anxious or worriers may enjoy engaging with thrilling material. The theory, which is going to require lots more testing, is not just that we are getting a natural high and shutting down our executive functioning but that our stress tolerance undergoes a kind of recalibration. When we push ourselves to the extreme, the everyday things that used to bother us just don't seem like that big of a deal anymore. If you can handle Death locking you in a coffin for a minute, having your mouth sewn shut in a church, and being sliced with an electrified knife, you can handle anything. Yes, all these things were experienced from inside what researcher Michael Apter calls the "protective frame" of safety, but the resilience, the confidence, and the break—even if just for a short while—from the constant mental chatter is real, and it feels good.

But there was one more thing. For the second year running, customers said it wasn't scary enough. I *knew* it was scary and could say so without bias. I had watched people scream and run out of scenes. I'd watched them reveal their own subjective boundaries and then have them pushed. What more could you ask a haunted house to do? At that moment, the beauty of our fear lab made itself apparent. Based on readouts from their EEG scans, and even just in talking to customers after the experience, it was obvious that our customers were in a completely different, more relaxed, more laid-back physical and mental space after their thrilling experience. They weren't being dishonest in the way they answered our survey questions, but they didn't feel fear upon leaving; the sheer pleasure and relief shifted their recall of the experience. In fact, this was a sign that we had accomplished what we had set out to do: to take people on an emotional, boundary-expanding growth adventure and bring them back safe and sound, feeling better than when they first arrived.

Greg and I still have lots more data to analyze and more questions to ask. But what a thrill it was to see it all in action. I'd been around the world in search of fear and then tried to put what I'd found into one big dark room—and it worked. I felt a familiar satisfaction, of the kid I'd been, dragging my friends to see the murdered man in the blacksmithing shed. Spreading fear and joy in equal measure.

Years ago, I became a sociologist because I wanted to make people's lives better. I wanted to find ways to end the hurtful and damaging impact of prejudice, discrimination, and abuse rooted in fear. I never thought I would accomplish that in a dusty basement, with a knife in one hand and a black bag in the other.

AFTERWORD

The humans who overcame their fears to kill the wild beasts and who ventured out to explore the great unknown were greatly rewarded with the gift of survival. These are our ancestors. We want to go on adventures; we want opportunities to challenge ourselves and overcome. Thrilling experiences and self-scaring all come with a moment of confrontation and resolution, leaving us feeling good, in control, confident, and secure in our abilities and ourselves. We can sail into a chaotic storm and navigate our way back out. All we have to do is be open to it, to *choose* to opt in. When we do, we become the driver, we guide the experience, and we decide what it means.

Your brain is amazing at simulation, but there is no substitute for the tactile, physical sensations that come with experience— even if it's just sitting in a forest by yourself. You never know what you might experience or feel. You don't have to hang off the CN Tower; you can start small: try a new food; watch a scary movie; go ice skating, roller skating, skiing; play a sport, any sport; do a handstand or a somersault. Make your own adventure map. Start with lots of totally achievable destinations and activities and a few reach activities and save up! I have gotten more pleasure and ful-fillment from walking around dark hallways and crawling through tunnels than I ever got from a new pair of boots.

Keep an adventure journal or blog, and take photos and write about how you felt during those experiences. Confront death.

Write about your fears. What are you really afraid of and why? Just pushing yourself, even in small ways, to step outside your comfort zone can bring a feeling of excitement, of growth and living life to the fullest.

ACKNOWLEDGMENTS

Realizing that who you are is an amalgamation of the people in your life is powerful. For me, this is an awe-inspiring realization because the people who surround me are amazing (everyone should write an acknowledgments section—it's a great chance for reflection). I want to thank Alia Hanna Habib and Ben Adams for agreeing to jump on, buckle up, and go with me on this adventure. I am incredibly grateful, inspired by, and thankful for Greg Siegle; never did I imagine my biggest adventure would start by going back into the lab.

To acknowledge the contributions of ScareHouse would be another book. The support, guidance, mentorship, faith, and trust of the Simmonses have been beyond belief, and I am forever grateful. ScareHouse gave me a whole new life. To the cast and crew of ScareHouse, thank you a thousand times over for scaring the hell out of me. And a special thanks to Crystal Rupp, Scott Simmons, and the cast of the Basement: we made people feel good and turned nightmares into a hero's journey. I want to acknowledge the incredible influence Hollins University had on my path. Women who are going places really do start at Hollins, and I would not have found my passion for exploration or my confidence without my amazing experience and incredible professors there.

I don't think anyone had a graduate school experience quite like ours at the University of Pittsburgh, and for that I am thankful. I thank Melissa Swauger Roberson, Lisa Huebner, Kat Bulger Gray, and Majo Álvarez Rivadulla.

I am forever thankful to my mom and dad, the ones who brought me into this world to experience this great adventure of life, not to mention grateful for their unwavering support of a daughter who makes a living scaring people. I know it's not easy.

I have to thank Laura Kingsley, Dan Kimmons, Jessica Manack, Chelly Johnson, and Angela Wilson, who have been so supportive and understanding.

Finally, I am so thankful for Amy Hollaman, who bridged that gap between my thinking brain and my emotional brain, who walked with me to the edge and made sure I made it back (literally, in a few cases), and who was there so many times when I turned and said, "Oh my God." As I learned, everything is better when we have someone to share it with. I couldn't ask for a better someone.

NOTES

PREFACE

6 **We live in an objectively safer world**: David Ropeik, "The Consequences of Fear," *EMBO Reports* 5 (2004); World Health Organization 2014 reports, who.int/en/.

6 **We are arguably consumed with fear:** Daniel Gardner, *The Sci-
ence of Fear: How the Culture of Fear Manipulates Your Brain* (New
York: Penguin, 2008); Peter Stearns, *American Fear: The Causes
and Consequences of High Anxiety* (New York: Routledge, 2006);
Barry Glassner, *The Culture of Fear: Why Americans Are Afraid of the
Wrong Things* (New York: Basic Books, 1999).

CHAPTER 1: THE STOMACH DROP

12 **In fact, the National Institutes of Health:** "Research Domain Crite-
ria for the National Institute of Mental Health," National Institutes
of Health, nimh.nih.gov/research-priorities/rdoc/nimh-research
-domain-criteria-rdoc.shtml#toc_product, accessed April 24, 2015.

13 **Paul Ekman identified six:** Paul Ekman, "Universals and Cul-
tural Differences in Facial Expressions of Emotion," in *Nebraska
Symposium on Motivation, 1971,* edited by J. Cole, vol. 19 (Lincoln:
University of Nebraska Press, 1972), 207–282.

13 **new research from Erika Siegel and Lisa Feldman Barrett:** Erika
H. Siegel, Molly Cannon, Paul Condon, Karen Quigley, and Lisa
Feldman Barrett, "Where in the Body Are Discrete Emotions?,"
poster presentation, Society for Affective Science, Bethesda, MD,
April 24–26, 2014; Maria Gendron, Debi Roberson, and Lisa Feld-
man Barrett, "Cultural Variation in Emotion Perception Is Real:

A Response to Sauter, Eisner, Ekman, and Scott," *Psychological Science* 26, no. 3 (2015).

13 **it's one of our survival circuits:** Joseph LeDoux, "The Slippery Slope of Fear," *Trends in Neuroscience* 36, no. 5 (2013): 275–284.

14 **LeDoux calls the "low road" and the "high road":** Joseph LeDoux, "Emotional Brain, Fear and the Amygdala," *Cellular and Molecular Neurobiology* 23, nos. 4–5 (2002): 727–738.

14 **Over 290 million people:** International Association of Amusement Parks and Attractions, *The Economic Impacts of the US Attractions Industry*, 2014, iaapa.org/iaapa-foundation/economic-impact -study.

16 **something called the Russian Ice Slides:** Robert Cartmell, *The Incredible Scream Machine: A History of the Roller Coaster* (Bowling Green, OH: Bowling Green State University Popular Press, 1987).

16 **The Centrifugal Railway:** David Bennett, *Roller Coaster: Wooden and Steel Coasters, Twisters and Corkscrews* (Edison, NJ: Chartwell Books, 1998).

17 **Electric trolley cars:** Adam Sandy, "Roller Coaster History," Ultimate Rollercoaster, 1999–2006, ultimaterollercoaster.com/coasters /history/.

18 **research from Arthur Aron:** Arthur Aron, Christina C. Norman, Elaine N. Aron, Colin McKenna, and Richard E. Heyman, "Couples' Shared Participation in Novel and Arousing Activities and Experienced Relationship Quality," *Journal of Personality and Social Psychology* 78, no. 2 (2000): 273–284.

18 **research by Garriy Shteynberg:** Garriy H. Shteynberg, Jacob B. Hirsh, Evan P. Apfelbaum, Jeff T. Larsen, Adam D. Galinsky, and Neal J. Roese, "Feeling More Together: Group Attention Intensifies Emotion," *Emotion* 14, no. 6 (2014): 1102–1114.

19 **Kyung Hwa Lee and Greg Siegle:** Kyung Hwa Lee and Greg J. Siegle, "Common and Distinct Brain Networks Underlying Explicit Emotional Evaluation: A Meta-Analytic Study," *Social Cognitive and Affective Neuroscience* 7, no. 5 (2012): 521–534.

19 **researchers like neuroscientist V. S. Ramachandran:** Lindsay M. Oberman and Vilayanur S. Ramachandran, "The Simulating Social Mind: The Role of the Mirror Neuron System and Simulation in the Social and Communicative Deficits of Autism Spectrum Disorders," *Psychological Bulletin* 133, no. 2 (2007): 310–327.

20 **mirror neurons:** Jason Marsh, "Do Mirror Neurons Give Us Empathy?," Greater Good: The Science of a Meaningful

Life, March 29, 2012, greatergood.berkeley.edu/article/item
/do_mirror_neurons_give_empathy.

19 **cognitive neuroscientist and science writer:** Christian Jarrett,
"A Calm Look at the Most Hyped Concept in Neuroscience: Mirror Neurons," *Wired*, December 13, 2013.

20 **Researchers James Kilner and Roger Lemon:** James Kilner and
Roger Lemon, "What We Know Currently About Mirror Neurons," *Current Biology* 23, no. 23 (2013): R1057–1062.

21 **our vestibular system and our proprioception:** Jason R. Carter
and Chester A. Ray, "Sympathetic Responses to Vestibular Activation in Humans," *American Journal of Physiology: Regulatory, Integrative and Comparative Physiology* 294, no. 3 (2008): R681–688;
Diane Deroualle and Christopher Lopez, "Toward a Vestibular
Contribution to Social Cognition," *Frontiers in Integrative Neuroscience* 8 (2014): 16; Stephen M. Highstein, Richard R. Fay, and
Arthur N. Popper, *The Vestibular System* (New York: Springer,
2004).

21 **US Air Force officer named John Stapp:** "International Space
Hall of Fame: John P. Stapp," New Mexico Museum of Space
History, nmspacemuseum.org/halloffame/detail.php?id=46,
accessed March 15, 2015.

22 **These are the sensations:** Suzanne Slade, *Feel the G's: The Science
of Gravity and G-Forces*, Headline Science (Mankato, MN: Com-
pass Point Books, 2009).

23 **You have to choose to relax:** Greg Siegle and I conducted an
experiment in the middle of a spinning light tunnel. While wearing a portable EEG, I alternated between trying to "regulate"
or control the dizzy feeling and just relaxing and enjoying the
disorientation. The EEG data showed that my brain waves were
indeed different when I was attempting to regulate versus relax.

23 **those who have poor postural control:** Julien Barra, Laurent
Auclair, Agnès Charvillat, Manuel Vidal, and Dominic Pérennou,
"Postural Control System Influences Intrinsic Alerting State,"
Neuropsychology 29, no. 2 (2015): 226–234.

24 **sent to your brain via the vagus nerve:** Christopher Berg-
land, "How Does the Vagus Nerve Convey Gut Instincts to the
Brain?," The Athlete's Way (blog), *Psychology Today*, May 23, 2014,
psychologytoday.com/blog/the-athletes-way/201405/how-does
-the-vagus-nerve-convey-gut-instincts-to-the-brain; Mela-
nie Klarer, Myrtha Arnold, Lydia Günther, Christine Winter,

Wolfgang Langhans, and Urs Meyer, "Gut Vagal Afferents Differentially Modulate Innate Anxiety and Learned Fear," *Journal of Neuroscience* 34, no. 21 (2014): 7067–7076.

24 **works with the parasympathetic system:** Robert W. Levenson, "The Autonomic Nervous System and Emotion," *Emotion Review* 6, no. 2 (2014): 100–112.

24 **responsible for making us feel *better*:** Pavel Mohr, Mabel Rodriguez, Anna Slavičková, and Jan Hanka, "The Application of Vagus Nerve Stimulation and Deep Brain Stimulation in Depression," *Neuropsychobiology* 64, no. 3 (2011): 170–181; Giuseppe Tisi, Angelo Franzini, Giuseppe Messina, Mario Savino, and Orsola Gambini, "Vagus Nerve Stimulation Therapy in Treatment-Resistant Depression: A Series Report," *Psychiatry and Clinical Neurosciences* 68, no. 8 (2014): 606–611.

25 **g-force can feel like a panic attack:** Klarer et al., "Gut Vagal Afferents."

27 **Screaming is part of our evolved survivor tool kit:** Roger Highfield, "Science: Why We Scream," *Telegraph* (London), June 17, 2008.

28 **release "bottled-up emotions":** Frederick Verbruggen, Maisy Best, William A. Bowditch, Tobias Stevens, and Ian P. L. McLaren, "The Inhibitory Control Reflex," *Neuropsychologia* 65 (2014): 263–278; Kai Hwang, Avniel S. Ghuman, Dara S. Manoach, Stephanie R. Jones, and Beatriz Luna, "Cortical Neurodynamics of Inhibitory Control," *Journal of Neuroscience* 34, no. 29 (2014): 9551–9561; Simon Chamberland and Lisa Topolnik, "Inhibitory Control of Hippocampal Inhibitory Neurons," *Frontiers in Neuroscience* 6 (2012): 165.

28 **While it's tempting to think:** Brad J. Bushman, Roy F. Baumeister, and Colleen M. Phillips, "Do People Aggress to Improve Their Mood? Catharsis Beliefs, Affect Regulation Opportunity, and Aggressive Responding," *Journal of Personality and Social Psychology* 81, no. 1 (2001): 17–32.

28 **"psychic" tears associated:** Nicholas M. Farandos, Ali K. Yetisen, Michael J. Monteiro, Christopher R. Lowe, and Seok Hyun Yun, "Contact Lens Sensors in Ocular Diagnostics," *Advanced Healthcare Materials*, November 17, 2014.

29 **dopamine is released:** Diana I. Tamir and Jason P. Mitchell, "Disclosing Information About the Self Is Intrinsically Rewarding," *Proceedings of the National Academy of Sciences* 109, no. 21 (2012): 8038–8043.

29 **James Coan:** James A. Coan and John J. B. Allen, eds., *The Handbook of Emotion Elicitation and Assessment* (New York: Oxford University Press, 2007); Lane Beckes and James Coan, "Social Baseline Theory and the Social Regulation of Emotion," in *The Science of the Couple,* edited by L. Campbell, J. La Guardia, J. M. Olson, and M. P. Zanna, Ontario Symposium on Personality and Social Psychology (New York: Psychology Press, 2012), 79–91.

CHAPTER 2: ACROPHOBIA

33 **A full 100 percent of humans:** T. Brandt and D. Huppert, "Fear of Heights and Visual Height Intolerance," *Current Opinion in Neurology* 27, no. 1 (2014): 111–117.

33 **People have been jumping out:** "Skydiving History," United States Parachute Association, uspa.org/AboutSkydiving/Sky divingHistory/tabid/118/Default.aspx, accessed March 15, 2015; "The History of Bungee Jumping," Bungee Zone, bungeezone .com/history, accessed March 15, 2015.

35 **Dachner Keltner, codirector:** Dacher Keltner, "Evolution of the Sublime: Toward a Science of Awe," presentation at the annual meeting of the Society of Affective Science, April 2015.

35 **Psychologist Candace Raio:** Candace M. Raio, Temidayo A. Orederu, Laura Palazzolo, Ashley A. Shurick, and Elizabeth A. Phelps, "Cognitive Emotion Regulation Fails the Stress Test," *Proceedings of the National Academy of Sciences* 110, no. 37 (2013): 15139–15144.

37 **part of our brain called the hippocampus:** Stefan G. Hofmann, Kristen K. Ellard, and Greg J. Siegle, "Neurobiological Correlates of Cognitions in Fear and Anxiety: A Cognitive-Neurobiological Information-Processing Model," *Cognition and Emotion* 26, no. 2 (2012): 282–299; Adam L. Lawson, Sarah Gauer, and Rebecca Hurst, "Sensation Seeking, Recognition Memory, and Autonomic Arousal," *Journal of Research in Personality* 46, no. 1 (2012): 19–25; Joshua P. Johansen, Christopher K. Cain, Linnaea E. Ostroff, and Joseph E. LeDoux, "Molecular Mechanisms of Fear, Learning and Memory," *Cell* 147, no. 3 (2011): 509–524.

40 **symptoms related to the fight or flight response:** Joseph E. LeDoux, "The Slippery Slope of Fear," *Trends in Neuroscience* 36, no. 5 (2013): 275–284.

40 **Vertigo occurs:** J. R. Carter and C. A. Ray, "Sympathetic Responses to Vestibular Activation in Humans," *American Journal*

of Physiology—Regulatory, Integrative and Comparative Physiology 294, no. 3 (2008): R681–688.

40 **full "go" mode:** Joseph E. LeDoux, "Emotional Brain: Fear and the Amygdala," *Cellular and Molecular Neurobiology* 23, nos. 4/5 (2002): 727–738.

41 **Our prefrontal cortex is responsible for sending:** Masamichi Sakagami, Xiaochuan Pan, and Bob Uttl, "Behavioral Inhibition and Prefrontal Cortex in Decision-Making," *Neural Networks* 19, no. 8 (2006): 1255–1265.

42 **diminish a feeling of disgust:** Peter J. de Jong, Mark van Overveld, and Charmaine Borg, "Giving In to Arousal or Staying Stuck in Disgust? Disgust-Based Mechanisms in Sex and Sexual Dysfunction," *Journal of Sex Research* 50, nos. 3–4 (2013): 247–262.

42 **Paul Slovic:** Daniel Vastfjall, Paul Slovic, and Marcus Mayorga, "Whoever Saves One Life Saves the World: Confronting the Challenge of Pseudoinefficacy," University of Oregon Global Justice Program, April 2014, globaljustice.uoregon.edu/files/2014/07 /Whoever-Saves-One-Life-Saves-the-World-1wda5u6.pdf.

46 **Researchers like David Zald:** David H. Zald, Ronald L. Cowan, Patrizia Riccardi, Ronald M. Baldwin, M. Sib Ansari, Rui Li, Evan S. Shelby, Clarence E. Smith, Maureen McHugo, and Robert M. Kessler, "Midbrain Dopamine Receptor Availability Is Inversely Associated with Novelty-Seeking Traits in Humans," *Journal of Neuroscience* 28, no. 53 (2008): 14372–14378.

46 **Oxytocin is the hormone:** Shelley E. Taylor, "Tend and Befriend: Biobehavioral Bases of Affiliation Under Stress," *Current Directions in Psychological Science* 15, no. 6 (2006): 273–277.

46 **Serotonin is the neurotransmitter:** Sara Shabani, Mohsen Dehghani, Mehdi Hedayati, and Omid Rezaei, "Relationship of Serum Serotonin and Salivary Cortisol with Sensation Seeking," *International Journal of Psychophysiology* 81, no. 3 (2011): 225–229; Masahiro Matsunaga, Hiroki Murakami, Kaori Yamakawa, Tokiko Isowa, Kunio Kasugai, Masashi Yoneda, Hiroshi Kaneko, Seisuke Fukuyama, Jun Shinoda, Jitsuhiro Yamada, and Hideki Ohira, "Genetic Variations in the Serotonin Transporter Gene-Linked Polymorphic Region Influence Attraction for a Favorite Person and the Associated Interactions Between the Central Nervous and Immune Systems," *Neuroscience Letters* 468, no. 3 (2010): 211–215.

47 **The story on endorphins:** Jon-Kar Zubieta, Yolanda R. Smith, Joshua A. Bueller, Yanjun Xu, Michael R. Kilbourn, Douglas M. Jewett, Charles R. Meyer, Robert A. Koeppe, and Christian S. Stohler, "Regional Mu Opioid Receptor Regulation of Sensory and Affective Dimensions of Pain," *Science* 293, no. 5528 (2001): 311–315; A. Vania Apkarian, M. Catherine Bushnell, Rolf-Detlef Treede, and Jon-Kar Zubieta, "Human Brain Mechanisms of Pain Perception and Regulation in Health and Disease," *European Journal of Pain* 9 (2005): 463–484.

47 **our endocannabinoid system:** James J. Burston and Stephen G. Woodhams, "Endocannabinoid System and Pain: An Introduction," *The Proceedings of the Nutrition Society* 73, no. 1 (2014): 106; Molly S. Crowe, Sara R. Nass, Kristin M. Gabella, and Steven G. Kinsey, "The Endocannabinoid System Modulates Stress, Emotionality, and Inflammation," *Brain, Behavior, and Immunity* 42 (2014): 1–5; Josee Guindon and Andrea Hohmann, "The Endocannabinoid System and Pain," *CNS & Neurological Disorders: Drug Targets* 8, no. 6 (2009): 403–421; John McPartland, Geoffrey W. Guy, and Vincenzo Di Marzo, "Care and Feeding of the Endocannabinoid System: A Systematic Review of Potential Clinical Interventions That Upregulate the Endocannabinoid System," *PLoS One* 9, no. 3 (2014).

48 **what is called "focused interoception":** A. D. "Bud" Craig, "How Do You Feel—Now? The Anterior Insula and Human Awareness," *Nature Reviews Neuroscience* 10, no. 1 (2009): 59–70; A. D. "Bud" Craig, "Interoception: The Sense of the Physiological Condition of the Body," *Current Opinion in Neurobiology* 13, no. 4 (2003): 500–505.

CHAPTER 3: ALONE IN THE DARK

54 **Erving Goffman:** Erving Goffman, *Asylums: Essays on the Social Situation of Mental Patients and Other Inmates* (Garden City, NY: Anchor Books, 1961).

54 **drawn to the novel:** Roy F. Baumeister, Ellen Bratslavsky, Catrin Finkenauer, and Kathleen D. Vohs, "Bad Is Stronger Than Good," *Review of General Psychology* 5, no. 4 (2001): 323–370; Nico Bunzeck and Emrah Düzel, "Absolute Coding of Stimulus Novelty in the Human Substantia Nigra/VTA," *Behavioral Medicine* 51, no. 3 (2006): 280–282; Gary Lewandowski Jr. and Arthur Aron, "Distinguishing Arousal from Novelty and Challenge in Initial

Romantic Attraction Between Strangers," *Social Behavior and Personality* 32, no. 4 (2004): 361–372; Adam L. Lawson, Sarah Gauer, and Rebecca Hurst, "Sensation Seeking, Recognition Memory, and Autonomic Arousal," *Journal of Research in Personality* 46, no. 1 (2012): 19–25.

56 **Philip Zimbardo's famous prison experiment:** Philip Zimbardo, *The Lucifer Effect: Understanding How Good People Turn Evil* (New York: Random House, 2008).

56 **To paraphrase Michel Foucault:** Michel Foucault, *Discipline and Punish: The Birth of the Prison*, vol. 2, translated by Alan Sheridan, 2nd ed. (New York: Vintage, 1995).

56 **Pennsylvania's Eastern State Penitentiary:** *History of Eastern State Penitentiary*, Eastern State Penitentiary Historic Site, 1994; *Eastern State Penitentiary: Historic Structures Report*, 2 vols., Philadelphia Historical Commission, July 21, 1994; B. Belbot, "Eastern State Penitentiary," in *Encyclopedia of Prisons & Correctional Facilities*, edited by Mary Bosworth (Thousand Oaks, CA: Sage Publications, 2005), 272–274; Mike Walsh, "Black Hoods and Iron Gags: The Quaker Experiment at Eastern State Penitentiary in Philadelphia," MissionCreep, missioncreep.com/mw/estate.html, accessed March 15, 2015.

59 **the "scolds bridle":** "Museum History Talk," Walsall Council, May 11, 2009, cms.walsall.gov.uk/museum_history_talk_sheds_light _on_the_scold_s_bridle.htm.

62 **Human interaction is fundamental:** Lane Beckes and James Coan, "Social Baseline Theory and the Social Regulation of Emotion," in *The Science of the Couple*, edited by L. Campbell, J. La Guardia, J. M. Olson, and M. P. Zanna, Ontario Symposium on Personality and Social Psychology (New York: Psychology Press, 2012), 79–91; Seth D. Pollak, Charles A. Nelson, Mary F. Schlaak, Barbara J. Roeber, Sandi S. Wewerka, Kristen L. Wiik, Kristin A. Frenn, Michelle M. Loman, and Megan R. Gunnar, "Neurodevelopmental Effects of Early Deprivation in Post-Institutionalized Children," *Child Development* 81, no. 1 (2010): 224–236; Harry T. Chugani, Michael E. Behen, Otto Muzik, Csaba Juhász, Ferenc Nagy, and Diane C. Chugani, "Local Brain Functional Activity Following Early Deprivation: A Study of Postinstitutionalized Romanian Orphans," *NeuroImage* 14, no. 6 (2001): 1290–1301.

62 **"In its intention I am well":** Charles Dickens, "Philadelphia, and Its Solitary Prison," chapter 7 in *American Notes* (1842; reprint, London: Chapman & Hall, 1913).

64 **Pennhurst Haunted House:** Patrick Walters, "Mental Health Pros Boo Haunted House at Pa. Asylum," *Boston Globe*, September 22, 2010; Jamie Tarabay, "Haunted House Has Painful Past as Asylum," National Public Radio News, October 29, 2010; "Pennhurst Asylum Haunted House," Pennhurst Asylum, pennhurstasylum .com, accessed March 13, 2015; "A Statement Regarding the Pennhurst Haunted Asylum," Pennhurst Memorial and Preservation Alliance, August 2010, preservepennhurst.org, accessed April 27, 2015.

71 **"I wish now to charge the Inspectors":** *Eastern State Penitentiary: Historic Structures Report*, Philadelphia Historical Commission, 1994, 1:220.

72 **"I went down and I found lying upon his cell":** Ibid., 1:221.

73 **French physician Philippe Pinel:** Michel Foucault, *The Birth of the Clinic: An Archaeology of Medical Perception* (New York: Vintage, 1994).

76 **Rumination is the practice:** Susan Nolen-Hoeksema, Blair E. Wisco, and Sonja Lyubomirsky, "Rethinking Rumination," *Perspectives on Psychological Science* 3, no. 5 (2008): 400–424.

77 **study from the University of Virginia:** "Most People Would Rather Shock Themselves Than Be Alone with Their Thoughts," *University Herald* [New York], July 6, 2014; Judy McGuire, "People Would Rather Shock Themselves Than Be Alone with Their Thoughts," *Today*, July 3, 2014.

77 **As James Gross found:** James Gross, "Emotion Regulation: Affective, Cognitive, and Social Consequences," *Psychophysiology* 39 (2002): 281–291.

78 **(somatosensory stimulation):** V. Legrain, F. Mancini, C. Sambo, D. M. Torta, I. Ronga, and E. Valentini, "Cognitive Aspects of Nociception and Pain: Bridging Neurophysiology with Cognitive Psychology," *Clinical Neurophysiology* 42, no. 5 (2012): 325–336; Valéry Legrain, Caroline Perchet, and Luis Garcia-Larrea, "Involuntary Orienting of Attention to Nociceptive Events: Neural and Behavioral Signatures," *Journal of Neurophysiology* 102, no. 4 (2009): 2423–2434; Geert Crombez, Chris Eccleston, Frank Baeyens, and Paul Eelen, "Attentional Disruption Is Enhanced by the Threat of Pain," *Behaviour Research and Therapy* 36, no. 2 (1998): 195–204.

78 **Russian scientists:** "Whipping Therapy Cures Depression and Suicide Crises," Pravda.ru, March 26, 2005, english.pravda.ru/health /26-03-2005/7950-whipping-0.

80 **The passage of time is a subjective experience:** Olga Pollatos, Jochen Laubrock, and Marc Wittmann, "Interoceptive Focus Shapes the Experience of Time," *PLoS One* 9, no. 1 (2014).

81 **(a "looming" threat):** Justine Cléry, Olivier Guipponi, Soline Odouard, Claire Wardak, and Suliann Ben Hamed, "Impact Prediction by Looming Visual Stimuli Enhances Tactile Detection," *Journal of Neuroscience* 35, no. 10 (2015): 4179–4189.

81 **Research from Marc Wittmann:** Marc Wittmann, Virginie van Wassenhove, A. D. "Bud" Craig, and Martin P. Paulus, "The Neural Substrates of Subjective Time Dilation," *Frontiers in Human Neuroscience* 4, no. 2 (2010); Marc Wittmann and Martin P. Paulus, "Decision Making, Impulsivity and Time Perception," *Trends in Cognitive Science* 12, no. 1 (2008): 7–12.

82 **Involuntary isolation:** Philip Solomon, Philip E. Kubzansky, Herbert Leiderman, Jack H. Mendelson, Richard Trumbull, and Donald Wexler, eds., *Sensory Deprivation: A Symposium Held at Harvard Medical School* (Cambridge, MA: Harvard University Press, 1961); Michael Bond, "How Extreme Isolation Warps the Mind," BBC, May 14, 2014.

82 **Dostoyevsky:** *The Yale Book of Quotations*, edited by Fred R. Shapiro (New Haven, CT: Yale University Press, 2006), 210.

CHAPTER 4: EXORCISING THE GHOST

87 **Tequendama Falls:** "Deserted Places: The Haunted Hotel at Tequendama Falls," Deserted Places: Abandoned Places and Urban Decay (blog), August 16, 2012, desertedplaces.blogspot.com/2012 /08/the-haunted-hotel-at-tequendama-falls.html.

88 **the Bible is full of monsters:** Stephen T. Asma, *On Monsters: An Unnatural History of Our Worst Fears* (New York: Oxford University Press, 2009).

88 **Claude Lévi-Strauss:** Claude Lévi-Strauss, *Myth and Meaning* (London: Routledge & Kegan Paul, 1978).

89 **Barbara Ehrenreich:** Barbara Ehrenreich, *Blood Rites: Origins and History of the Passions of War* (New York: Holt, 1998).

89 **"Though it may seem a remote":** Asma, *On Monsters*, 24.

89 **"a triple row of teeth like a comb":** Ibid., 33.

90 **"the Far East was a land":** Ibid., 37.

91 **Modern monsters continue:** Jason Zinoman, *Shock Value: How a Few Eccentric Outsiders Gave Us Nightmares, Conquered Hollywood, and Invented Modern Horror* (New York: Penguin, 2011).

91 **the supernatural is extremely popular:** Lee Speigel, "Spooky

Number of Americans Believe in Ghosts," *Huffington Post*, February 2, 2013.

94 **some people, like monks:** Mario Beauregard and Vincent Paquette, "Neural Correlates of a Mystical Experience in Carmelite Nuns," *Neuroscience Letters* 405, no. 3 (2006): 186–190.

96 **Richard Lord, an acoustic scientist:** "Infrasound Linked to Spooky Effects," Associated Press, September 7, 2003.

96 **Michael A. Persinger:** Michael A. Persinger, "Infrasound, Human Health, and Adaptation: An Integrative Overview of Recondite Hazards in a Complex Environment," *Natural Hazards* 70, no. 1 (2013): 501–525.

96 **Vic Tandy:** Vic Tandy, "The Ghost in the Machine," *Journal of the Society for Psychical Research* 62, no. 851 (1998).

97 **the Hum:** Marc Lallanilla, "Mysterious Hum Driving People Around the World Crazy," *LiveScience*, July 25, 2013, livescience .com/38427-the-hum-mystery-taos-hum.html.

97 **the God Helmet:** Michael A. Persinger, "Religious and Mystical Experiences as Artifacts of Temporal Lobe Function: A General Hypothesis," *Perceptual and Motor Skills* 57 (1983): 1255–1262; Michael A. Persinger, "The Neuropsychiatry of Paranormal Experiences," *Journal of Neuropsychiatry and Clinical Neurosciences* 13, no. 4 (2001).

98 **found God (and ghosts):** Jack Hitt, "This Is Your Brain on God," *Wired*, November 7, 1999.

98 **psychologist Pehr Granqvist:** Pehr Granqvist, Mats Fredrikson, Patrik Unge, Andrea Hagenfeldt, Sven Valind, Dan Larhammer, and Marcus Larsson, "Sensed Presence and Mystical Experiences Are Predicted by Suggestibility, Not by the Application of Transcranial Weak Complex Magnetic Fields," *Neuroscience Letters*, 379, no. 1 (2005): 1–6.

98 **transcranial magnetic stimulation (TMS):** Vaughan Bell, Venu Reddy, Peter W. Halligan, George Kirov, and Hadyn Ellis, "Relative Suppression of Magical Thinking: A Transcranial Magnetic Stimulation Study," *Cortex* 43, no. 4 (2007): 551–557; Marco Sandrini, Carlo Umiltà, and Elena Rusconi, "The Use of Transcranial Magnetic Stimulation in Cognitive Neuroscience: A New Synthesis of Methodological Issues," *Neuroscience & Biobehavioral Reviews* 35, no. 3 (2011): 516–536.

98 **article by Shahar Arzy:** Shahar Arzy, Margitta Seeck, Stephanie Ortigue, Laurent Spinelli, and Olaf Blanke, "Induction of an Illusory Shadow Person," *Nature* 443, no. 7109 (2006): 287.

98 **"sense a presence":** Anne-Marie Landtblom, "The 'Sensed Presence': An Epileptic Aura with Religious Overtones," *Epilepsy & Behavior* 9, no. 1 (2006): 186–188; Anne-Marie Landtblom, H. Lindehammer, H. Karlsson, and A. D. Craig, "Insular Cortex Activation in a Patient with 'Sensed Presence'/Ecstatic Seizures," *Epilepsy & Behavior* 20, no. 4 (2011): 714–718; Christine Le and Daniel H. Silverman, "Neuroimaging and EEG-Based Explorations of Cerebral Substrates for Suprapentasensory Perception: A Critical Appraisal of Recent Experimental Literature," *Psychiatry Research* 194, no. 2 (2011): 105–110; Michael Trimble and Anthony Freeman, "An Investigation of Religiosity and the Gastaut-Geschwind Syndrome in Patients with Temporal Lobe Epilepsy," *Epilepsy & Behavior* 9, no. 3 (2006): 407–414; Norman Geschwind, "Personality Changes in Temporal Lobe Epilepsy," *Epilepsy & Behavior* 15, no. 4 (2009): 425–433; Kara O'Connell, Joanne Keaveney, and Raymond Paul, "A Novel Study of Comorbidity Between Schizoaffective Disorder and Geschwind Syndrome," *Case Reports in Psychiatry* 2013 (2013): 1–3.

99 **Gastaut-Geschwind syndrome:** Trimble and Freeman, "An Investigation of Religiosity and the Gastaut-Geschwind Syndrome," 407–414.

103 **ASMR:** Rhodri Marsden, "'Maria Spends 20 Minutes Folding Towels': Why Millions Are Mesmerised by ASMR Videos," *Independent* [London], July 21, 2012; Harry Cheadle, "ASMR: The Good Feeling No One Can Explain," *Vice*, July 31, 2012; Nitin K. Ahuja, "It Feels Good to Be Measured: Clinical Role-Play, Walker Percy, and the Tingles," *Perspectives in Biology and Medicine* 56, no. 3 (2013): 442–451; Steven Novella, "ASMR," NeuroLogica (blog), March 12, 2012, theness.com/neurologicablog/index.php/asmr.

104 **Professor David Huron:** David Huron, "Biological Templates for Musical Experience: From Fear to Pleasure," International Symposium on the Neurobiology of Music, Rice University, November 18, 2006.

CHAPTER 5: THE LITTLE HOUSE OF HORRORS

110 **Celtic festival of Samhain:** Elizabeth A. Grater, "The Rise of 'Slut-o-ween': Cultural Productions of Femininity in Halloween Costumes," master's thesis, George Washington University, 2012.

111 **season starts as soon as the temperature:** Antoni Slodkowski, "As Temperatures Soar, Japanese Turn to Ghost Houses," Reuters, September 2, 2010.

114 **story starts with Ivan Pavlov:** Chris Beckett and Hilary Taylor, *Human Growth and Development*, 2nd ed. (Los Angeles: Sage, 2010).

116 **Uncanny Valley:** Ayse Pinar Saygin, Thierry Chaminade, Hiroshi Ishiguro, Jon Driver, and Chris Frith, "The Thing That Should Not Be: Predictive Coding and the Uncanny Valley in Perceiving Human and Humanoid Robot Actions," *Social Cognitive and Affective Neuroscience* 7, no. 4 (2012): 413–422.

116 **Researchers like Sandra Soares:** Sandra C. Soares, Björn Lindström, Francisco Esteves, and Arne Öhman, "The Hidden Snake in the Grass: Superior Detection of Snakes in Challenging Attentional Conditions," *PLoS One* 9, no. 12 (2014).

116 **Lynne Isbell:** Lynne A. Isbell, "Snakes as Agents of Evolutionary Change in Primate Brains," *Journal of Human Evolution* 51, no. 1 (2006): 1–35.

117 **a study by Vanessa LoBue:** Vanessa LoBue, David H. Rakison, and Judy S. DeLoache, "Threat Perception Across the Life Span: Evidence for Multiple Converging Pathways," *Current Directions in Psychological Science* 19, no. 6 (2010): 375–379.

117 **researchers like Isabelle Blanchette:** Isabelle Blanchette, "Snakes, Spiders, Guns, and Syringes: How Specific Are Evolutionary Constraints on the Detection of Threatening Stimuli?," *Quarterly Journal of Experimental Psychology* 59, no. 8 (2006): 1484–1504.

117 **Elaine Fox:** Elaine Fox, Laura Griggs, and Elias Mouchlianitis, "The Detection of Fear-Relevant Stimuli: Are Guns Noticed as Quickly as Snakes?" *Emotion* 7, no. 4 (2007): 691–696.

118 **As Hayao Kawai:** Kathryn Schulz, "Did Antidepressants Depress Japan?," *New York Times Magazine*, August 22, 2004.

118 **A study of college students:** Mary Picone, "Suicide and the Afterlife: Popular Religion and the Standardisation of 'Culture' in Japan," *Culture of Medical Psychiatry* 36, no. 2 (2012): 391–408.

118 **As Mary Picone states:** Ibid.

118 **Real estate agents:** Cara Clegg, "Living with Ghosts: The Rising Popularity of 'Death Rooms' in Japan," *Rocket News*, April 9, 2014.

122 **Every social interaction:** Paul J. Whalen, Hannah Raila, Randi Bennett, Alison Mattek, Annemarie Brown, James Taylor, Michelle van Tieghem, Alexandra Tanner, Matthew Miner, and Amy Palmer, "Neuroscience and Facial Expressions of Emotion:

The Role of Amygdala-Prefrontal Interactions," *Emotion Review* 5, no. 1 (2013): 78–83; Abigail A. Marsh, Megan N. Kozak, and Nalini Ambady, "Accurate Identification of Fear Facial Expressions Predicts Prosocial Behavior," *Emotion* 7, no. 2 (2007): 239–251; Matthew Botvinick, Amishi P. Jha, Lauren M. Bylsma, Sara A. Fabian, Patricia E. Solomon, and Kenneth M. Prkachin, "Viewing Facial Expressions of Pain Engages Cortical Areas Involved in the Direct Experience of Pain," *NeuroImage* 25, no. 1 (2005): 312–319; David Matsumoto and Hyisung C. Hwang, "Judgments of Subtle Facial Expressions of Emotion," *Emotion* 14, no. 2 (2014): 349.

122 **our physical environment, and our genetics:** Bernard M. C. Stienen and Beatrice de Gelder, "Fear Detection and Visual Awareness in Perceiving Bodily Expressions," *Emotion* 11, no. 5 (2011): 1182–1189; David Matsumoto, and Paul Ekman, "American-Japanese Cultural Differences in Intensity Ratings," *Motivation and Emotion* 13, no. 2 (1989); Koji Akiyama, "A Comparative Study of Facial Expressions and Emblems Between Japanese and Americans" *Intercultural Communication Studies* 1, no. 1 (1991): 147; Paul Ekman, "Universals and Cultural Differences in Facial Expressions of Emotion," in *Nebraska Symposium on Motivation, 1971*, edited by J. Cole, vol. 19 (Lincoln: University of Nebraska Press, 1972), 207–282; Jan B. Engelmann and Marianna Pogosyan, "Emotion Perception Across Cultures: The Role of Cognitive Mechanisms," *Frontiers in Psychology* 4 (2013): 118; Dawn T. Robinson, "The Role of Cultural Meanings and Situated Interaction in Shaping Emotion," *Emotion Review* 6, no. 3 (2014): 189–195.

124 **and as Maria Gendron:** Maria Gendron, Debi Roberson, Jacoba Marieta van der Vyver, and Lisa Feldman Barrett, "Cultural Relativity in Perceiving Emotion from Vocalizations," *Psychological Science* 25, no. 4 (2014): 911–920.

126 **In terms of physical gestures:** Jessica Tracy, Azim F. Shariff, Wanying Zhao, and Joseph Henrich, "Supplemental Material for Cross-Cultural Evidence That the Nonverbal Expression of Pride Is an Automatic Status Signal," *Journal of Experimental Psychology: General* 142, no. 1 (2013): 163–180.

126 **represents a collectivist orientation:** Joan Y. Chiao, "Current Emotion Research in Cultural Neuroscience," *Emotion Review* 7, no. 3 (2015), 280–293. Kimberly B. Rogers, Tobias Schröder, and Christian von Scheve, "Dissecting the Sociality of Emotion: A

Multilevel Approach," *Emotion Review* 6, no. 2 (2013): 124–133; Engelmann and Pogosyan, "Emotion Perception Across Cultures."

127 **it felt like forever:** Yair Bar-Haim, Aya Kerem, and Dominique Lamy, "When Time Slows Down: The Influence of Threat on Time Perception in Anxiety," *Cognition & Emotion* 24, no. 2 (2010): 255–263.

128 **David Eagleman:** David M. Eagleman, "Human Time Perception and Its Illusions," *Current Opinion in Neurobiology* 18, no. 2 (2008): 131–136.

CHAPTER 6: MEMENTO MORI

137 **Fear of death and dying is layered:** Researchers use many different scales. The Multidimensional Fear Scale breaks our fear of death into eight categories: Fear of the Dying Process, Fear of the Dead, Fear of Being Destroyed, Fear for Significant Others, Fear of the Unknown, Fear of Conscious Death, Fear for the Body After Death, and Fear of Premature Death. Each of these eight categories can be further broken down. For example, Victor Florian and Shlomo Kravetz's 1983 Fear of Personal Death Scale separately measures our intrapersonal concerns (loss of self-fulfillment, self-annihilation), our interpersonal concerns (loss of social identity, consequences to family and friends), and our transpersonal concerns (transcendental consequences, punishment in the hereafter). The most widely used scale, developed by Lora-Jean Collett and David Lester in 1969, attempts to simplify the scale by measuring our fear of Death of Self (e.g., total isolation of death, shortness of life, never thinking or experiencing), Dying of Self (e.g., pain involved in dying, intellectual degeneration, lack of control over process, grief of others), Death of Others (e.g., losing someone close, never being able to communicate again, feeling lonely without the person), and Dying of Others (e.g., watching the person suffer, having to be with someone who is dying).

137 **"This is the terror":** Ernest Becker, *The Denial of Death* (New York: Simon & Schuster, 1973), 87.

138 **terror management theory:** Brian L. Burke, Andy Martens, and Erik H. Faucher, "Two Decades of Terror Management Theory: A Meta-Analysis of Mortality Salience Research," *Personality and Social Psychology Review* 14, no. 2 (2010): 155–195.

138 **In America, dying has changed dramatically:** Peter Berger, Anthony Giddens, Michel Foucault, and Bryan S. Turner have

contributed to the conversation about how death and dying have changed, providing historical backgrounds and theoretical frameworks for understanding how our relationships with mortality affect our lives.

138 **sociologists Philip Mellor and Chris Shilling:** Philip A. Mellor and Chris Shilling, "Modernity, Self-Identity and the Sequestration of Death," *Sociology* 27, no. 3 (1993): 411–431.

139 **"Never before have people died":** Norbert Elias, *Loneliness of the Dying*, translated by Edmund Jephcott (New York: Blackwell, 1985), 23.

139 **Jaya Rao found that:** Jaya K. Rao, Lynda A. Anderson, Feng-Chang Lin, and Jeffrey P. Laux, "Completion of Advance Directives Among U.S. Consumers," *American Journal of Preventive Medicine* 46, no. 1 (2014): 65–70.

139 **Our workplaces, homes, water, and food are safer:** David Ropeik, "The Consequences of Fear," *EMBO Reports* 5 (2004); World Health Organization 2014 reports, who.int/en/.

139 **a study of Canadians:** Trinda L. Power and Steven M. Smith, "Predictors of Fear of Death and Self-Mortality: An Atlantic Canadian Perspective," *Death Studies* 32, no. 3 (2008): 253–272.

140 **the scarier the ones remaining become:** Fenna Van Marle and Shadd Maruna, "'Ontological Insecurity' and 'Terror Management': Linking Two Free-Floating Anxieties," *Punishment & Society* 12, no. 1 (2009): 7–26.

141 **Aokigahara Jukai Forest:** Rob Gilhooly, "Inside Japan's 'Suicide Forest,'" *Japan Times*, June 26, 2011; Peter Hadfield, "Japan Struggles with Soaring Death Toll in Suicide Forest," *Telegraph* [London], November 5, 2000.

143 **As Susan Sontag famously stated:** Susan Sontag, *Regarding the Pain of Others* (New York: Farrar, Straus and Giroux, 2003).

143 **dark tourism:** Michael S. Bowman and Phaedra C. Pezzullo, "What's So 'Dark' About 'Dark Tourism'? Death, Tours, and Performance," *Tourist Studies* 9, no. 3 (2010): 187–202; Philip R. Stone, "Dark Tourism and Significant Other Death," *Annals of Tourism Research* 39, no. 3 (2012): 1565–1587; Tracey J. Potts, "'Dark Tourism' and the 'Kitschification' of 9/11," *Tourist Studies* 12, no. 3 (2012): 232–249; Söndra Brand and Nina Platter, "Dark Tourism: The Commoditisation of Suffering and Death," in *The Long Tail of Tourism: Holiday Niches and Their Impact on Mainstream Tourism*, edited by Alexis Papathanassis (New York: Springer, 2011), 7–15.

145 *Complete Manual of Suicide*: Wataru Tsurumi, *Kanzen Jisatsu Manyuaru* [*Complete Suicide Manual*], 1993.

145 *Sea of Trees*: Seicho Matsumoto, *Kuroi Jukai (Sea of Trees* [Tokyo: Kodansha]), 1960.

145 **practice called *ubasute***: Rosie Goldsmith, "Suicide 'Epidemic' Among Japan's Elderly," BBC, March 19, 2003.

146 **In 2013 the United States was ranked**: World Health Organization 2014 reports, who.int/en/.

146 **lowest level of violence**: Ibid.

147 **the governor of Tokyo publicly called**: Erin Petrun, "Suicide in Japan," *CBS News*, July 12, 2007.

147 **prominent doctor, Yoshiki Sasai**: Alexander Martin, "Japanese Stem-Cell Scientist Yoshiki Sasai Commits Suicide," *Wall Street Journal*, August 5, 2014.

147 **Japanese culture is more collectivist**: Mary Picone, "Suicide and the Afterlife: Popular Religion and the Standardisation of 'Culture' in Japan," *Culture of Medical Psychiatry* 36, no. 2 (2012): 391–408; Jennifer R. Reimer, "Kokoro no kaze: The Creation of 'Depression' in Japan," *Practice of Madness Magazine*, March 2010.

148 **Things are changing in Japan**: Justin McCurry, "Japan Vows to Cut Suicide Rate by 20% over 10 Years," *Guardian* [London], September 4, 2014; Cameron Allan McKean, "How Blue Lights on Train Platforms Combat Tokyo's Suicide Epidemic," *Next City*, March 20, 2014.

149 **"death reflection" task**: Philip J. Cozzolino, Angela Dawn Staples, Lawrence S. Meyers, and Jamie Samboceti, "Greed, Death, and Values: From Terror Management to Transcendence Management Theory," *Personality and Social Psychology Bulletin* 30, no. 3 (2004): 278–292; Laura E. R. Blackie and Philip J. Cozzolino, "Of Blood and Death: A Test of Dual-Existential Systems in the Context of Prosocial Intentions," *Psychological Science* 22, no. 8 (2011): 998–1000; Oona Levasseur, Mark R. McDermott, and Kathryn D. Lafreniere, "The Multidimensional Mortality Awareness Measure and Model: Development and Validation of a New Self-Report Questionnaire and Psychological Framework," *OMEGA—Journal of Death and Dying* 70, no. 3 (2015): 317–341.

151 **Debra Bath found**: Debra M. Bath, "Separation from Loved Ones in the Fear of Death," *Death Studies* 34, no. 5 (2010): 404–425.

152 **Kenneth Vail and colleagues**: Kenneth E. Vail III, Jacob Juhl, Jamie Arndt, Matthew Vess, Clay Routledge, and Bastiaan T. Rutjens, "When Death Is Good for Life: Considering the Positive

Trajectories of Terror Management," *Personality and Social Psychology Review* 16, no. 4 (2012): 303–329.

153 **negative social consequences of bringing up death:** Victor Florian and Mario Mikulincer, "Fear of Death and the Judgment of Social Transgressions: A Multidimensional Test of Terror Management Theory," *Journal of Personality and Social Psychology* 73, no. 2 (1997): 369–380; Abram Rosenblatt, Jeff Greenberg, Sheldon Solomon, Tom Pyszczynski, and Deborah Lyon, "Evidence for Terror Management Theory: I. The Effects of Mortality Salience on Reactions to Those Who Violate or Uphold Cultural Values," *Journal of Personality and Social Psychology* (1989): 10–1037; Linda Simon, Jeff Greenberg, Eddie Harmon-Jones, Sheldon Solomon, and Tom Pyszczynski, "Mild Depression, Mortality Salience and Defense of the Worldview Evidence of Intensified Terror Management in the Mildly Depressed," *Personality and Social Psychology Bulletin* 22, no. 1 (1996): 81–90.

153 **mindfulness training:** Fadel Zeidan, Nakia S. Gordon, Junaid Merchant, and Paula Goolkasian, "The Effects of Brief Mindfulness Meditation Training on Experimentally Induced Pain," *Journal of Pain* 11, no. 3 (2010): 199–209.

153 **Molly Maxfield and colleagues found that:** Molly Maxfield, Sheldon Solomon, Tom Pyszczynski, and Jeff Greenberg, "Mortality Salience Effects on the Life Expectancy Estimates of Older Adults as a Function of Neuroticism," *Journal of Aging Research* (2010): 1–8.

156 **Resilient individuals bounce right back:** Gina O'Connell Higgins, *Resilient Adults: Overcoming a Cruel Past* (San Francisco: Jossey-Bass, 1994); Scott J. Russo, James W. Murrough, Ming-Hu Han, Dennis S. Charney, and Eric J. Nestler, "Neurobiology of Resilience," *Nature Neuroscience* 15, no. 11 (2012): 1475–1484.

156 **"What happens when we are traumatized?":** Thomas Greening, "PTSD from the Perspective of Existential-Humanistic Psychology," *Journal of Traumatic Stress* 3, no. 2 (1990): 323–326.

156 **Tom Pyszczynski conducted studies:** Tom Pyszczynski and Pelin Kesebir, "Anxiety Buffer Disruption Theory: A Terror Management Account of Posttraumatic Stress Disorder," *Anxiety, Stress & Coping* 24, no. 1 (2011): 3–26.

157 **Research on post-trauma growth:** Christopher Peterson, Nansook Park, Nnamdi Pole, Wendy D'Andrea, and Martin E. P. Seligman, "Strengths of Character and Posttraumatic Growth," *Journal of Trauma Stress* 21, no. 2 (2008): 214–217.

157 **feel emotionally numb:** Wendy D'Andrea, Nnamdi Pole, Jonathan DePierro, Steven Freed, and D. Brian Wallace, "Heterogeneity of Defensive Responses After Exposure to Trauma: Blunted Autonomic Reactivity in Response to Startling Sounds," *International Journal of Psychophysiology* 90, no. 1 (2013): 80–89.

CHAPTER 7: WRONG TURN

161 **The US Department of State's travel warning:** *Colombia 2014 Crime and Safety Report: Bogotá*, US Department of State, 2014.

162 **Bogotá these days is an up-and-coming:** "A Tourist Revival in the Heart of Bogotá," *New York Times*, September 14, 2012.

162 **Bogotá was characterized:** Christoffer Frendsen, "Bogota's Most Dangerous Places," *Colombia Reports*, August 11, 2014; John Quiñones, "Radio Shows Help Colombia Kidnap Victims," ABC News, May 17, 2014; Alan Gilbert, "Urban Governance in the South: How Did Bogotá Lose Its Shine?" *Urban Studies* 52, no. 4 (2014): 665–684.

164 **little over half . . . of all Americans:** *Post-Traumatic Stress Disorder* (brochure), Arlington, VA: National Alliance on Mental Illness, 2011.

165 **Kerry Ressler and colleagues:** Kerry J. Ressler, Barbara O. Rothbaum, Libby Tannenbaum, Page Anderson, Ken Graap, Elana Zimand, Larry Hodges, and Michael Davis, "Cognitive Enhancers as Adjuncts to Psychotherapy," *Archives of General Psychiatry* 61, no. 11 (2004): 1136–1144.

165 **Genes play a role as well:** Negar Fani, David Gutman, Erin B. Tone, Lynn Almli, Kristina B. Mercer, Jennifer Davis, Ebony Glover, Tanja Jovanovic, Bekh Bradley, Ivo D. Dinov, Alen Zamanyan, Arthur W. Toga, Elisabeth B. Binder, and Kerry J. Ressler, "FKBP5 and Attention Bias for Threat: Associations with Hippocampal Function and Shape," *Archives of General Psychiatry* 70, no. 4 (2013): 392.

166 **Other genetic differences:** Lynn M. Almli, Negar Fani, Alicia K. Smith, and Kerry J. Ressler, "Genetic Approaches to Understanding Post-Traumatic Stress Disorder," *International Journal of Neuropsychopharmacology* 17, no. 2 (2014): 355; Masahiro Matsunaga, Hiroki Murakami, Kaori Yamakawa, Tokiko Isowa, Kunio Kasugai, Masashi Yoneda, Hiroshi Kaneko, Seisuke Fukuyama, Jun Shinoda, Jitsuhiro Yamada, and Hideki Ohira, "Genetic Variations in the Serotonin Transporter Gene-Linked Polymorphic Region Influence Attraction for a Favorite Person and

the Associated Interactions Between the Central Nervous and Immune Systems," *Neuroscience Letters* 468, no. 3 (2010): 211–215.

166 **easily produce neuropeptide Y:** Research at the Indiana University School of Medicine in Indianapolis found that rats injected with NPY before being stressed interacted with other rats afterwards without any sign of stress, while those not injected avoided their cage mates for ninety minutes. Tammy J. Sajdyk, Philip L. Johnson, Randy J. Leitermann, Stephanie D. Fitz, Amy Dietrich, Michelle Morin, Donald R. Gehlert, Janice H. Urban, and Anantha Shekhar, "Neuropeptide Y in the Amygdala Induces Long-Term Resilience to Stress-Induced Reductions in Social Responses but Not Hypothalamic-Adrenal-Pituitary Axis Activity or Hyperthermia," *Journal of Neuroscience* 28, no. 4 (2008): 893–903.

166 **our ability to deal with trauma:** Mark Gapen, Dorthie Cross, Kile Ortigo, Allen Graham, Eboni Johnson, Mark Evces, Kerry J. Ressler, and Bekh Bradley, "Perceived Neighborhood Disorder, Community Cohesion, and PTSD Symptoms Among Low-Income African Americans in an Urban Health Setting," *American Journal of Orthopsychiatry* 81, no. 1 (2011): 31–37.

169 **house in which about seventy kids and adults:** Molly Born, "Woodland Hills Schools, Swissvale Police Investigate Bus-Stop Fights," *Pittsburgh Post Gazette*, January 9, 2013.

172 **violent mugging and sexual assault of an American:** Jim Glade, "Tourists to Bogota Sexually Assaulted, Held Hostage in Series of Hotel Robberies," *Colombia Reports*, April 19, 2011. Hostels are a popular target for robbery and muggings; in 2011 there were at least twelve muggings inside hostels, ranging from single intruders to entire groups of robbers storming the hostel and holding everyone hostage until all their belongings were collected. Many of these crimes go unreported because hostels fear bad press, and tourists are unfamiliar with and fearful of the justice system.

173 **living in a constant state of fear:** Lisa M. McTeague and Peter J. Lang, "The Anxiety Spectrum and the Reflex Physiology of Defense: From Circumscribed Fear to Broad Distress," *Depression and Anxiety* 29, no. 4 (2012): 264–281; Desmond J. Oathes, Greg J. Siegle, and William J. Ray, "Chronic Worry and the Temporal Dynamics of Emotional Processing," *Emotion* 11, no. 1 (2011): 101–114; *Post-Traumatic Stress Disorder* (brochure).

174 **PTSD in residents of certain violent parts:** Jen Christensen, "PTSD from Your ZIP Code: Urban Violence and the Brain,"

CNN, March 27, 2014; Schwartz et al., "Posttraumatic Stress Disorder Among African Americans."

174 **Judy Cameron:** Interview with Judy Cameron, July 2015; Cynthia L. Bethea, Kenny Phu, Arubala P. Reddy, and Judy L. Cameron, "The Effect of Short-Term Stress on Serotonin Gene Expression in High and Low Resilient Macaques," *Progress in Neuropsychopharmacology & Biological Psychiatry* 44 (2013): 143–153.

176 **pharmacological interventions:** Brian G. Dias, Sunayana B. Banerjee, Jared V. Goodman, and Kerry J. Ressler, "Towards New Approaches to Disorders of Fear and Anxiety," *Current Opinion in Neurobiology* 23, no. 3 (2013): 346–352; Giuseppe Tisi, Angelo Franzini, Giuseppe Messina, Mario Savino, and Orsola Gambini, "Vagus Nerve Stimulation Therapy in Treatment-Resistant Depression: A Series Report," *Psychiatry and Clinical Neurosciences* 68, no. 8 (2014): 606–611; Marco Sandrini, Carlo Umiltà, and Elena Rusconi, "The Use of Transcranial Magnetic Stimulation in Cognitive Neuroscience: A New Synthesis of Methodological Issues," *Neuroscience & Biobehavioral Reviews* 35, no. 3 (2011): 516–536.

177 **memory reconsolidation theory:** Cristina M. Alberini and Joseph E. LeDoux, "Memory Reconsolidation," *Current Biology* 23, no. 17 (2013): R746–R750; Joshua P. Johansen, Christopher K. Cain, Linnaea E. Ostroff, and Joseph E. LeDoux, "Molecular Mechanisms of Fear, Learning and Memory," *Cell* 147, no. 3 (2011): 509–524; Thomas Agren, Jonas Engman, Andreas Frick, Johannes Björkstrand, Elna-Marie Larsson, Tomas Furmark, and Mats Fredrikson, "Disruption of Reconsolidation Erases a Fear Memory Trace in the Human Amygdala," *Science* 337, no. 6101 (2012): 1550–1552.

178 **Emily Holmes:** Emily A. Holmes, Ella L. James, Thomas Coode-Bate, and Catherine Deeprose, "Can Playing the Computer Game 'Tetris' Reduce the Build-Up of Flashbacks for Trauma? A Proposal from Cognitive Science," *PLoS One* 4, no. 1 (2009).

178 **beta-blockers such as propranolol:** Elise Donovan, "Propranolol Use in the Prevention and Treatment of Posttraumatic Stress Disorder in Military Veterans: Forgetting Therapy Revisited," *Perspectives in Biology and Medicine* 53, no. 1 (2010): 61–74.

179 **researcher Elise Donovan:** Ibid.

180 **experience called "Extreme Kidnapping":** Drew Magary, "What It's Like to Be Kidnapped," *GQ*, April 2013.

183 **Americans are a paranoid bunch:** Daniel Gardner, *The Science of Fear: How the Culture of Fear Manipulates Your Brain* (New

York: Penguin, 2008); Peter Stearns, *American Fear: The Causes and Consequences of High Anxiety* (New York: Routledge, 2006); Barry Glassner, *The Culture of Fear: Why Americans Are Afraid of the Wrong Things* (New York: Basic Books, 1999).

183 **"From transgenic food to industrial chemicals":** David Ropeik, "The Consequences of Fear," *EMBO Reports* 5 (2004).

184 **According to the Pew Research Center:** *Gun Homicide Rate Down 49% Since 1993 Peak; Public Unaware*, Pew Research Center, 2013; "Study: Gun Homicides, Violence Down Sharply in Past 20 Years," CNN, May 9, 2013. For a review of statistics on Americans' misperception of risk see Stearns, *American Fear.*

185 *The State of the News Media*: *The State of the News Media*, Pew Research Center, 2013.

186 **overprotective or "helicopter" parents:** Hannah Rosin, "The Overprotected Kid," *Atlantic*, April 2014.

186 **critical skill called "distress tolerance":** C. W. Lejuez, Anne N. Banducci, and Katherine Long, "Commentary on the Distress Tolerance Special Issue," *Cognitive Therapy Research* (2013).

186 **researcher Roger Hart:** Rosin, "The Overprotected Kid."

187 **Stress management is a skill:** Virginia Hughes, "Stress: The Roots of Resilience," *Nature* 490 (October 10, 2012): 165–167; Scott J. Russo, James W. Murrough, Ming-Hu Han, Dennis S. Charney, and Eric J. Nestler, "Neurobiology of Resilience," *Nature Neuroscience* 15, no. 11 (2012): 1475–1484; Aliza P. Wingo, Kerry J. Ressler, and Bekh Bradley, "Resilience Characteristics Mitigate Tendency for Harmful Alcohol and Illicit Drug Use in Adults with a History of Childhood Abuse: A Cross-Sectional Study of 2024 Inner-City Men and Women," *Journal of Psychiatric Research* 51 (2014): 93–99; Bekh Bradley, Telsie A. Davis, Aliza P. Wingo, Kristina B. Mercer, and Kerry J. Ressler, "Family Environment and Adult Resilience: Contributions of Positive Parenting and the Oxytocin Receptor Gene," *European Journal of Psychotraumatology* 4 (2013): 1–9.

CHAPTER 8: BUILDING THE BASEMENT

197 **the concept of extreme haunts:** Ricky Brigante, "Most Extreme Haunted Houses," Fox News, October 10, 2014.

198 *Sleep No More*: Ben Brantley, "'Sleep No More' Is a 'Macbeth' in a Hotel," *New York Times*, April 13, 2011.

198 *STRATA*: Bill O'Driscoll, "Bricolage Offers Immersive, Interactive Theatrical Experience *STRATA*," *Pittsburgh City Paper*, July 25, 2012.

199 **Immanuel Kant:** Immanuel Kant, *Kant's Critique of Judgement*, translated by J. H. Bernard (London: Macmillan, 1914).

199 **As Pat Konopelski:** Pat Konopelski, personal conversation, summer 2014.

209 **First, you can suppress it:** Gal Sheppes and Ziv Levin, "Emotion Regulation Choice: Selecting Between Cognitive Regulation Strategies to Control Emotion." *Frontiers in Human Neuroscience* 7 (2013): 179.

209 **the New School's Wendy D'Andrea:** Wendy D'Andrea, Nnamdi Pole, Jonathan DePierro, Steven Freed, and D. Brian Wallace, "Heterogeneity of Defensive Responses After Exposure to Trauma: Blunted Autonomic Reactivity in Response to Startling Sounds," *International Journal of Psychophysiology* 90, no. 1 (2013): 80–89.

209 **vigilant/avoidant response:** Christine L. Larson, Hillary S. Schaefer, Greg J. Siegle, Cory A. B. Jackson, Michael J. Anderle, and Richard J. Davidson, "Fear Is Fast in Phobic Individuals: Amygdala Activation in Response to Fear-Relevant Stimuli," *Biological Psychiatry* 60, no. 4 (2006): 410–417; Michael W. Schlund, Greg J. Siegle, Cecile D. Ladouceur, Jennifer S. Silk, Michael F. Cataldo, Erika E. Forbes, Ronald E. Dahl, and Neal D. Ryan, "Nothing to Fear? Neural Systems Supporting Avoidance Behavior in Healthy Youths," *NeuroImage* 52, no. 2 (2010): 710–719.

210 **introducing social support:** Olivia L. Conner, Greg J. Siegle, Ashley M. McFarland, Jennifer S. Silk, Cecile D. Ladouceur, Ronald E. Dahl, James A. Coan, and Neal D. Ryan, "Mom—It Helps When You're Right Here! Attenuation of Neural Stress Markers in Anxious Youths Whose Caregivers Are Present During fMRI," *PLoS One* 7, no. 12 (2012).

210 **James Coan:** James A. Coan, Hillary S. Schaefer, and Richard J. Davidson, "Lending a Hand: Social Regulation of the Neural Response to Threat," *Psychological Science* 17, no. 12 (2006): 1032–1039.

210 **Candace Raio:** Candace M. Raio, Temidayo A. Orederu, Laura Palazzolo, Ashley A. Shurick, and Elizabeth A. Phelps, "Cognitive Emotion Regulation Fails the Stress Test," *Proceedings of the National Academy of Sciences* 110, no. 37 (2013): 15139–15144.

210 **James Gross and Gal Sheppes have shown:** Sheppes and Levin, "Emotion Regulation Choice"; James Gross, "Emotion Regulation: Affective, Cognitive, and Social Consequences," *Psychophysiology* 39 (2002): 281–291.

211 **Tibetan Buddhist monks:** B. Rael Cahn and John Polich, "Meditation States and Traits: EEG, ERP, and Neuroimaging Studies," *Psychology Bulletin* 132, no. 2 (2006): 180–211; Christine Le and Daniel H. S. Silverman, "Neuroimaging and EEG-Based Explorations of Cerebral Substrates for Suprapentasensory Perception: A Critical Appraisal of Recent Experimental Literature," *Psychiatry Research* 194, no. 2 (2011): 105–110; John Thomas, Graham Jamieson, and Marc Cohen, "Low and Then High Frequency Oscillations of Distinct Right Cortical Networks Are Progressively Enhanced by Medium and Long Term Satyananda Yoga Meditation Practice," *Frontiers in Human Neuroscience* 8 (2014): 197.

212 **researcher Fadel Zeidan:** Fadel Zeidan, Nakia S. Gordon, Junaid Merchant, and Paula Goolkasian, "The Effects of Brief Mindfulness Meditation Training on Experimentally Induced Pain," *Journal of Pain* 11, no. 3 (2010): 199–209; Fadel Zeidan, Susan K. Johnson, Bruce J. Diamond, Zhanna David, and Paula Goolkasian, "Mindfulness Meditation Improves Cognition: Evidence of Brief Mental Training," *Consciousness and Cognition* 19, no. 2 (2010): 597–605.

213 **(BDSM) community:** Andreas A. J. Wismeijer and Marcel A. L. M. van Assen, "Psychological Characteristics of BDSM Practitioners," *Journal of Sexual Medicine* 10, no. 8 (2013): 1943–1952; Ali Héber and Angela Weaver, "An Examination of Personality Characteristics Associated with BDSM Orientations," *Canadian Journal of Human Sexuality* 23, no. 2 (2014): 106–115; Juliet Richters, Richard O. De Visser, Chris E. Rissel, Andrew E. Grulich, and Anthony M. A. Smith, "Demographic and Psychosocial Features of Participants in Bondage and Discipline, 'Sadomasochism' or Dominance and Submission (BDSM): Data from a National Survey," *Journal of Sexual Medicine* 5, no. 7 (2008): 1660–1668.

214 **marker of anxiety in children:** Linda Gilmore and Marilyn Campbell, "Scared but Loving It: Children's Enjoyment of Fear as a Diagnostic Marker of Anxiety?" *Australian Educational and Developmental Psychologist* 25, no. 1 (2008): 24–31.

217 **Catherine Hartley and colleagues:** Catherine Hartley, Alyson Gorun, Marianne Reddan, Franchesca Ramirez, and Elizabeth A. Phelps, "Stressor Controllability Modulates Fear Extinction in Humans," *Neurobiology of Learning and Memory* 113 (2014): 149.

222 **as Vincent Felitti:** Laura Starecheski, "10 Questions Some Doctors Are Afraid to Ask," National Public Radio, March 3, 2015; Robert Anda, "The Health and Social Impact of Growing Up

with Adverse Childhood Experiences: The Human and Economic Costs of the Status Quo," Anna Institute, theannainstitute.org /ACE%20folder%20for%20website/50%20Review_of_ACE _Study_with_references_summary_table_2_.pdf, accessed April 20, 2015.

224 **they left the Basement feeling** *wonderful***:** "A Haunted House Turned Scientists' Lab," *Science Friday*, National Public Radio, October 2014; "Adventures in the Upside of Fear," *Essential Pittsburgh*, WESA Radio, October 2014; Margee Kerr, "Scared and Loving It: Improved Mood Following Voluntary Engagement with Negative Stimuli," poster presentation, Society for Affective Science, April 2015.

225 **Michael Apter calls the "protective frame":** Michael J. Apter, *The Dangerous Edge: The Psychology of Excitement* (New York: Free Press, 1992).

INDEX

Photo courtesy ScareHouse. Copyright Rachellynn Schoen.

Margee Kerr has a PhD in sociology from the University of Pittsburgh, where she currently teaches. She is also a nationally recognized expert on professional haunted houses and works year-round for the ScareHouse haunted house, analyzing data on customers and employees to make its attractions scarier. Her work has been featured in the *Washington Post*, *Parade*, *Atlantic Monthly*, and NPR's Science Friday, among other places. She is also the coinvestigator on the country's first-of-its-kind study measuring fear in the real world, collecting data on how the brain and body respond in real-life threatening situations. She lives in Pittsburgh.

PublicAffairs is a publishing house founded in 1997. It is a tribute to the standards, values, and flair of three persons who have served as mentors to countless reporters, writers, editors, and book people of all kinds, including me.

I. F. STONE, proprietor of *I. F. Stone's Weekly*, combined a commitment to the First Amendment with entrepreneurial zeal and reporting skill and became one of the great independent journalists in American history. At the age of eighty, Izzy published *The Trial of Socrates*, which was a national bestseller. He wrote the book after he taught himself ancient Greek.

BENJAMIN C. BRADLEE was for nearly thirty years the charismatic editorial leader of *The Washington Post*. It was Ben who gave the *Post* the range and courage to pursue such historic issues as Watergate. He supported his reporters with a tenacity that made them fearless and it is no accident that so many became authors of influential, best-selling books.

ROBERT L. BERNSTEIN, the chief executive of Random House for more than a quarter century, guided one of the nation's premier publishing houses. Bob was personally responsible for many books of political dissent and argument that challenged tyranny around the globe. He is also the founder and longtime chair of Human Rights Watch, one of the most respected human rights organizations in the world.

• • •

For fifty years, the banner of Public Affairs Press was carried by its owner Morris B. Schnapper, who published Gandhi, Nasser, Toynbee, Truman, and about 1,500 other authors. In 1983, Schnapper was described by *The Washington Post* as "a redoubtable gadfly." His legacy will endure in the books to come.

Peter Osnos, *Founder and Editor-at-Large*